The Representation of Women's Emotions
in Medieval and Early Modern Culture

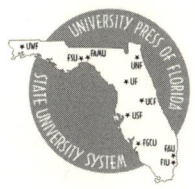

Florida A&M University, Tallahassee
Florida Atlantic University, Boca Raton
Florida Gulf Coast University, Ft. Myers
Florida International University, Miami
Florida State University, Tallahassee
University of Central Florida, Orlando
University of Florida, Gainesville
University of North Florida, Jacksonville
University of South Florida, Tampa
University of West Florida, Pensacola

The Representation of Women's Emotions in Medieval and Early Modern Culture

Edited by Lisa Perfetti

University Press of Florida
Gainesville/Tallahassee/Tampa/Boca Raton
Pensacola/Orlando/Miami/Jacksonville/Ft. Myers

Copyright 2005 by Lisa Perfetti
Printed in the United States of America on recycled, acid-free paper
All rights reserved
10 09 08 07 06 05   6 5 4 3 2 1

A record of cataloging-in-publication data is available from the Library of Congress.

ISBN 0-8130-2829-9

The University Press of Florida is the scholarly publishing agency for the State University System of Florida, comprising Florida A&M University, Florida Atlantic University, Florida Gulf Coast University, Florida International University, Florida State University, University of Central Florida, University of Florida, University of North Florida, University of South Florida, and University of West Florida.

University Press of Florida
15 Northwest 15th Street
Gainesville, FL 32611–2079
http://www.upf.com

Contents

Acknowledgments vii

Introduction 1
Lisa Perfetti

1. Theories of the Passions and the Ecstasies of Late Medieval Religious Women 23
E. Ann Matter

2. The Allegorical Construction of Female Feeling and *Forma*: Gender, Diabolism, and Personification in Hildegard of Bingen's *Ordo Virtutum* 43
James J. Paxson

3. The Spiritual Role of the Emotions in Mechthild of Magdeburg, Angela of Foligno, and Teresa of Avila 63
Elena Carrera

4. "Us for to wepe no man may lett": Resistant Female Grief in the Medieval English Lazarus Plays 90
Katharine Goodland

5. Constant Sorrow: Emotions and the Women Trouvères 119
Wendy Pfeffer

6. A Pugnacious Pagan Princess: Aggressive Female Anger and Violence in *Fierabras* 133
Kristi Gourlay

7. Calefurnia's Rage: Emotions and Gender in Late Medieval Law and Literature 164
Sarah Westphal

8. Waxing Red: Shame and the Body, Shame and the Soul 191
Valerie Allen

Contributors 211
Index 215

Acknowledgments

While completing my book on women's laughter in medieval literature, I chanced to meet Leslie Abend Callahan, who was working on an article on women's lament in the Middle Ages. We discovered that laughter and lament had much in common and that a study of women's emotions more broadly would make an important contribution to medieval studies. I would like to thank Leslie for helping with this project in its initial stages; her suggestions and enthusiasm were a key part of the process of writing this book. Friends and colleagues gave helpful suggestions on the introduction: Mary Coffey, Deborah McGrady, and Brenda Risch. The readers at the University Press of Florida were particularly helpful with their comments and suggestions on the entire manuscript. Amy Gorelick, our editor at the University Press of Florida, was a wonderful shepherd throughout the whole process. Copy editor Ann Marlowe did an outstanding job of making all necessary corrections and asking the right questions. Finally, many thanks to the contributors for the thought and emotion that they devoted to the queries and comments on their essays.

Introduction

Lisa Perfetti

One moment she's singing, the next she's thinking;
Now she laughs, and then she'll cry.
Her mood changes greatly in the blink of an eye![1]

Emotionally unstable, moody, subject to emotional outbursts, unpredictable, cause of social upheaval: this was a common medieval view of woman. Medical, philosophical, and theological traditions conspired to create this portrait of the weaker, more emotional sex, one that is so familiar to us that we have come to take it for granted. Stereotypes about emotional women endure today, but the understanding of emotions in the Middle Ages differed in significant ways from our own, and we must attend to cultural differences in order to interpret representations of emotion in their proper context. While emotions have emerged as an important and lively subject of concern among medievalists in recent years, gender has only occasionally been applied as a primary category of analysis.[2] As the first study devoted specifically to women's emotions in the medieval and early modern period, this volume is intended to initiate discussion among scholars through an examination of case studies demonstrating the range of factors that shape the representation of women's emotions.

The essays of this collection examine the importance of factors like class and ethnicity in determining attitudes toward emotions and consider the impact of the belief in female emotional volatility upon women's participation in public and private life. The contributors also explore how the assumption of female emotionality might have influenced women's perceptions of their own emotions. Attention to these issues promises to bring particularly valuable new insights to bear on our understanding of several subjects that have recently been of interest to medievalists, such as women's roles in family relationships and friendships, the place of conduct or courtesy literature in female socialization and education, and same-sex love or friendship among women, just to name a few. An awareness of the various contexts that shape the representation of emotions like love, hate, sadness, or anger will enable us to gain more insight into women's experiences as wives, mothers, daughters, sisters, and friends.

It goes without saying that texts written more than five hundred years ago inform us more about emotional conventions and standards than about actual emotions. The poems, epics, plays, legal texts, devotional prose, and other texts the authors analyze give us insights into whether women were encouraged to express particular emotions like anger or grief and in what contexts, but are less helpful for telling us whether emotions were qualitatively different for medieval women.[3] Emotional standards do, however, affect personal judgments about our emotions and therefore influence how we feel. Thus, representations of women's emotions in medieval and early modern texts indicate the stereotypes and expectations about proper emotional expression and behavior that would have circumscribed how individual women processed their feelings and allow us to imagine how medieval women might "navigate" the complicated web of social norms and cultural values that define and give meaning to emotions.[4]

An obvious challenge to our investigation is that few texts of the medieval period are known to have been authored by women, and so in many cases we are looking at emotions described by men; patriarchal ideology and ideas about masculinity are also at stake in these accounts. Some of the essays of this collection consider whether female authors were more likely to resist stereotypical discourse on women's emotions in their own writing. Another challenge is the enormous time span of the period in question. The primary texts studied in this volume range from the twelfth through the seventeenth century, and theoretical background reaches back to classical authors such as Aristotle. For convenience, in this introduction I use the term "medieval" to refer to material that reaches into the early modern period. Historians of emotion have often sought to establish turning points in emotional standards, arguing that such shifts illuminate other forms of social change, such as changes in family structure or labor practices.[5] Although not the central focus of this book, historical shifts in the representation of emotion within the medieval period or between the Middle Ages and the early modern era are addressed in several of the essays. Ann Matter traces the increasingly interiorized understanding of emotion that begins to resemble modern psychology, and the essays by Elena Carrera, Katharine Goodland, and Valerie Allen explore the impact of various emerging Christian doctrines and movements on the conceptualization of emotion.

Whether or not medieval and early modern views of emotion differ in any significant way, what is clear from these essays is that the Middle Ages were far from emotionally primitive and childlike, as Norbert Elias and others had imagined them to be prior to the "civilizing process" of the sixteenth century.[6] The diverse genres and sociocultural contexts engaged by these essays give us a picture of a complex period with competing discourses at work in the shaping of attitudes toward women's emotions, discourses that cannot be reduced to a unitary system or code.[7]

The essays have been chosen for the diversity of their material and have been arranged in a way that brings out connections between them. The first two essays of the volume provide theoretical background on medical, philosophical, and theological traditions at the heart of medieval conceptions of emotion. Ann Matter discusses theories of the passions and humors and traces their influence on the affective piety of several female religious leaders of the sixteenth and seventeenth centuries. James Paxson analyzes gendered aspects of classical and medieval rhetoric as a context for understanding Hildegard of Bingen's use of female personification in the *Ordo Virtutum*.

The next two essays also focus on religious literature: Elena Carrera studies the use of emotions by Mechthild of Magdeburg, Angela of Foligno, and Teresa of Avila, and Katharine Goodland examines the representation of grieving women in several British Lazarus plays. Following Goodland's discussion of grief, Wendy Pfeffer's essay looks at the sorrow expressed in a quite different context: the twelfth- and thirteenth-century French lyrics written in women's voices. Anger is the focus of the next two essays: Kristi Gourlay's on *Fierabras*, a late twelfth-century French chanson de geste, and Sarah Westphal's on medieval German legal and fictional texts. The final essay, by Valerie Allen, considers the medieval Christian understanding of shame both in the theoretical writings of thinkers such as Augustine and Aquinas and in penitential manuals and literary texts.

While each study bases its conclusions on specific contexts, the essays taken as a whole lay much-needed groundwork for exploring why beliefs about women's emotionality were so prevalent and what implications these beliefs had for women's participation in public and private life. Two thematic strands running throughout the essays are the fundamental importance of medieval views about the body in understanding how emotions were gendered and the importance of class and ethnicity in determining the particular values attributed to women's emotion. Another theme recurring in several essays is the key function of emotions as indicators of communal identity, which also determined how specific emotional expression or behavior in women could be either valued or denigrated. Finally, all of the essays go beyond an explanation of stereotypes about female emotionality or emotion standards to consider how women responded to such stereotypes and how they understood and used their own emotions.

Emotions and the Body

Emotions are popularly understood in terms of a binary separating passion from reason and feeling from thinking. Anyone studying emotion today, whether in the field of anthropology, sociology, psychology, history, or literary theory, understands how oversimplified this binary is, for cognition and emotion are processes that are highly interdependent.[8] The popular view of emotion as the opposite of reason has its roots in medieval and classical conceptions of the body. Under the influence of Aristotle and others, medieval philosophers and theologians viewed sexual difference according to a binary that defined the body as female and the mind as male.[9] Thought to be less endowed with the rational faculties that enable one to control the passions, women were considered to be more emotional than men, a belief that persists in many respects today.[10] One might even say that in the medieval way of thinking, emotions *were* female. In his essay on medieval personification, James Paxson argues that the tendency to personify abstract concepts like emotions as female came from the deep structure of classical rhetoric that hinges on a series of associations: since the body is female, and since the use of rhetorical figures is associated with the body because they give form to (or "embody") abstract thought, then rhetorical figures are associated with femininity.

The belief in women's bodily predisposition to emotionality was also based upon the notion that the human body is composed of four qualities (hot, cold, moist, and dry) that produce a certain "complexion," a notion related to the theory of the four humors determining both physical health and character. While the humors were found in both sexes—a man and a woman whose dominant humor was black bile would both be "melancholic," for example—it was thought that the female body was colder and moister than the male body. This inferior heat in women, which was used to explain many female "imperfections," tended to produce the notion that women were more emotionally volatile than men, whose hot and dry constitution kept them more stable. While both men and women could suffer physical and character defects from a lack of balance of the four humors, woman's generally cold and moist complexion was viewed as the cause of her weakness and susceptibility to passions, which she was less able to control.[11] The humoral conception of emotion explains why tears and laughter, which we commonly think of as opposite behaviors, were both attributed more often to women.[12] A belief that a woman's uterus (Greek *hyster*) could wander about her body further contributed to the idea that women were hysterical.[13]

Because emotions were seen as connected to the heavily gendered body, specific emotions were also likely to be represented differently according to gender. Kristi Gourlay's essay discusses the belief that women's anger was not brief and easily extinguishable like men's, but longer-lasting, smoldering because of women's cold and wet constitution. This belief had important consequences for women's legal status. Whereas men could plead innocence because their crime was committed in a heated moment of anger ("chaude colle"), women had to look for other mitigating circumstances since their "cold" anger was seen to be smoldering and enduring, thus more likely to lead to a premeditated murder than to a crime of passion. While the ability of men to claim "hot anger" as a defense seems to contradict the overall view of "cold" women as more emotional, anger was by nature a "hot" emotion, associated with choler; the distinction in this case is primarily between the brief duration of male anger, or *temporary loss of reason*, and the enduring, perpetually irrational state of the angry woman.

Beliefs about female embodiment also meant that women's emotions were often sexually coded. In her essay Valerie Allen contrasts the representation of male shame, which encompasses a broad range of behavior related to social estate, with the almost exclusively sexual nature of women's shame. Similarly, in Sarah Westphal's discussion of the *Sachsenspiegel*, a body of German customary law, the shameful behavior of the female defendant Calefurnia in a court of law is explicitly characterized as sexual: her angry challenge is visually displayed in the exposure of her "shameful parts" before her male audience, a sexual display that the *Sachsenspiegel* uses to justify denying women legal subjecthood.

As with the popular understanding of emotions today, in the Middle Ages emotions seemed to have a spontaneous power and force of their own. Ann Matter's essay describes the premodern view of emotions (or "passions") that considered humans as a microcosm reflecting larger forces in the cosmos. Accordingly, the position of the stars, the cardinal directions, the essential elements of all creation and the humors of the body all served to influence human nature. The word "emotion," although not used until the nineteenth century to describe feelings, contains in its etymology the idea of movement: it comes from the Latin *movēre*, "to move out from."[14] Both medieval and modern views of emotion thus include an idea of the force of movement, a kind of passion exerting its force on the body.

But Matter reminds us that in the Middle Ages, before the development of modern psychology, these forces were seen as coming from the outside rather than from within. Whereas today we tend to validate emotions as purely felt, as authentic sources of self-knowledge, some states such as envy and anger could be considered sins, which would have important implications for medieval views of the relationship between emotions and behavior (see below). Christian teaching instructed the faithful to channel the passions appropriately and vigilantly through conscious and rational meditation and prayer. For example, in the *Psychomachia*, a popular Latin text of the fifth century, opposing virtues and vices (such as patience and anger) go to war in the individual's soul. While representing the individual's emotional life as a battlefield between forces from outside the self, the *Psychomachia* also teaches that the individual who understands and attends to this cosmic battle is armed with the spiritual weapons to prevail. Paxson notes in his essay that Hildegard of Bingen's personified Joyful Soul (Felix Anima) falls from her joyful state to become unhappy ("infelix") upon being reminded by the devil (Diabolus) of her embodiment. It is the personified virtues such as humility, charity, and faith that enable the soul to fight off the attacks of Diabolus. So, although the bodily passions were seen as coming from outer forces, they were not viewed as fixed, predetermined, or beyond control. Concerted efforts of the mind could even alter the body's humors. As Ann Matter points out, although a melancholic woman was believed to be predisposed to mystical rapture by nature, a woman who dedicated herself to constant and intense mental activity could actually develop melancholy.

In late medieval piety, beliefs about female embodiment allowed for a certain privileging of women's emotions. In her essay Matter notes that, ironically, women's presumed embodiment, which generally resulted in their lower social status, actually led to the widespread assumption that women's sanctity was inherent because their embodiment predisposed them to participate mystically in the Passion of Christ. Carrera also discusses the positive associations with women's bodily expressions of mysticism, pointing out that the Church Fathers taught that the Scriptures must not only be understood intellectually but also experienced emotionally. All Christians, whether men or women, were taught to experience and emulate Christ's suffering and to cultivate a knowledge of God through intense feelings of love and joy.

Class and Ethnicity

The association between the feminine and the body meant that women, regardless of social class or status, were to some extent viewed as a group apart from men, a "fourth estate." In medieval penitential manuals, as Valerie Allen explains in her study, the primary distinction made among penitents was gender, and confessors were urged to be particularly careful when confessing female penitents. But other questions of status could either reinforce or obviate the negative associations between women and emotion. Elena Carrera remarks that access to education was limited for women, but also for the majority of men; differences in emotional expression in devotional literature may have had as much to do with the level of formal training as to expectations about gender. Sarah Westphal describes how Roman law denied certain legal rights to an entire group, comprised of women, sexual deviants, outlaws, blind men, and those who fight beasts by profession. Westphal comments that this odd group seems to be defined by association with taboos concerning the body, sexuality, and animal contact. The stigma against women is thus based in a larger concern about embodiment and animality, shared by other low-status groups.

Psychological studies today show that the perceived excessive emotionality of women continues to be attributed both to lower classes and to ethnic others.[15] In medieval texts, noblewomen are more likely to be represented as emotionally stable and rational compared to women of lower birth.[16] Katharine Goodland observes in her essay that the one Lazarus play that does not portray women as mourning extravagantly is also the one in which the women are of noble birth. The most stoic of female figures in the religious dramas, these aristocratic women are also represented as the most heroic. Laughter, like lament, was also attributed more often to lower classes and ethnic others (and children, it could be added), and conduct literature made clear that noblewomen in particular should control movements of the body and avoid excessive laughter, which ill befitted their noble station.[17] When emotional behavior in women was justified, it was often by reason of class or status. For example, a woman's anger or sorrow upon being forced to marry against her wishes was likely to be viewed with sympathy when the man was of lower social station, as a case discussed by Wendy Pfeffer indicates.

The association between ethnic others and emotionality is explored in essays by Gourlay and Westphal. Gourlay documents how medieval didactic and literary texts repeatedly imagined Saracens as innately violent and prone to fits of rage. Gourlay explains that this view stemmed in part from the notion that because Arabs lived in hot and dry climates, they were correspondingly hot-tempered by nature.[18] Gourlay argues that it is because of her Saracen identity that the heroine of *Fierabras* is permitted to display violent outbursts of rage, normally considered ill suited to a medieval princess, who is expected to be modest, quiet, and passive. Gourlay adds, however, that the heroine's anger, while permissible, is also laughable, and may have provided high entertainment value for medieval audiences. Sarah Westphal, too, points to the shaping force of ethnicity in *Die Mörin* (The Moorish Woman), a "trial poem." Whereas the white queen defendant is able eventually to cool her anger, the black queen holds to her anger, compromising a communal accord negotiated by the other plaintiffs in the fictional trial.

Emotion, Behavior, and Community

Emotions serve the key function of enabling the individual to adapt to environmental conditions and to feel a sense of belonging to a community defined by certain standards of behavior. As one anthropologist has defined them, emotions are "self-concerning, partly physical responses that are at the same time aspects of a moral or ideological attitude; emotions are both feelings and cognitive constructions, linking person, action, and sociological milieu."[19] Emotions have an adaptive social function in all cultures, where standards of behavior shape how individuals perceive and express their emotions. Where medieval and modern views of the social function of emotions most differ is in the way that they view the situation or direction of the emotions. In the Middle Ages, emotions are not inner feelings that serve to constitute a highly individuated self with a unique personality. They are oriented outward and define the individual's relationship to a community. In his well-known study on honor and humiliation in early Icelandic sagas, William Ian Miller explains that emotions function more as a "social state" or condition. For example, the proclaimed grief of a man whose murdered father has been unavenged functions as a "justificatory argument" enabling the son to take punitive action.[20] The man may well be experiencing the pain we commonly feel when losing our loved ones, but the saga's concern is to assess how his feelings position him relationally to others and what social outcomes they will produce. His grief is not a private feeling whose significance resides in the moment; it is part of the "habitus" of the warrior and as such situates him within an ethos where the performance of grief demonstrates that death demands retribution.[21] More recently, Daniel Smail has emphasized a similar performative aspect of emotion in the court records of late medieval Marseille. The key emotions of love and hate, which could determine the legitimacy of a legal grievance or the reliability of a witness called to testify, were seen not as internal states of mind but rather "as patterned behaviors and performances."[22] What is emphasized is not an individual psychological state but rather the relationships that define one's position relative to other individuals, families, and groups.

The court records Smail examines also indicate the medieval tendency to blur the line between affect and behavior. The prosecutors sought not to establish whether individuals had feelings of love or hate for another but rather whether they existed in a *state* of affection or enmity; the behaviors (such as having a meal together or sleeping in the same house) were seen less as consequences of emotion than as constitutive of it. In his essay on the virtues in the *Ordo Virtutum*, Paxson notes the difficulty of separating emotions like love, fear, and happiness from behavioral states like chastity. All serve as "emotional regulators" that properly situate the individual in the larger ethical and moral universe.

This is not to say that there was no distinction made between inner feeling and outer behavior. Penitential manuals instructed people to feel truly contrite in their hearts; they must not simply speak words of remorse without feeling them. In medieval misogynistic discourse, women were often accused of faking emotion, and their tears were particularly suspect. An especially interesting emotion is shame, perhaps the most social of emotions, as Valerie Allen notes in her essay. For Aquinas, shame was an involuntary passion, evidenced in the sudden blush when the blood rushes to the face, but also rationally motivated and consciously cultivated because it was related to the virtue of temperance, which protected one from sinning. Women, stigmatized by their inherent carnality, were particularly burdened by the need to demonstrate that their shame was "naked" and their confession sincere. Yet, however problematic the link between the display of behavior and the sincerity of emotion, medieval texts clearly indicate that the concern is with what the emotions reveal about the individual's relationship to a community, whether defined in political, religious, or other terms.[23]

Attention to this "outward-orienting" social function of emotions can help us to interpret moments of highly charged emotions in medieval texts without imposing our own values. A good example is the medieval French poems, discussed by Pfeffer, where women experience pain as a result of being married to men chosen for them by their families. Commonly thought of as poems about "unhappily" married women, the *chansons de malmariée* are more literally songs about *poorly* or *inappropriately* married women whose spouses are too old, are of inferior social status, or mistreat them. Are we justified in labeling these women "unhappy"? What would it mean for them to be "happy"? The most obvious problem in answering this question is that emotion words rarely convey the same semantic field across cultures.[24] The modern English word "happy" encompasses a different semantic range than the Latin *felix*, and Old French *joie* is quite different from our sense of either "happiness" or "joy." Even though all cultures have some concept of happiness, this concept varies according to the beliefs and values of each culture. Here we touch upon the ongoing debate over whether any emotions can be said to be universal, or whether all emotion is always socially constructed and culturally contingent.[25]

Perhaps one of the most important distinctions made by those who argue for the primacy of culture is the difference between collectivistic and individualistic societies.[26] According to the standards of individualistic cultures, a woman who marries a man chosen by her family might be viewed as sacrificing her personal happiness, whereas she would be viewed as feeling emotionally fulfilled in collectivistic cultures where "happiness" comes from feeling one has played one's proper role in achieving collective goals. Given the debate over how the "individual" or the "self" was understood in the Middle Ages, the "collectivist" label should probably not be applied to medieval society in the way it is used to refer to societies in non-Western cultures today.[27] The distinction does, however, offer a helpful way to reframe our approach to the question of the unhappy women of the Old French lyric.

In addition to the *chanson de malmariée*, Pfeffer discusses a *jeu-parti* (debate poem) in which a woman and man debate the relative merits of marrying a spouse chosen by one's family. The woman affirms that she would rather marry the man her friends and family (her "privez") had chosen for her than a man she loved but whom her family did not approve. The respect and love of her community are more important to her than "true love." To view her as an unhappy victim is to misunderstand her sense of identity. The lady's intellectual speech on the rational reasons for her choice does differ quite markedly from the emotional complaints of the women in the contemporaneous *chanson de malmariée*. These women who describe their husbands and family with insulting words and vividly name their pain or sorrow seem more clearly "unhappy." Yet even though they express what we could fairly call unhappiness, other emotions seem even more important, such as their anger at the family who chose poorly for them, their devotion to their secret lovers, or their feeling of satisfaction that they will make their husbands cuckolds. Putatively about the woman's unhappiness, the poems elevate the woman's depth of love and fidelity to her lover, and highlight the imminent shame of the husband. The women's unhappiness is thus intertwined with a range of other emotions, beliefs, thoughts, and expectations (including expectations of literary genre) that make this emotion culturally distinct.

The important social regulatory function attributed to emotions had particular implications for women's participation in public life. Women's greater emotional volatility was cited as the primary reason why they needed men as guardians and protectors who could act in their economic, political, or legal interest. Sarah Westphal shows how the *Sachsenspiegel* uses the fictional story of the female defendant Calefurnia as justification for forbidding women to plead their own case in court. It is noteworthy that Calefurnia's anger resembles the standard and approved legal disposition of *zorn* belonging to the epic male hero, whose anger is righteous and requires action. Yet Calefurnia's act of mooning the emperor relegates her *zorn* to the bodily realm and empties it of any legal efficacy. Her anger, affirms the *Sachsenspiegel*, is only private, lacking the gravitas of male anger; it thus disqualifies women from acting publicly on their own behalf.

In her essay on anger, Kristi Gourlay points to similar concerns about women's agency. Expressions of anger by a woman could be positive; for example, a woman should react angrily if her chastity is threatened, since this is her most valuable asset, to be zealously guarded. However, any public action should be taken by the men in the family, who would act on her behalf. Female anger, then, is valorized as a force that motivates the male to action. When it does not, it is castigated as an affront to male authority and a threat to social harmony, as the Calefurnia story vividly shows. Valerie Allen draws similar conclusions about the need for male guardianship in her discussion of shame. The association between shame and sexuality meant that women, naturally more prone to shameful acts and thoughts, needed men to control them and monitor their behavior. Moreover, using the example of Arthur and Gawain in *Sir Gawain and the Green Knight*, Allen points out how the men's shame is viewed positively since it spurs them on to actions that will recover the honor of the whole court. By contrast, when female characters experience shame in literary texts, they generally shrink back in silence.

Katharine Goodland's study on grieving women is particularly noteworthy in explaining how a specific emotion can change valence depending on prevailing social norms. In pre-Christian times, when women were in charge of performing ritual lamentation for the dead, their wailing, tears, and rending of garments had the positive function of ensuring the safe passage of the soul to the afterlife and perpetuating the memory of the dead among the living. Their tears not only were sanctioned by men but were necessary to a culture of male heroism. With the advent of Christianity, and its emphasis on a stoic acceptance of death as a passage to a higher life with God, women's lament takes on negative associations. The grieving women of the Lazarus plays are criticized by men for their ungodly tears. In one play the women are urged to at least do their weeping in private. The women's potentially blasphemous displays of emotion must be reined in by the men, whose more levelheaded adherence to Christian doctrine entitles them to play a more public and visible role. Yet it should be noted that women were often thought to be naturally compassionate, and their emotional sensitivity was often valued, particularly in the private sphere. In his *Manual for Confessors* (ca. 1215), Thomas of Chobham urged wives to use their persuasive powers (especially in bed) to "soften the heart" of any husband who was neglecting his duties as a Christian. Her power to provoke feelings of generosity and mercy in him could be more effective than the words of the priest.[28] The wife's "preaching" in private could thus lead to better public behavior on the part of the husband.

Women's Understanding and Use of Their Emotions

The concern that men showed over women's public display of emotion raises questions about the extent to which women could make use of their own emotions and, more fundamentally, the extent to which they consciously understood their own emotions as connected to their status as female. In the texts studied in this volume, there are no examples of women who refer directly to stereotypes of female emotionality or who speak of their emotions as particularly feminine. The religious women discussed by Matter and Carrera embrace their emotional displays of piety, but do not overtly announce such displays as uniquely feminine gifts. Carrera does note that female mystics generally displayed more visual and theatrical manifestations of emotion such as weeping, tearing at their garments, or proclaiming aloud their mystical visions. Male religious writers recounted the emotional experiences that brought them closer to God, but they did not include such visual displays in their accounts. Wendy Pfeffer argues that women who composed love poetry also spoke with more emotion than their male counterparts; while both male and female poets use words to describe their pain, the women express their pain more vociferously. Other literary examples bear out the notion of women's greater intensity of emotional expression.[29]

Written accounts of women's emotional displays cannot be taken at face value, but they may reflect some actual differences according to gender. Current studies on gender and emotion suggest that women tend to express themselves in more visibly emotional ways because they have internalized stereotypes about women's emotionality.[30] An example of a medieval text that points to a similar internalizing effect is in Pfeffer's essay, which discusses the topos in courtly love poetry of the haughty and cruel lady who rejects her devoted suitor. Pfeffer notes that whereas the male poet directs his suffering outward by blaming the pitiless lady for not granting him her love, songs in women's voices often direct their suffering inward, such as one lyric in which the lady castigates herself for her "cold heart" and regrets that she did not show mercy to her suitor. This blame of self is taken even further in other poems where a distraught woman entertains thoughts of suicide, a motif that is shared by romance heroines such as Chrétien's Enide and that seems to be more common among female characters than males. Carrera also notes that Angela of Foligno, upon gaining some prominence for her religious teachings (which made her an object of envy), began to internalize accusations of fraud leveled against her. She reproached herself for hypocritically posing as a holy woman when she was full of her own hidden sins, and condemned herself for misleading and endangering other souls. Although in one sense a simple imitation of the model of Christian humility, Angela's rhetoric of self-loathing also suggests particular anxiety about how the increasing public attention she was receiving was at odds with expectations that women not preach in public. A study of self-reproach, suicide, and other forms of hatred of self as they are found in literary and devotional texts in women's voices would be quite useful in helping us to think further about this internalizing of emotion stereotypes.

While medieval women may have internalized stereotypes about women's emotionality, other examples in this book suggest ways that women resisted them. Pfeffer demonstrates that women trouvères exhibit not extreme or erratic shifts in emotion but rather emotional constancy. Women who suffer as the result of being unloved or of having lost their lovers suffer consistently and swear that their pain will endure. As conduct manuals and literary texts amply illustrate, women were instructed to mold their emotions to the needs of their husbands.[31] The cobbler of a French farce, for example, brags that his wife is "like made of wax: I have only to ask her to laugh and she does. If I feel like crying, she cries. She can laugh and cry simultaneously. I do with her what I like."[32] As Carrera points out in her essay, Teresa of Avila explicitly rejected this ideology of wifely malleability; rather, she extolled the religious life by reminding her nuns that they are brides of Christ, who unlike a mortal husband will adapt to *their* emotional states, accepting their joy or their sorrow.

A particularly interesting case of a revision of paradigms about female emotionality is suggested in Paxson's discussion of Hildegard of Bingen. Although Hildegard grants epistemological privilege to the male Diabolus, who has knowledge that the virtues themselves do not possess, her drama creates a space to reconfigure dominant views of women's embodiment. The *Ordo Virtutum* demonstrates that the arrogant kind of knowledge flaunted by the male devil in his salacious taunts about women's embodiment is no match for the superior experiential wisdom to be achieved by aligning one's emotions with the virtues. While not explicit about this inversion, Hildegard shows that female emotion, or emotional engagement, triumphs over male reason; the binary so common to misogynistic discourse undergoes a revision in which embodied emotion is redefined as a kind of reason, one potentially empowering to the female religious community for whom the drama was written.

While Hildegard was highly educated and the author of learned works, the *Ordo* itself provides for its female religious community a model for self-understanding where the affective realm is given special prominence, and where intellect is cultivated alongside emotion. In the Middle Ages, few women enjoyed Hildegard's access to formal education or were able to express themselves in writing; women's perceived emotional sensitivity provided an alternative avenue for self-understanding and self-expression. Elena Carrera points out that women like Mechthild of Magdeburg and Angela of Foligno lacked the intellectual training of writers like Augustine or Bernard and were not permitted to preach in public; for them, affective piety offered a way to communicate their sense of belonging to a Christian community. Even Teresa of Avila, who was educated and wrote her own works, actively cultivated an affective approach to prayer, reminding her nuns that any creature, regardless of intellect, could feel deep love for God.

Conclusion

By engaging with a range of social and cultural contexts, these essays demonstrate how the belief in excessive female emotion was used to limit women's participation in public life. At the same time, the authors argue that women's emotions contest forms of gender ideology.[33] Westphal and Gourlay show that women's emotionality was used as a rationale for their exclusion from legal and political institutions, but it can also be argued that these fictional accounts of female plaintiffs portray their rage as a *result* of this exclusion. While the *Sachsenspiegel* uses its example of female anger to justify the subordination of women to men, it may also have served to suggest the legitimacy of women's anger. Carrera and Matter discuss the marginalization of women in medieval theological institutions, yet note the respect given to female mystics, whose bodily expressions of sorrow and joy align them with Christ's life and Passion, an affective language less accessible to the male theological establishment. Goodland argues that while the Lazarus plays criticize women's grieving, it is the women's tears that have the power both to summon Jesus and to move audiences, thus engaging them in the story of Christ's miracle.

Medieval attitudes toward women's emotions were complex, and whether a woman's emotion was represented as positive or negative depended on factors related to her status within a given community as well as to the discourses shaping the written text itself. Paying attention to these factors and especially keeping in mind the medieval emphasis on the social performative function of emotion will help to illuminate moments of emotional complexity that require a closer look. A better understanding of the cultural specificity of emotions in the Middle Ages will be particularly helpful for teaching students how to engage medieval texts on their own terms. When students say that the feelings or behavior of a romance heroine are not "realistic," we can challenge them to think about how the woman's sorrow, anger, or shame is a clue to how she sees herself in relation to her family, to her friends, and to her broader community.

The findings of this collection invite a number of interesting lines of inquiry that promise to tell us yet more about women's emotions in the premodern period. First, while there was clearly overlap in the way literary and historical documents represented emotions, it would be useful to think more about how records of public proceedings like court trials were likely to differ from other forms of discourse, such as didactic or literary texts.[34] A related question is how representation differs according to literary genre. Some genres are virtually defined by women's emotion, such as the *chanson de malmariée*. How and why does this genre represent the unhappily married woman differently from other genres treating this topos, such as the fabliau? More studies on single emotions across genres would thus be very helpful. A recent approach to emotion combining cognitive science with literary criticism argues that people understand what they are feeling by appraising how their feelings match emotion prototypes, or stories about emotion.[35] Medieval narratives thus offer us insight into the different prototypes available and also suggest the kinds of models available to female audiences and storytellers. It would be quite interesting to consider how the creative process of storytelling might foster in women a greater self-reflective awareness of their own emotions.

Other productive avenues to explore involve the relationship between emotions and social change. As women's economic and political status shifts in particular places and times, what new emotion standards develop? Does an increased access to certain professions or trades produce discourses that either describe or proscribe new emotions for women? What role do changes in courtship, marriage, or family structure play in shaping women's emotional expression? How do emerging forms of social distinction make certain emotions fashionable? The suffering elevated so lyrically in courtly love poetry served to assert the superior sensibilities of the nobility and appears to have been embraced equally by male and female poets. Other examples of emotions "in vogue" might suggest how distinctions of class played out specifically along gender lines.

The territory still to be examined is considerable and promises to yield many new insights into the lived experiences of women in the Middle Ages. One of the traditional challenges for medieval feminist scholarship has been how to acknowledge the multiple forms of women's oppression without viewing women as passive victims. While stereotypes about the inferiority of female feeling dominated, views of women's emotions were far from monolithic, and medieval texts suggest how women navigated through a maze of competing social standards and cultural norms, in some ways conforming to standards denigrating women's feelings as irrational, in other ways contesting them. Whether tears of grief, a cry of joy, or a red flush of shame or anger, representations of emotions point to the things that mattered for medieval women and help us to imagine the everyday dimension of women's sense of belonging to the world in which they lived—what they thought and how they felt.

Notes

1. "Or chante, or pense, or rit, or pleure; / Moult mue son cuer en pou de heure!" *Three Medieval Views of Women: "La Contenance des Fames," "Le Bien des Fames," "Le Blasme des Fames,"* ed. and trans. Gloria K. Fiero, Wendy Pfeffer, and Mathé Allain (New Haven: Yale University Press, 1989), lines 109–10. The translation is my own.

2. Notable studies on medieval and early modern emotion include Barbara H. Rosenwein, ed., *Anger's Past: The Social Uses of an Emotion in the Middle Ages* (Ithaca: Cornell University Press, 1998), and C. Stephen Jaeger and Ingrid Kasten, eds., *Codierungen von Emotionen im Mittelalter / Emotions and Sensibilities in the Middle Ages* (New York: de Gruyter, 2003). Two studies devoted specifically to gender are Gwynne Kennedy, *Just Anger: Representing Women's Anger in Early Modern England* (Carbondale: Southern Illinois University Press, 2000), and Jennifer C. Vaught, ed., with Lynne Dickson Bruckner, *Grief and Gender: 700–1700* (New York: Palgrave, 2003).

3. For a discussion of "emotionology" or the emotional standards of a particular society, see Peter N. Stearns and Carol Z. Stearns, "Emotionology: Clarifying the History of Emotions and Emotional Standards," *American Historical Review* 90.4 (1985): 813–36. Noteworthy is their distinction between the history of ideas and emotionology, which is more concerned with the everyday interaction between values and behavior (833). Also see Peter N. Stearns and Jan Lewis, eds., *An Emotional History of the United States*, History of Emotions 4 (New York: New York University Press, 1998).

4. I take the term "navigate" from William Reddy, *The Navigation of Feeling: A Framework for the History of Emotions* (Cambridge: Cambridge University Press, 2001). Reddy defines emotion as "an array of loosely linked thought material" that is activated virtually simultaneously so that it exceeds the capacity for attention to translate it into a succinct action or talk in a short period of time (111). The individual "navigates" this tangle of thought material, sometimes fitting "emotional regimes" or standards, sometimes not, mostly unconsciously.

5. Stearns and Stearns, "Emotionology," 814, argue, "Changes in emotional standards can in turn reveal much about other aspects of social change and may even contribute to such change."

6. Norbert Elias, *The Civilizing Process: The History of Manners and State Formation and Civilization*, trans. Edmund Jephcott, 2 vols. (Oxford: Blackwell, 1994). The original German work was published in 1939. For a discussion of Elias's work as it applies to medieval anger, see Rosenwein, *Anger's Past*. The essays of her volume, she comments, "suggest that historical change takes us from one set of conventions and restraints to another rather than through a process of civilizing" (241) and that "an entire repertory of conflicting norms persisted side-by-side throughout the Middle Ages" (242–43).

7. In the introduction to their edited volume *Language and the Politics of Emotion* (Cambridge: Cambridge University Press, 1990), 9, Lila Abu-Lughod and Catherine Lutz comment that studies of emotion fall into the error of essentialism in their use of the term "culture," which "seems to connote a certain coherence, uniformity, and timelessness in the meaning systems of a given group" and "tends to divert us from looking for contests for meaning and at rhetoric and power, contradictions, and multiple discourses. . . ." The authors consequently reject the word "culture" in favor of "discourses." The multiple, often conflicting discourses at work in the representation of women's emotions in the Middle Ages are evident in this collection. We use the term "medieval culture" with full recognition of the anything but unitary nature of that culture.

8. Indicative of the trend among scientists to investigate the cognitive component of emotion is the existence of the journal *Cognition and Emotion*, published annually since 1986. For a sociological perspective on the emotion/cognition divide, see the introduction by Gillian Bendelow and Simon J. Williams to their edited volume *Emotions in Social Life: Critical Themes and Contemporary Issues* (London and New York: Routledge, 1998). A distinction is sometimes made between feeling (somatic experiences of the body) and emotion (the psychological processing of feelings). But the neuroscientist Antonio Damasio, whose work has become widely influential, has argued that this distinction is untenable. Reversing the conventional understanding of emotion and feeling, and recognizing the unorthodoxy of this move, he comments in *The Feeling of What Happens: Body and Emotion in the Making of Consciousness* (New York: Harcourt Brace, 1999), 284: "First, I am suggesting that there is no central feeling state before the respective emotion occurs, that expression (emotion) precedes feeling. Second, I am suggesting that 'having a feeling' is not the same as 'knowing a feeling,' that reflection on feeling is yet another step up. . . . But all of these processes—emotion, feeling, and consciousness—depend for their execution on representations of the organism. Their shared essence is the body." In this introduction, I use the terms "emotion" and "feeling" without any particular distinction between the two.

9. On the way that the Middle Ages categorized and valued qualities of masculine and feminine, see Joan Cadden, *Meanings of Sex Difference in the Middle Ages:*

Medicine, Science, and Culture (Cambridge: Cambridge University Press, 1993), 205–8.

10. In a 1988 essay, Catherine Lutz actually blamed the tendency to understand emotion as a biological rather than a cultural phenomenon on the Western bias against women. Paraphrasing her claim, William Reddy in *Navigation*, 40–41, comments that "the notion that emotions are biologically based is not simply erroneous, it is part of a larger, insidious, gender-biased Western view of the self that privileges alleged male rationality over the supposedly natural emotionalism of women."

11. See Cadden, *Meanings*, 170–73, for a discussion of complexion and the fundamental role of heat in medieval views of sexual difference.

12. The sixteenth-century physician Laurent Joubert, in *Treatise on Laughter*, trans. Gregory David de Rocher (Tuscaloosa: University of Alabama Press, 1980), 103, explained: "Now the soft, such as women and children, are not only less conscious and less wise, but are also easily moved by every occasion, be it sad or happy." Related to the humors is the idea that some emotions have their "seat" in particular parts of the body. Laughter, for instance, was thought by Joubert (104–105, 110–13) and others to come from the heart, liver, or spleen because these organs circulate or purify the blood, the humor that produces joy. Today the organ we look to for a biological explanation of emotions is the brain. It is interesting to note that neuroscientists have demonstrated that there are only a small number of brain sites involved in emotions, most of them subcortical, and that different emotions are found in the same area of the brain. Rather than being "seated" in specific sites of the brain, emotions appear to result from the activation *patterns* of a number of sites of the brain (Damasio, *Feeling*, 62).

13. On the wandering uterus, see Cadden, *Meanings*, 14–15.

14. *Oxford English Dictionary*, 2nd ed., s.v. "emotion."

15. Kay Deaux, "Gender and Emotion," in *Gender and Emotion: Social Psychological Perspectives*, ed. Agneta H. Fischer, Studies in Emotion and Social Interaction, 2nd ser. (Cambridge: Cambridge University Press, 2000), 308. For the importance of class in medieval attitudes toward anger, see Rosenwein, *Anger's Past*, 244–45.

16. A famous exception to this rule is the lowborn Griselda, the heroine lauded by Boccaccio, Petrarch, and Chaucer for her virtual lack of emotion as she endures the cruel tests of her husband. An implicit message of the text, however, is that if a woman such as Griselda could have such nobility of character, surely women of gentler birth could aspire to her model. The Griselda story was widely used in conduct literature for women in the later Middle Ages. In the *Ménagier de Paris*, written by a husband for his young wife, the story appears in a section on wifely obedience; see *Le Ménagier de Paris*, ed. Georgine E. Brereton and Janet M. Ferrier (Oxford: Clarendon, 1981), 72–73.

17. On attitudes toward women's laughter as it relates to class, see my *Women and Laughter in Medieval Comic Literature* (Ann Arbor: University of Michigan Press, 2003), 11, 25.

18. The view of climatic "heat" creating emotional volatility and violence appears to be at odds with humoral theory's view of heat and dryness as qualities associated with men's more rational constitution. This conflict is indicative of the competing learned and popular theories circulating in the Middle Ages. As Cadden remarks, medical knowledge was often fragmented and illustrated "synchretism and compromise" (*Meanings*, 55).

19. Michelle Z. Rosaldo, "Toward an Anthropology of Self and Feeling," in *Culture Theory: Essays on Mind, Self, and Emotion*, ed. Richard A. Shweder and Robert A. Le Vine (Cambridge: Cambridge University Press, 1984), 137–57. For a discussion of the *evolutionary* adaptive role of human feelings, see Damasio, *Feeling*, 31.

20. William Ian Miller, *Humiliation: And Other Essays on Honor, Social Discomfort, and Violence* (Ithaca: Cornell University Press, 1993), 108.

21. In using "habitus" I am referring to the idea, known best through the work of Pierre Bourdieu, that social structures are not only internalized by the individual but *incorporated* through generally unconscious mimetic and habitual repetitions. The habitus includes a scheme of dispositions including perceptions, emotions, thoughts, and actions that provide a "feeling for the game," in a given social context or field. See Pierre Bourdieu, *Outline of a Theory of Practice* (Cambridge: Cambridge University Press, 1977).

22. Daniel Lord Smail, *The Consumption of Justice: Emotions, Publicity, and Legal Culture in Marseille, 1264–1423* (Ithaca: Cornell University Press, 2003), 100–101. Smail notes the interesting exception of anger, which was at times said to be motivated by the devil. For a discussion of demonic influences on emotion, see chapter one of this volume.

23. It should be added that interest in the social function of emotion is not confined to the Middle Ages. Many theorists today who study the contemporary period focus on the "public face" of emotion. See Abu-Lughod and Lutz, *Language*, 11; Julie Ellison, *Cato's Tears and the Making of Anglo-American Emotion* (Chicago: University of Chicago Press, 1999) includes an interesting discussion of the public discourse on sympathy as it relates to views of the proper role of government.

24. In her essay "Emotion, Language, and Cultural Scripts," Anna Wierzbicka argues that because language is so culturally specific, we should avoid language-bound concepts such as happiness and anger and seek instead "conceptual primitives such as good and bad, or want, know, say, and think, [which] are not cultural artifacts of the English language but belong to the universal alphabet of human thoughts; they appear to have their semantic equivalents in all, or nearly all, languages of the world." In *Emotion and Culture: Empirical Studies of Mutual Influence*, ed. Shinobu Kitayama and Hazel Rose Markus (Washington, D.C.: American Psychological Association, 1994), 133–96, at 139.

25. Happiness is often considered one of the six "basic" emotions shared by people regardless of culture, along with sadness, fear, anger, disgust, surprise. For an early discussion of this claim, see Keith Oatley and P. N. Johnson-Laird, "Toward a Cognitive Theory of Emotions," *Cognition and Emotion* 1.1 (1987): 29–50. For a

more recent discussion of the basic or "primary" emotions and their relationship to "secondary" emotions such as embarrassment, jealousy, or pride, see Damasio, *Feeling*, 51. Recently, Patrick Colm Hogan has argued that there has been too much emphasis on cultural difference. Using a wide range of examples from literature, he develops the idea that there are "narrative universals" shared by literary texts in almost every culture and generated from emotion prototypes. Happiness, he argues, is the fundamental narrative universal and it produces the two primary literary genres found in most cultures: romantic comedy (based on achievement of personal happiness through reuniting with a lover) and heroic tragicomedy (based on the social happiness where an individual or group is restored to political and social power). See his *The Mind and Its Stories: Narrative Universals and Human Emotion* (Cambridge: Cambridge University Press, 2003), esp. 121.

26. Harry C. Triandis argues in "Major Cultural Syndromes and Emotion," in *Emotion and Culture* (see note 24), 285–306, that individualism versus collectivism is the most important factor resulting in variation in emotions across cultures. He notes that the collective can include "the family, the work group, a political or religious group, a social class, or an ideological or national entity that is centrally important to the individual's self-definition" (287). The relevance of individualism to gender has been discussed by Agneta H. Fischer and Antony S. R. Manstead in "The Relation between Gender and Emotions in Different Cultures," in *Gender and Emotion* (see note 15), 71–94. They argue that gender differences in emotion are strongest in individualistic societies, where the importance of achieving and maintaining independence from others threatens the stability of the most important social unit, the family. A kind of "psychological task differentiation" results whereby women are encouraged to express emotions that maintain social relations to compensate for men's tendency to separate from the family, as they are socialized to do.

27. Stephen Greenblatt, *Renaissance Self-Fashioning: From More to Shakespeare* (Chicago: University of Chicago Press, 1980), famously located the emergence of Western individuality in the Renaissance. Medievalists before and after him have debated the status of "self" or "individual" in the Middle Ages. For a useful discussion of this debate, see Susan Crane, "Knights in Disguise: Identity and Incognito in Fourteenth-Century Chivalry," in *The Stranger in Medieval Society*, ed. F. R. P. Akehurst and Stephanie Can Van D'Elden (Minneapolis: University of Minnesota Press, 1997), 63–79. Another recent work that investigates premodern personhood and touches on the emotions is Timothy J. Reiss, *Mirages of the Selfe: Patterns of Personhood in Ancient and Early Modern Europe* (Stanford: Stanford University Press, 2003).

28. For a discussion of Thomas of Chobham and other writers who valued women's ability to influence their husbands positively, see Sharon Farmer, "Persuasive Voices: Clerical Images of Medieval Wives," *Speculum* 61.3 (1986): 517–42.

29. For example, Ann Marie Rasmussen, "Clovis's Grief, Tristan's Anger, and Kriemhild's Restless Corpse: Emotions, Gender, and Lordship in Medieval Literature," in *Codierungen* (see note 2), 174–91, argues that in the German poem *The*

Lament, men and women share some of the outer signs of grief like weeping and screaming, but "men do not wring their hands, tear their hair, rend their garments, or hug corpses. This is women's work, just as the most violent and truly involuntary, somatic expressions of grief—losing the ability to speak, going mad, and dying from grief—are enacted by women" (186). My own preliminary study of the lays of Marie de France (presented at the 39th International Congress on Medieval Studies at Kalamazoo, Michigan, May 9, 2004) also finds a more dramatic display of emotion in women. Emotion words like *dolent* or *liez* are used as frequently with male as with female characters (in fact they are used somewhat more frequently for males), but female characters are more likely to shed tears, cry out "Lasse!," grow pale, faint, and attempt suicide.

30. Deaux, "Gender and Emotion," 302–303. On the more intense emotional displays of women in Western cultures, see also Fischer and Manstead, "Relation," 73–74.

31. Christine de Pizan, who in other respects challenges misogynistic discourse, urges wives to put on a cheerful countenance to greet their husbands after a hard day's work; see *A Medieval Woman's Mirror of Honor: "The Treasury of the City of Ladies,"* ed. Madeleine Pelner Cosman, trans. Charity Cannon Willard (New York: Persea Books, 1989), 187.

32. The original reads:
    . . . est faicte comme de cire
    Et si ne demande que rire.
    Si je vueil plourer, elle pleure,
    Rire et plourer tout à une heure,
    Je fais d'elle ce que je veulx.

Farce Nouvelle Tresbonne et fort joueuse a quattre personnages: Le savetier, le moyne, la femme, le portier, in *Recueil de farces françaises inédites du XVe siècle,* ed. Gustave Cohen (Cambridge, Mass.: Medieval Academy of America, 1949), 261, vv. 112–16.

33. Abu-Lughod and Lutz affirm that "emotion discourses establish, assert, challenge, or reinforce power or status differences" (*Language*, 14). Discourses on fear, they point out, have been used by colonial powers, and marginalized groups have used emotion discourses to demonstrate rebellion against or equality with higher status groups.

34. For example, Smail, *The Consumption of Justice*, 94, argues that the legal records he analyzes show little indication of gender difference either in the kinds of emotion expressed or in the way they were expressed in public. In her essay, Gourlay also notes the less gendered account of emotions in legal records compared with literary texts.

35. See especially Hogan, *The Mind and Its Stories*.

1

Theories of the Passions and the Ecstasies of Late Medieval Religious Women

E. Ann Matter

It is well known to those of us who share a passion for the reconstruction of the lives and actions and thoughts—the gestures, behaviors, and emotions—of medieval men and women that the people we study did not necessarily understand themselves the way we understand ourselves. This is especially true with regard to the interpretations given to emotions and passions. Even the way I began the first sentence, with the assertion that we share "a passion," evokes a modern psychological conception of how human beings work. It can, however, be instructive to remember that medieval Christians categorized much of what we think of as "passions"—anger, jealousy, lust—among the Seven Deadly Sins![1] Our common assumption about human passions, like almost all post-Freudian ideas about human nature, is essentially interior, consisting of concepts that begin within the human psyche—or heart—or soul. In contrast, people in the premodern world, from classical antiquity and continuing through "the long Middle Ages" into the middle of the seventeenth century, understood human nature in a different way—if not exactly as a result of, then at least intrinsically allied to, external forces. This "humoral theory" of human nature explains human existence as linked to an enormous, cosmic series of interrelated phenomena: the stars, the cardinal directions, the essential elements of all creation, and the essential humors of the human body.

While a review of theories of microcosm and macrocosm from the first century to the dawn of the modern era is not possible here, I would like to make some observations on this philosophical and theological tradition. Suffice it to say that many cosmological theories influenced the Latin West; they mostly originated in the Greek world, with Plato as a starting point; and they were directly influential at least through the sixth century, with a secondary effect from the ninth century onward.[2] The basic concept is a parallelism between small, finite humans and larger, more lasting entities, such as the relationship between humans and the World-Soul in Plato's *Timaeus*, or Augustine's understanding of the human soul as a small reflection of the Trinity.[3] By the time of the twelfth-century author Bernardus Silvestris, as Winthrop Weatherbee put it, "The ideal of a harmony between macrocosm and microcosm was becoming a cliché."[4] Bernardus thus tries to say something more sophisticated about this issue. His *Cosmographia* is divided into two books entitled "Macrocosmos" and "Microcosmos"; like the contemporary *De planctu naturae* of Alan of Lille, it explains the creation of human beings. In Bernardus this is done by Physis, in Alan by Natura, and exactly in the image of the macrocosm.[5]

Books 4 and 11 of Isidore of Seville's *Etymologiae* are a major source for the transmission of Greek medical thought into the Christian Middle Ages, especially with respect to the correspondence between macrocosmic elements and the human microcosm that is characteristic of Hippocratic medicine.[6] Such a "humoral" understanding of human nature links our emotions and passions with far greater forces. Perhaps this link gives a particular importance to what we moderns understand as human emotion, and helps to explain the stubborn persistence of some aspects of the Galenic cosmology into the modern world. One example of this is the role the humors played in Baroque art, as Zirka Filipczak explains in her lavishly illustrated book on the far-reaching aesthetic consequences of a general knowledge and acceptance of these theories into the seventeenth century.[7]

Although the title of my essay refers specifically to the later Middle Ages, I would actually like to focus my remarks on examples from a slightly later part of "the long Middle Ages," the sixteenth and seventeenth centuries, to investigate how theories of the passions changed as they survived.

This diagram, based on the cosmology of Isidore of Seville, is adapted from Barbara Newman's wonderful study of Hildegard of Bingen, *Sister of Wisdom*, and from the analysis of medieval sexuality and medicine by Danielle Jacquart and Claude Thomasset.[8] It shows a conception of a connection between the elements (clockwise from the top: fire, earth, water, air), the seasons (summer, autumn, winter, spring), and the four essential humors of human beings outlined by Galenic and Hippocratic medicine:

choleric (related to yellow bile), melancholic (black bile), phlegmatic (phlegm), and sanguine (blood).[9] These qualities are further related to the cardinal directions (again clockwise): south, west, north, east.

What were the consequences of the fact that humans were understood in relationship to the four elements, directions, humors? As a number of modern scholars have pointed out—here I am thinking of Dyan Elliott and Joan Cadden, as well as of Jacquart and Thomasset and of Newman—one

	South	
	Summer	
	Fire	
	Choler	
	(dry and hot)	
East		West
Spring		Autumn
Air		Earth
Blood		Melancholy
(moist and hot)		(dry and cold)
	North	
	Winter	
	Water	
	Phlegm	
	(moist and cold)	

result of this set of assumptions was a cosmic explanation of the differences between the sexes. From Aristotle on, it was a premise of philosophy as much as of medical theory that women were by nature cold and wet, as opposed to the hot, dry character of men. As Newman quotes William of Conches, "The warmest woman is colder than the coldest man."[10] No less a figure than Hildegard of Bingen understood herself—one could almost say mediated her own difficult self for others—through this language of the humors: the sanguine woman, Hildegard says, is soft, tender, fertile; phlegmatic women are hardworking, practical, lusty; choleric women are discreet, kindhearted, loyal; and the melancholic woman is the only kind of woman who is actually better off without a man, since such women are gaunt in body, susceptible to sickness and exhaustion, "wandering in their thoughts," in short, intellectual. Newman points out that Hildegard most likely understood herself this way because of her "unusually susceptible constitution" and her openness to the winds of God that blow through her and sound her like a lyre, making her God's prophet.[11]

In its use of the ancient humoral language, this sounds very traditional. Yet Hildegard's descriptions of these female characteristics, including her own self-description, have already been pointed to as examples of a major change in the understanding of the humors. Peter Dronke says about Hildegard: "What is particularly new and startling in her procedure is that she interprets the four humors fundamentally in terms of sexual behavior, and that she gives a separate detailed account for four temperaments of women as well as for those of men. Such predictive physiological sketches of women are not previously attested."[12] "What is unprecedented about Hildegard's characterology," Newman says, "is its emphasis on psychosexual traits."[13] Jacquart and Thomasset, without specific reference to Hildegard, see something similar as characteristic of a broader change in medieval humoral theory: "The originality of the Middle Ages lay in their bringing together the facts provided by psychology and physiology, so as to constitute a model capable of accounting in detail for the overlapping of physical and mental states."[14] Quoting this passage, Dyan Elliott adds, "Thus the passions, which in classical times were chiefly *disturbances* or accidents which raged through the soul, develop a 'hybrid status as both *physical* and *mental* states.'"[15]

Elliott goes on to discuss the ecstatic raptures of late medieval women in terms of the embodied female spirituality described so well by Caroline Walker Bynum.[16] Since Bynum's work has significantly changed the terms of the discussion, many scholars of medieval Christianity now look for the bodily manifestations of the ecstasies of medieval women.[17] Of course, all mystical experience in human beings is ultimately mediated through the body, just for lack of any other way to express ourselves. But the humoral theory of human nature, with the strong distinction between male and female essences, emphasized the bodily nature of female mystics in contradistinction to their male counterparts. Perhaps this is a consideration that could be added to the debate over the characterization of "male" and "female" forms of spirituality and mysticism.[18]

The reintroduction of Aristotle to Western thought starting in the late twelfth century spurred another level of philosophical debate about the relationship of macrocosm and microcosm, for two reasons. First, it was Aristotle who had coined the terms and set up the problem, writing in the *Physics*: "If this [here Aristotle is talking about the eternity of motion] can happen in the living being, what hinders it from happening also in the All? For if it happens in the little world (it happens) also in the great [ei gar en mikro cosmo ginetai, kai en megalo]. And if in the world, also in the Infinite, if it is possible for the Infinite to move itself."[19] The great number of commentaries on the *Physics* written between 1200 and 1650—twice the number of commentaries on other books of Aristotle[20]—shows the importance of these ideas to scholastic thinkers. It set an intellectual background for what might be called "an imitation of the Cosmic Christ" or, perhaps better put, "a cosmic imitation of Christ."

Christian philosophers of the late Middle Ages and early modern period used, and furthered, these cosmological concepts while pursuing their own philosophical and theological concerns. Nicholas of Cusa, the great mystical theologian (or philosophical mystic?) of the fifteenth century, came to terms most clearly with the problem of macrocosm and microcosm in his work *De docta ignorantia*. The work is the result of a vision Cusa reports having as he sailed back to Venice from Constantinople, where he had been a member of a papal delegation in negotiations with the Eastern Church. Cusa says here that human beings are especially suited for union with God because of our special place in the universal order of creation: "Truly, human nature is such that it is elevated above all the works of God and is slightly less than the angels, embracing [both] the intellectual and the sensible nature, and binding the universe within itself, and so was reasonably called a microcosm, or a little world, by the ancients."[21] The mystical nature of Cusa's theory of macrocosm and microcosm lies in the fact that "human nature" does not exist except in individual people, so that union between the microcosm and the universal macrocosm can take place only on an individual basis, between one person and God.[22] As Elliott has shown, there was a close link between theories of the passions and medieval Christian theories of demonic possession. One of her more colorful examples comes from the *De universo* of William of Auvergne, who explains in detail how the devil can actually cause certain physical responses, such as seizures, by pressing on certain organs. Elliott says that William "excoriates certain medical experts who argue that such disorders have a simple physical origin."[23]

Given all of this, it should come as no surprise to see how the burst of visionary and mystical activity by women that began in the High Middle Ages and continued into the seventeenth century was analyzed by the learned clerics whose task it was to keep such expressions of piety in check and within the norms of orthodoxy. These clerics would naturally turn to the theories of the passions for some clues about how to explain the phenomenon. William of Auvergne thought that a woman constitutionally given to melancholia (as Hildegard had described herself) would have a *physical* predisposition to mystical rapture, and even that the reverse is possible—that is, that a woman given to vehement prayer and devotions can actually *develop* melancholia.[24]

A number of well-known medieval mystical and visionary women fit these parameters. Elliott mentions Hildegard, Elisabeth of Schönau, Marie of Oignies, Lutgard of Aywières, the aptly named Christine the Marvelous, Vanna of Orvieto, Margaret of Cremona, Brigit of Sweden.[25] For most of this period, she argues, women's sanctity was a given, assumed to be a natural, if paradoxical, result of women's inherent inferiority. Bynum has suggested that women were considered to be more of the body and, by this very embodiment, were then predisposed to participate mystically in the Passion of Christ. But by the fourteenth century one can see a "progressive caution" in the hagiographical writings about holy women; Elliott says this "reflects a dangerous collapse in the representation of the familiar polarities of female spirituality."[26] As shown most vividly by the case of Joan of Arc, the mystical raptures of women were increasingly seen to be the result of demonic influence. This is something new, and yet, as we have seen, its seeds can already be found in the theories of the humors, where demonic possession is linked to "inherent" human qualities. Elliott ends with the *Malleus maleficarum*, the infamous late fifteenth-century Inquisitors' handbook that associates women with the bodily in an exclusively negative way, in which women, because of their corporeality, are intimately associated with the devil. The emphasis of this text is definitely on the intimate, as is expressed in the famous conclusion about women's superstition: "All witchcraft comes from carnal lust, which is in women insatiable."[27] "Here," Elliott says, "is the terminus of a previously auspicious and vindicatory current in the assessment of female spirituality."[28]

But was it? I would like to examine this premise forward another 150 years by looking at the lives and the contexts of those lives, and the writings and the reception of the writings, of three women visionaries and religious leaders who were very well known in their own worlds. They are Lucia Brocadelli da Narni (1476/77–1544), a Dominican Tertiary and the court prophet of Ercole I "il Magnifico" of Ferrara; Maria Maddalena de' Pazzi (1566–1607), a Carmelite of Florence closely tied to the new world of Jesuit spirituality; and Maria Domitilla Galluzzi (1595–1671), a Capuchin of Pavia whose life and spirituality strongly echo the spiritual patterns of her medieval predecessors even though she lived in the golden age of Borromean Lombard spirituality and was, in fact, an exact contemporary of Descartes. I will speak about them in chronological sequence and then conclude with some effort to see if there has been another major shift in theories of the passions, like the one in the twelfth century described by Dronke, Newman, and Jacquart and Thomasset and the one in the High Middle Ages explained by Elliott.

Lucia Brocadelli da Narni

Over half a millennium ago, in March of 1500, Ercole d'Este, Duke of Ferrara, "Ercole il Magnifico," wrote a letter about the admiration and respect due to certain women of spiritual gifts. Later expanded into a short treatise and published as a pamphlet in both Latin and German under the Latin title *Spiritualium personarum feminei sexus facta admiratione digna*, it circulated rather widely among a pious courtly elite of early modern Europe.

Ercole, who had earlier undertaken a searching correspondence with the Dominican apocalyptic prophet Girolamo Savonarola, here set forth a theory that every prince needed a "court prophet" to advise him of God's will. The prophets, Ercole explained, are more usually than not women, and the one recently installed at his court, Lucia Brocadelli, was especially holy. Lucia Brocadelli, for one thing, bore stigmata, the marks of the Passion of Christ. As Ercole put it, "These things are shown by the Supreme Craftsman in the bodies of His servants to conform and strengthen our Faith, and to remove the incredulity of impious men and hard of heart."[29]

Ercole wanted to boast of his court prophet because Lucia Brocadelli's presence at the court of Ferrara had not been easily accomplished. The story of Lucia's arrival in Ferrara is a Renaissance intrigue almost comical in its details, involving the complicity of Pope Alexander VI, whose daughter, Lucrezia Borgia, was soon to marry Ercole's son, and reaching a climax when Lucia was smuggled out of Viterbo in a basket of linen, on the back of a mule, and whisked through the Papal States to Ferrara, where she arrived on May 7, 1499. In the next year, Ercole built Lucia a house, the Convent of Santa Caterina, and established around her a community of Dominican Tertiaries.

Ercole's letter on the importance of female prophecy may reflect some uneasiness about the way he found a woman prophet for his court, or a concern to appear orthodox in the wake of the burning of Savonarola in 1498. Nevertheless, Ercole here describes a number of other women, the *sante vive* studied by Gabriella Zarri, who served the same function in other Italian cities: Osanna Andreasi in Mantua, Stefana Quinzani in Crema, Colomba da Rieti in Perugia. In this context, to the religious and political elite of the Italian city-states at the turn of the sixteenth century, Lucia Brocadelli's role in Ferrara made perfect sense.

Upon Ercole's death, however, Lucia's position in Ferrara changed dramatically, essentially because, for reasons we cannot fully understand, the new duke, Alfonso, did not share his father's enthusiasm for this figure of sanctity.[30] From 1505, when she was just twenty-nine years old, for nearly the next four decades until her death at sixty-eight on November 15, 1544, Lucia Brocadelli was kept under close supervision, a virtual prisoner in the house that had been built as a testimony to her spiritual gifts.

In these years Lucia Brocadelli continued to have visions. An account of seven visions written in her own hand in the year of her death was widely attested by secondary sources, but had been missing since the nineteenth century until I found it in the library of another north Italian city, Pavia, and edited it for publication with Armando Maggi and Maiju Lehmijoki-Gardner. For the first time, modern scholars can now hear the voice of Lucia Brocadelli.

The visions involve a series of guided tours of Paradise, usually led by Jesus, the Virgin Mary, or Saints Paul and Jerome. Lucia calls Jesus "mio dolce Jesu" [my sweet Jesus] or "mio solazzo" [my consolation], while Jesus habitually addresses Lucia as "fiola" or "filia" [daughter], often with accompanying adjectives such as "dilecta" [beloved] or "dolcisima" [sweetest]. Lucia's guides point out palaces, gardens, angels, maidens carrying cups, altars covered with cloths, heavenly seats, often in groups of four or seven.

In the third revelation, Jesus explains the four heavenly seats: one is for her father confessor, one for Jesus, one for a Franciscan friar (not specified), and the last one for Lucia herself. Lucia gets a chair, Jesus says, because:

My sweet daughter, you have been in the burning fire, and then beaten by the waves of the stormy sea. And the great adornment of your crown and your seat signify the great alms and charity that you have shown to the poor for my love. Your hand has done every thing for love of me and my mother Mary, and ... you have borne various tribulations with such constancy and true patience, and voluntarily, with much adversity, with such sufferance and tolerance, for my love. And I know you have abandoned life, possessions, dignity, and creatures who loved you so much for my love.[31]

It is clear from this passage, and many others like it in this remarkable tour of the palaces and gardens of Paradise, that the infamy and sufferings of Lucia have been understood and psychologically processed in relation to those of Christ. This is very personal love language. An understanding of the Passion of Christ as a model for human love is not new, of course, but it is striking how Lucia repeats this information over and over, insisting on her identification with the figure of Christ.

Lucia Brocadelli's seven revelations are patterned quite closely on a vision book of another important Dominican spiritual leader, Girolamo Savonarola, the text known in Latin and Italian as *The Compendium of Revelation*.[32] The palaces and gardens of Lucia's spiritual journey follow Savonarola so closely that there can be little doubt that she knew his work. But what Savonarola also included in his account is a philosophical framework that includes a rejection of the humors as a motivation, or perhaps an excuse, for sin. In contrast to the thirteenth century, here we see an increased degree of emphasis and a gradually increasing, explicit theorizing of these spiritual insights and theological/psychological habits.

In the *Compendium*, Savonarola meets the devil in the form of an elderly, bearded hermit, and engages him in a lively spiritual debate. At one point the Tempter suggests that Savonarola has such a strong sense of sin because he is possessed by "the spirit of melancholy that makes you think and speak in this manner," or else "this is due to the fact that you are born under a certain constellation that inclines you in this manner, or it is the influence of some planet or some fixed star that makes you talk this way." "Father," Savonarola replies, "I feel nothing in my heart and spirit but the highest joy.... I mean the natural light of reason.... Only fools believe in the influence of the heavens."[33]

We have already seen that Lucia's patron, Ercole d'Este, understood her spiritual powers as coming from God. Her biographer, Fra Serafino Razzi of Florence, also explained her trials as external, saying "she had many persecutions, even from the devil, who appeared to her often and beat her hard."[34] Lucia Brocadelli's story suggests that women's spiritual gifts were indeed, as Elliott suggests, no longer totally "auspicious and vindicatory." Even though Lucia had been a person of enormous spiritual and political power, she was, nevertheless, shut away by Alfonso when he came to power in Ferrara. It does seem that her visionary career is evidence that the locus of that spiritual power Elliott saw changing in the thirteenth century had continued to shift.

Maria Maddalena de' Pazzi

In the second half of the sixteenth century, a Carmelite nun in the convent of Santa Maria degli Angeli in Florence began to experience mystical raptures. Like Lucia Brocadelli and the other *sante vive* of the generation before, this young woman, Maria Maddalena de' Pazzi, acted out the Passion of Christ in her own embodied experience. Unlike Lucia Brocadelli and the other "living saints," however, Maria Maddalena's spirituality was intensely private. She never wanted her raptures to be recorded or read by anyone in the outside world. Had it not been for the teams of her sister nuns (as many as four at a time) who were assigned to record her words and the acts that accompanied them, we would not have any record of Maria Maddalena de' Pazzi's mysticism. The transcriptions made by her companions did not circulate widely and were not even published until the middle of the twentieth century.[35] Until the work of Armando Maggi in the past decade, there has been no secondary work in English on this figure.[36] It would be easy to get the feeling that scholars have rather been avoiding Maria Maddalena de' Pazzi.

When one turns to the visions transcribed in her name, it is not difficult to see why. The few historians who have written on Maria Maddalena de' Pazzi all comment on the intensely oral nature of her texts and its performative quality. The transcriptions preserve not only her words but also the gestures, movements, sighs, mumblings, and silences that frame and give meaning to her mystical vocabulary. Maria Maddalena's raptures are recorded not at all in her own hand, or even in her own words, but through a sort of sacred eavesdropping. As Giovanni Pozzi characterizes the experience of reading Maria Maddalena's works, we hear: "Prolixity, discontinuity, disorder, interruption, digressions, symbolic monstrosities, fallacies, [which] continually stalk the steps of the reader on this itinerary;

on the other hand, the reader is consoled by lyrical effusions, rushes of vehement and eternal passion, ardent speculation, abysmal descent into the core of the human soul, elevations to the threshold of the sublime."[37]

The context of Maria Maddalena's spirituality is the dramatic representations and recreations of Jesuit spirituality, specifically the spirituality of Ignatius of Loyola, the founder of the order. Through the intervention of Ignatius, Jesuits came to replace Carmelite friars as the confessors of Carmelite women's houses, and thus came to have direct influence on Maria Maddalena de' Pazzi.[38] This is a spirituality strongly oriented toward drama and mimesis. Loyola's "Spiritual Exercises" is not a philosophical treatise as much as a how-to book by Ignatius the pragmatic soldier, who knew what motivates human actions. Ideally the exercises are to be experienced, not studied—acted out over the course of a month. Right in the middle, on the fourth day of the second week, Ignatius placed the "Meditation of the Two Standards," a psychodrama in which the soul imagines "a great plain in the region of Jerusalem, where the supreme commander of the good people is Christ our Lord; the other plain in the region of Babylon, where the leader of the enemy is Lucifer." Each leader has a standard, a banner with followers massed under it, and the soul, with the help of the Virgin Mary, is called to make a decision about which side it will choose.[39] At the end of the *Spiritual Exercises* the soul, who presumably has chosen the standard of Christ rather than that of Lucifer, engages in a dramatic mimesis of the earthly life of Jesus, from the Annunciation to Mary to the Ascension.[40]

This type of Ignatian mimetic spirituality is especially visible in one of Maria Maddalena's late works, entitled "Probation." Here we get a description of

> two terrible visions that were always before the eyes of her mind, that is, the vision of the devils and that of the offenses given to God; and sometimes she saw the devils with her corporeal eyes as well. ... God himself had allowed these devils to afflict her body. Indeed, they often pushed her down the stairs, made her fall down; and other times, like venomous vipers, they wrapped around her flesh, biting her with a great cruelty. She was besieged by all kinds of afflictions, sufferings, torments.[41]

It should be noted that one major contrast between this account and the revelations of Lucia Brocadelli is the role of demonic figures. Lucia does not mention persecution by demons, although she does call her brother-in-law "demonio" in the last revelation, and is told by Jesus in the fourth revelation that visions may come from demons.[42] Maria Maddalena de' Pazzi is far more involved with demonic presences than was Lucia Brocadelli.

After staving off the devils, and through the intercession of the Virgin Mary, Maria Maddalena entered into a mimesis of the events of Holy Week, from washing the feet of the disciples on Maundy Thursday to a simulation of the Crucifixion. This was also deeply embodied; when she carried the cross, for example, the recorded account says:

> And it was the thirteenth hour. And she carried [the cross] for a half-hour, walking back to where she had come from. Along the way she suffered very much because sometimes we saw that she was being pushed down with such a violence that she almost fell down. And sometimes she did fall down, but she showed that someone forced her to stand up with vehement blows. This was clear by her exterior acts, as we had imagined it had been done to Jesus. So eloquent were this soul's gestures."[43]

By the middle of the sixteenth century, then, and especially under the influence of Ignatian mimetic spirituality, the external influences on a soul's journey were understood in personified terms. I do not mean to claim that this period of early modern Christianity is the first time in the history of Christian spirituality that an acting out of the Passion of Christ was an important component of Christian devotion. Indeed, as McGinn notes, this is "part of a long trajectory in medieval spirituality."[44] It is, for one thing, an intrinsic part of Franciscan spirituality as it develops, and becomes highly influential, in the later Middle Ages.[45] Similar personal recreation of moments of the Passion of Christ can be seen in what McGinn terms the "new mysticism" that begins around 1200, and is especially characteristic of the Dominican women whose ecstasies and raptures are recorded in the *Sister Books* of late medieval Germany.[46] This "new mysticism" may even be seen to be congruent with the psychologizing tendency of late medieval letters described by Dyan Elliott.

My claim here, however, is that the early modern period takes this a step further. Although neither Ignatius of Loyola nor Maria Maddalena de' Pazzi was exactly a speculative thinker, their graphic descriptions of spiritual experiences give a potent cast of characters: Lucifer, the devil, the Virgin Mary, Christ, caught up in a profoundly theoretical battle. This is not a cosmic battle, in the sense of earlier medieval views of external good and evil at work in the human soul, but deeply interior and psychologized. The soul's struggle to accept or reject these influences was acted out in what we can begin to discern as psychological terms, even though, in contrast to modern psychological theory, it is still understood as part of a divine psychodrama.

Maria Domitilla Galluzzi

The last figure I want to consider, Maria Domitilla Galluzzi, is the least well known to us today. Unlike Lucia Brocadelli (beatified in the eighteenth century) and Maria Maddalena de' Pazzi (canonized in the seventeenth), Maria Domitilla was never officially recognized for her sanctity. But in her own world she was a noted figure, and her autobiography, books of spiritual exercises, writings on the religious life, and collections of letters remain in northern Italian libraries as testimony to her local fame. Very little of this material has yet been published in full or in the original Italian.[47]

Born Severetta Galluzzi in the town of Acqui, Piedmont, Maria Domitilla fulfilled her girlhood ambition to become an enclosed nun on October 19, 1615, at the age of twenty, when she entered the monastery of Capuchin women dedicated to the Blessed Sacrament in Pavia.[48] Her religious vocation had been both encouraged and to some extent stifled by her family, and the autobiographical *Vita* goes to some lengths to portray the devil as the enemy trying to keep her in the world. In chapter 16, Maria Domitilla portrays this as an internal struggle, but one that stems from an external enemy:

> My stomach filled with venom because of the great excitement (I cannot describe it any other way) that God gave me permission to become totally his. But this was not all—if I thought, or reasoned, or heard discussion of becoming a nun, such sharp arrows pierced my soul that I became so breathless that I had leave the discussion, so that I felt less of this most bitter pain and anguish. Then the Enemy took the occasion to suggest to me that I was unworthy of God since I could not hear talk of such good things, except bitterly.[49]

This passage again shows the growth of interiorized human experience of spiritual gifts between the later Middle Ages and the early modern period. Even as a member of the community, Maria Domitilla continues to struggle with her interior life in graphic bodily terms. Early in the novitiate, she fights physically with the devil.[50] Praying before the crucifix one day, she is levitated in conjunction with the wounded Christ: hands to hands, feet to feet, head to head.[51] We can see here influences of many strands of the religiosity of early modern Catholicism, notably the self-scrutiny (and reportage) of Teresa of Avila,[52] and the mimetic devotional practices we have already noted in Ignatian spirituality. In fact, two of Maria Domitilla's works, the *Forty Hours* devotional treatise and the series of visions and spiritual experiences called the *Passione*, are essentially guided devotions based on the events of Christ's Passion.[53] Much like the "Mysteries of the Life of Christ Our Lord" at the end of Loyola's *Spiritual Exercises*,[54] these are not so much visions as exercises, even though the soul can be totally taken up in rapture while carrying them out. Maria Domitilla too had an amanuensis who was assigned to watch her and write down her words.[55] A comparison of the accounts given with the records of the transports of Maria Maddalena de' Pazzi would be very interesting.

Maria Domitilla's cosmology seems to have interiorized the concept of the human microcosm that reflects the cosmic macrocosm. The cosmic is totally identified with the human life of Christ, especially the Passion, and the human participation in this life has become a mimesis of the life of God Incarnate. This interior drama is subject to some outside influences, mostly the pricks and temptations of the devil. By the seventeenth century, of course, there had developed a very elaborate Christian demonology, including the linguistic demonology, "Satan's rhetoric," that has been described recently by Armando Maggi.[56]

The persistence of a firm belief in the powers of the devil can be seen in the description of the 1630 plague of Milan by Maria Domitilla Galluzzi's contemporary Cardinal Federigo Borromeo of Milan. Throughout his plague treatise Borromeo credits demonic forces with the instigation of the "Untori," the poisoners who spread the plague through deliberate malice (and demonic inspiration). Nevertheless, Borromeo's treatise also shows the increased tendency to understand evil as interiorized and psychologized that I have been describing. This outside evil works in conjunction with interior forces, says Borromeo, speaking particularly of the local people in their most ancient name: "The Insubrians incline to anger [*habitu faciles ad iram*] in both body and spirit, they were not able to tolerate those hardships [of a recent famine] and so reduced themselves to accept shameful proposals in order to find an end to their misery."[57]

Here we are confronted with an etiology of the plague (the "Untori," spurred on by the devil) that offends modern sensibilities, but nevertheless there is something almost modern about the scenario in general: the Insubrians have their national character, they have been badly pressed by circumstances, they seek revenge or at least self-expression by spreading the plague.

Cardinal Federigo Borromeo's story about the plague, like the visionary activities of Lucia Brocadelli and Maria Maddalena de' Pazzi and Maria Domitilla Galluzzi, shows us the distance between the cosmologies of the ancient world and of the early modern era. It can be understood, I think, as a continuation of the change noted by so many scholars about the interiorization of cosmology in the twelfth century, and the second shift toward internalizing, especially evil influences, described by Elliott in the late Middle Ages. Indeed, I think it helps us to understand the growth of demonology and the theology of blame (especially of women) at the turn of the modern era. It is important to note that the women studied here never represent themselves as uniquely spiritually gifted because of their female nature and have no explicit idea of feminine spiritual gifts. This is a characteristic accorded them by their male admirers, patrons, and confessors, and by feminist scholars in the twentieth and twenty-first centuries! But their spiritual lives do show a development that is especially, if not uniquely, characteristic of Christian visionary women—the symbolic movement, one might say, from a cosmic drama to psychodrama.

Notes

This paper was presented at the Illinois Medieval Association meeting at the Newberry Library, Chicago, in February of 2001, and published in a slightly different form in the online journal of the Association, *Essays in Medieval Studies* 18 (2001). Many thanks to Alan Frantzen for his generous permission to republish in this venue.

1. For the Seven Deadly Sins, see Morton W. Bloomfield, *The Seven Deadly Sins: An Introduction to the History of a Religious Concept* (East Lansing: Michigan State College Press, 1952); Richard Newhauser, *The Early History of Greed: The Sin of Avarice in Early Medieval Thought and Literature* (Cambridge: Cambridge University Press, 2000); and Jean Leclercq, *The Love of Learning and the Desire for God: A Study of Monastic Culture*, trans. Catharine Misrahi (New York: Fordham University Press, 1961). For a recent study of the multiple contexts of anger in the Middle Ages, see *Anger's Past: The Social Uses of an Emotion in the Middle Ages*, ed. Barbara H. Rosenwein (Ithaca: Cornell University Press, 1998).

2. See George Perrigo Conger, *Theories of Macrocosms and Microcosms in the History of Philosophy* (New York: Columbia University Press, 1922), and Edward

Grant, *Planets, Stars, and Orbs: The Medieval Cosmos, 1200–1687* (Cambridge: Cambridge University Press, 1994). The latter work is clearly more sophisticated and inclusive, although neither gives sufficient attention to the period between 500 and 1000, when some notable thinkers (Boethius, John Scotus Eriugena, Ratramnus of Corbie) were clearly aware of such cosmic ideas as the World-Soul. Grant dismisses early medieval theories of microcosm as "meager, superficial, and often unreliable" (12).

3. Conger, *Macrocosms and Microcosms*, 8–9 for Plato; Augustine, *Confessions* XIII.11.

4. *The "Cosmographia" of Bernardus Silvestris*, trans. Winthrop Weatherbee (New York: Columbia University Press, 1973).

5. Alan of Lille, *The Complaint of Nature*, trans. Douglas M. Moffat (1908; Hamden, Conn.: Archon Books, 1972).

6. Book 4 of the *Etymologiae* discusses diseases and their cures; Book 11 is a compendium of anatomical description. See *Isidori Hispalensis Episcopi Etymologiarum sive Originum Libri XX*, ed. W. M. Lindsay (Oxford: Clarendon Press, 1911) and the discussions in Danielle Jacquart and Claude Thomasset, *Sexuality and Medicine in the Middle Ages*, trans. Matthew Adamson (Princeton: Princeton University Press, 1985), 10–15, and Joan Cadden, *The Meanings of Sex Difference in the Middle Ages: Medicine, Science, and Culture* (Cambridge: Cambridge University Press, 1993), 49.

7. Zirka Filipczak, *Hot Dry Men, Cold Wet Women: The Theory of Humors in Western European Art: 1575–1700* (New York: American Federation of Arts, 1997).

8. Barbara Newman, *Sister of Wisdom: St. Hildegard's Theology of the Feminine* (Berkeley and Los Angeles: University of California Press, 1987), 127; Danielle Jacquart and Claude Thomasset, *Sexualité et savior médical au Moyen Age* (Paris: Presses Universitaires de France, 1985).

9. *Galen on the Passions and Errors of the Soul*, trans. Paul W. Harkins, intro. Walther Riese (Columbia: Ohio State University Press, 1963).

10. Newman, *Sister of Wisdom*, 127–128; William of Conches, *Philosophia* I.23, PL 172:56.

11. Newman, *Sister of Wisdom*, 132, 129.

12. Peter Dronke, *Women Writers of the Middle Ages: A Critical Study of Texts from Perpetua (†203) to Marguerite Porete (†1310)* (Cambridge: Cambridge University Press, 1984), 180.

13. Newman, *Sister of Wisdom*, 131–32; see also her "Hildegard of Bingen: Visions and Validations," *Church History* 54 (1985): 163–75.

14. Jacquart and Thomasset, *Sexuality and Medicine*, 83–84.

15. Dyan Elliott, "The Physiology of Rapture and Female Spirituality," in *Medieval Theology and the Natural Body*, ed. Peter Biller and A. J. Minnis (Rochester, N.Y.: York Medieval Press, 1997), 141–73, at 147 (emphases mine).

16. See especially Bynum, *Holy Feast and Holy Fast:The Religious Significance*

of Food to Medieval Women (Berkeley and Los Angeles: University of California Press, 1987), 238–44, 290–94.

17. One scholar who has extended the terms of this discussion significantly is Ulrike Wiethaus. See her *Ecstatic Transformation: Transpersonal Psychology in the Work of Mechthild of Magdeburg* (Syracuse: Syracuse University Press, 1996), and "Sexuality, Gender, and the Body in Late Medieval Women's Spirituality: Cases from Germany and the Netherlands," *Journal of Feminist Studies in Religion* 7 (1991): 35–52.

18. Bynum's understanding of the connection between a specifically female spirituality and embodiment has been criticized by Bernard McGinn; see his review of *Holy Feast and Holy Fast* in *History of Religion* 28 (1988): 90–92, and his *The Presence of God: A History of Western Christian Mysticism*, vol. 3 of *The Flowering of Mysticism: Men and Women in the New Mysticism (1200–1350)* (New York: Crossroad, 1998), 15–17. This ongoing discussion has also raised the issue of how much of "women's spirituality" is mediated through male confessors and spiritual directors; see especially Catherine M. Mooney, ed., *Gendered Voices: Medieval Saints and Their Interpreters* (Philadelphia: University of Pennsylvania Press, 1999).

19. Aristotle, *Physics* VIII.2.252b, quoted in Conger, *Macrocosms and Microcosms*, 11.

20. This according to Grant, *Planets, Stars, and Orbs*, 31.

21. "Humana vero natura est illa, quae est supra omnia Dei opera elevata et paulo minus angelis minorata, intellectualem et sensibilem naturam complicans ac universa inter se constringens, ut microcosmos aut parvus mundus a veteribus rationabiliter vocitetur." Nicholas of Cusa, *De docto ignorantia* 3.3, in *Opera Omnia*, ed. E. Hoffmann and R. Klibansky (Leipzig: Felix Meiner, 1932), 126–27. See also Pauline Moffitt Watts, *Nicolaus Cusanus: A Fifteenth-Century Vision of Man* (Leiden: E. J. Brill, 1982), 76.

22. Nicholas of Cusa, *Opera Omnia*, 127; Watts, *Nicolaus Cusanus*, 76.

23. Elliott, "Physiology of Rapture," 147, quoting from *De universo*, pt. 2, 3, chap. 13.

24. *De universo* chaps. 20 and 21; Elliott, "Physiology of Rapture," 159.

25. Elliott, "Physiology of Rapture," 159–66.

26. Elliott, "Physiology of Rapture," 167.

27. Heinrich Kramer and Jacob Sprenger, *Malleus maleficarum*, quoted from the translation of Edward M. Peters in *Witchcraft in Europe, 400–1700: A Documentary History*, ed. Alan Charles Kors and Edward Peters, 2nd ed. (Philadelphia: University of Pennsylvania Press, 2001), 188.

28. Elliott, "Physiology of Rapture," 173.

29. Letter of Ercole I, dated March 4, 1500 (Modena, Archivio di Stato, Iurisdizione Sovrano, Santi e Beati 430 A), printed as *Spiritualium personarum feminei sexus facta amiratione digna* (Nuremberg 1501), a tract of twelve unpaginated leaves (six in Latin, six in German). For Lucia Brocadelli, see E. Ann Matter, "Political

Prophecy as Repression: Lucia Brocadelli da Narni and Ercole d'Este," in *Christendom and Its Discontents: Exclusion, Persecution, and Rebellion, 1000–1500*, ed. Scott L. Waugh (Cambridge: Cambridge University Press, 1995), 168–76, and E. Ann Matter, Armando Maggi, Maiju Lehmijoki-Gardner, and Gabriella Zarri, "Le Rivelazioni di Lucia Brocadelli da Narni," *Bollettino della Società Pavese di Storia Patria* 100 (2000): 3–32. The critical edition of Lucia's *Revelations* is "'Le Rivelazioni' of Lucia Brocadelli da Narni," ed. E. Ann Matter, Armando Maggi, and Maiju Lehmijoki-Gardner, *Archivum Fratrum Praedicatorum* 71 (2001): 311–44. The English translation is by E. Ann Matter, "Lucia Brocadelli, *Seven Revelations*," in *Dominican Penitent Women*, ed. Maiju Lehmijoki-Gardner (New York: Paulist Press, 2005), 212–305.

30. This antipathy seems to have been related to Lucia's known connections with Savonarola and his circle; cf. Tamar Herzig, "The Rise and Fall of a Savonarolan Visionary: Lucia Brocadelli's Contribution to the Piagnone Movement," *Archiv für Reformationsgeschichte/Archive for Reformation History* 95 (2004): 34–60.

31. Lucia Brocadelli, "Le Rivelazioni," 325.

32. Girolamo Savonarola, *Compendio di Rivelazioni*, ed. Angela Crucitti (Rome: Angelo Belardetti, 1974); English translation by Bernard McGinn in *Apocalyptic Spirituality* (New York: Paulist Press, 1979), 183–275. I thank Bernard McGinn for pointing out the similarities between this text and Lucia's visions.

33. Ibid., 32 (Italian), 158 (Latin), 213–14 (English).

34. Fra Serafino Razzi, *Seconda parte delle vite de' santi e beati dell'ordine de' frati predicatori nelle quale si raccontano le vita, & opere, di molte Sante, e Beate Donne del medesimo ordine* (Florence: Bartolomeo Sermartelli, 1577), 153.

35. Maria Maddalena de' Pazzi, *Tutte le opere di Santa Maria Maddalena de' Pazzi dai manoscritti originali*, ed. Bruno Nardini, Bruno Visentin, Carlo Catena and Giulio Agresti, 7 vols. (Florence: Nardini, 1960–66).

36. Armando Maggi, *Uttering the Word: The Mystical Performances of Maria Maddalena de' Pazzi, a Renaissance Visionary* (Albany: State University of New York Press, 1998); Maria Maddalena de' Pazzi, *Selected Revelations*, trans. Armando Maggi (New York: Paulist Press, 2000).

37. Giovanni Pozzi, introduction to *Le parole dell'estasi*, by Maria Maddalena de' Pazzi (Milan: Adelphi, 1984), 21, translation mine.

38. Maggi, *Uttering the Word*, 6.

39. Ignatius of Loyola, "A Meditation on the Two Standards," in *Ignatius of Loyola: The Spiritual Exercises and Selected Works*, ed. George E. Ganss et al. (New York: Paulist Press, 1991), 154–55.

40. Ibid., 183–200.

41. de' Pazzi, "Probation," in *Selected Revelations*, 289.

42. Brocadelli, "Le Rivelazioni," 338, 328.

43. de' Pazzi, "Probation," 324.

44. McGinn, *The Flowering of Mysticism*, 59.

45. McGinn, *The Presence of God: A History of Western Christian Mysticism*,

vol. 2, *The Growth of Mysticism* (New York: Crossroad, 1994), 141–42, 174–77; Ewert Cousins, "The Humanity and Passion of Christ," in *Christian Spirituality: High Middle Ages and Reformation*, ed. Jill Raitt (New York: Crossroad, 1987), 375–91; Giles Constable, *Three Studies in Medieval Religious and Social Thought* (Cambridge: Cambridge University Press, 1995), 191–217.

46. McGinn, *The Flowering of Mysticism*, 304–19.

47. For Maria Domitilla Galluzzi see, all by E. Ann Matter: "Per la morte di Suor Maria Domitilla Galluzzi: Una poesia anonima del seicento Pavese," *Poesia: Mensile di cultura politica* 2.12 (1989): 11–14; "The Personal and the Paradigm: The Spiritual Autobiography of Maria Domitilla Galluzzi," in *The Crannied Wall: Women, Religion, and the Arts in Early Modern Europe*, ed. Craig A. Monson (Ann Arbor: University of Michigan Press, 1992), 87–103; "Interior Maps of an Eternal External: The Spiritual Rhetoric of Maria Domitilla Galluzzi d'Acqui," in *Maps of Flesh and Light: The Religious Experience of Medieval Women Mystics*, ed. Ulrike Wiethaus (Syracuse: Syracuse University Press, 1993), 60–73; "The Commentary on the Rule of Saint Clare by Maria Domitilla Galluzzi," in *Creative Women in Medieval and Early Modern Italy: A Religious and Artistic Renaissance*, ed. E. Ann Matter and John Coakley (Philadelphia: University of Pennsylvania Press, 1994), 201–11. And see, most recently, the entry by M. Belardini in the *Dizionario biografico degli Italiani* (Rome, 1998), 51:769–71.

48. Galluzzi, *Vita* 1.20–21 (Milano, Biblioteca Ambrosiana D77 suss., fol. 98r, and H47 suss., fol. 68r).

49. Galluzzi, *Vita* 1.16 (Milano, Biblioteca Ambrosiana G97 suss., fol. 41v): "mi si riempiva lo stomacho di velleno per il gran stimolo (non so dir altro) solo che Dio era quello cio mi permetteva per farmi tutta sua. Ma questo non bastò, s'aggionse che se pensavo o ragionavo o sentivo ragionar d'esser monaca m'erano tante accute saette che mi trafigevano il cuore, si che arivò a tal segno il mio affano ch'ero sforzata partirmi da dove si ragionava di queste cose, ultimamente mi sentivo venir meno da questo mio accerbissirno dolore et affano. Pigliò occasione il nemico di suggerirmi ch'ero indegna di Dio, puoiche non puotevo sentire raggionare di cose tanto buone, si che amaramente."

50. Galluzzi, *Vita* 1.23 (1616) (Biblioteca Ambrosiana G97 suss., fols. 65v–70r; also in D77 suss., H47 suss., A276 suss., and I41 suss.).

51. Pavia, Biblioteca Universitaria, MS Aldini 3069–*Passione*, fols. 3r–4r. This account is also found, with minor variants, at the beginning of book 2 of the *Vita* in the Biblioteca Ambrosiana G97 suss., fols. 234v–235v. For further analysis of this passage, see Matter, "Interior Maps."

52. The best example of this is her autobiography, Teresa of Avila, *Libro de la vida*, ed. Dámaso Chicharro (Madrid: Cátedra, 1982), translated by E. Allison Peers as *The Life of Teresa of Jesus: The Autobiography of St. Teresa of Avila* (Garden City, N.Y.: Doubleday, 1960).

53. The treatise entitled *Quarant'hora di meditatione mentale* is known only in one manuscript, Biblioteca Ambrosiana B199 suss. The *Passione*, which also is copied

as book 2 of the *Vita*, is found in Biblioteca Ambrosiana G97 suss.; Milano, Biblioteca Trivulziana 268 and 490; Pavia, Biblioteca Universitaria 145 and 306; and in private collections in Pavia and Acqui Terme.

54. Ignatius of Loyola, *Spiritual Exercises*, 183–200.

55. These raptures are known from the written testimony of Maria Domitilla Galluzzi's assistant, Suor Beatrice Avite, in letters appended as book 3 of the *Vita*, in Biblioteca Ambrosiana G97 suss.; Milano, Biblioteca Trivulziana 268; and Pavia, Biblioteca Universitaria 306.

56. Armando Maggi, *Satan's Rhetoric: A Study of Renaissance Demonology* (Chicago: University of Chicago Press, 2001).

57. "... cumque Insubri animi simul et corporis habitu faciles ad iram haec feree mala diutius non possent consilio attroci animum adiecere ut miseris suis per scelera finem invenirent." Federigo Borromeo, *La Peste di milano del 1630 (De pestilentia, quae Mediolani anno MDCXXX magnam stragem edidit)*, ed. Armando Torno (Milano: Rusconi, 1998), 64.

2

The Allegorical Construction of Female Feeling and *Forma*

Gender, Diabolism, and Personification in Hildegard of Bingen's *Ordo Virtutum*

James J. Paxson

The thematic or historical study of women's emotions in medieval representation must come to grips with the almost universal fact that, from early on, human emotions had to be embodied or personified *as* women. The massive literary and pictorial record of allegorical personifications cast as women provides grounds for theorizing the rhetorical agency of gender and emotions. We might find it convenient to schematize these grounds and their relations as an antimetabole or chiasmus in our own critical discourse through structural and semiotic analysis of the *gender of emotions*, a new model of the *emotions of gendered human subjects*—of women, in this book's case—can possibly emerge. That personified emotions and faculties of the human mind have female gender inflects or constructs mutually the actual emotions of female-gendered persons. The paralogical energy of antimetabole, the master trope of inverted cola in a sentence or logical expression (AB→BA), empowers this rhetorical possibility *par la dissémination*, as Derrida would put it.[1] We must look to the representational nature of these female personifications as closely as we look to the representations of women who enjoy or suffer emotions in the literary and artistic record of the Middle Ages, for if women could be defined in medieval thought in terms of strong emotions, tendencies, and even organs or localities in the body,[2] the overarching logic (or paralogic) of reification, personification, embodiment in rhetorical troping might serve as an important intellectual or conceptual adjunct to the sorts of historical studies collected in this volume. Although rhetorical deconstruction and structural semiotics have been passed by in the fashions of current literary theory, they still hold promise for very unusual medieval works engorged with the semiosis of allegory. This may be especially so for the dramatically simple though theologically rich narratives or dramas by a mystical writer such as Hildegard of Bingen.

From Prudentius's warring Ira in *Psychomachia* to Deguileville's Anger in *Pèlerinage de la Vie Humaine* (known well in late Middle English through an anonymously translated version, *Pilgrimage of the Lyfe of the Manhode*, and through John Lydgate's early fifteenth-century "Englished" version), allegory presents its personified viragos or sibyls in flamboyant form, just as all literature seems to overdetermine the emotions of women in ideologically, psychically, or rhetorically significant ways. The actions of personificational women and especially of female personified emotions must perforce be excessive; the *effictiones* and *notationes* that constitute their characterizations seem always overdetermined according to literary habit, as the examples of Anger from Prudentius and from Deguileville show.[3] Indeed, their own semiotic characters exceed the forms stamped on them, conforming eventually to actual gender-bending as witnessed within an historically late allegory such as Langland's *Piers Plowman*.[4] But another kind of gender transformation obtains historically as well—one traditionally treated only in descriptive literary history: personification allegory gradually shifts away from all-female personifications to a mix of male and female ones through the High Middle Ages, until male figures even outnumber female ones, certainly in the English literary tradition as witnessed in the late medieval Langland and in early modern allegorists such as Bunyan or Gray.

I cannot trace the historical and ideological vectors that make up this particular problem—the masculinization of personified character in late medieval and early modern poetics—in this short essay on Hildegard of Bingen's allegorical poetics. But I intend to help frame that problem, and to pursue further the antimetabolaic paralogic central to my essay's place in this volume, by taking up what could be thought of as a programmatic, indeed inaugural, moment in the literary history of female personifications—Hildegard's dramatically stark but musically beautiful *Ordo Virtutum* that dates to the 1150s. Hildegard's antiphonal play of the Virtues can serve as a test case for the normativity of didactic personification allegory. Its stark plot structure tells the medieval audience or readership (Hildegard's own nuns in her abbey, on the most local of scales) just what embodied and dramatized abstractions are supposed to teach them about their inner selves, and about what women in particular should embrace as their spiritual models of behavior.

In taking up this inaugural text which served as a didactic moral model for nuns, however, we might be still more taken by the intransigent force framed by Hildegard's representation of the virtues: the character Diabolus. The figure is the only male (with the exception of the Patriarchs who actually frame the starting action of the play), the only non-singing and the only nonpersonified character in the play.[5] He thereby represents a domain of knowledge and an ontological status sharply cut off from those of the Virtues and other female personified faculties or experiences while he turns out to be somehow aware of their semiotic structures but in subaltern terms. Maleness should represent the height of cosmic order and normativity in the medieval ontotheological picture, while femaleness might typically represent the subaltern. Personification too stands as a trope of absolute otherness, as the favorite trope of "allegory"—the *allos* of *allegorein* (*allos agoreuein*, "*other*-speak") being invoked here—given what might be expected about the conventional literary or dramatic representation of actual human character (human character being represented via the devices *effictio*, *notatio*, and *ethopeia* or *eidolopeia*). Yet Hildegard's programmatic play upsets as it tries to uphold these systemic values. Even brief focus on the play's characterizations will begin to show the strangeness in Hildegard's otherwise heterodox allegorical poetics, while my treatment of this strange dramatical specimen sets the stage for some theoretical pronouncements about the rhetorical and semiotic forces at work in "personification's gender" broadly construed in medieval representation. The minimal problem of categorizing Hildegard's female protagonists—as "emotions," "experiences," "faculties of mind," "virtues"—obtains in *Ordo virtutum*; yet self-reflective *knowledge* of such categorical status compounds this minimal but not infrequent confusion. Our task as reader of the *Ordo* seems more difficult than at first sight.

In carrying out these tasks, I will test the limits of Hildegard's allegorical poetics by testing the historical limits of the master trope prosopopeia itself (*prosopopeia* being the rhetorical term for personification). That is to say, I will employ one of the historically "terminal" theories of personification, Paul de Man's theory of the master trope of poetic discourse which dissipates ontological solidity and disrupts epistemological stability rather than ensuring it, in order to understand the relation of the numinous female personifications to the salacious and vulgar Diabolus. The tactic will support conclusions not just about what I find is the very font of late medieval dramatical personification allegory—the dramatically static *Ordo virtutum*—but about the seeming dead end of theory's long absorption in prosopopeia as it was theorized by (or, dare I say, embodied in) the thought of de Man.[6]

*   *   *

Whereas the bulk of critical work done on the *Ordo virtutum* (Play of the Virtues) has been on Hildegard's pioneering musical forms and, more recently, on the phenomenology of female creativity as realized through the author's social and biographical context,[7] little has as yet been said about the dramatic characterology realized as a semiotic sign system. Hildegard's secretary Volmar, well known as the only male person who lived among the nuns of Hildegard's order, has been analogized to the singular male devil in the play;[8] and this has been about as far as the gender theorization has gotten. Readers seem comfortable with the straightforward meanings of the human mental faculties and emotions embodied in the play's characters. But the rhetorical and semiological model I shall propose should clarify the relationship between Diabolus and the Virtues in ways that seem simple on first inspection but that set up for us the intensely self-reflexive turns that would come to characterize the great allegories following the twelfth century.

The action of the *Ordo virtutum* comes off as simple, static, perhaps algebraically reductive, though an action with structural precedent in allegorical poetics: somewhat as in Prudentius's *Psychomachia*, a formal division corresponds to an ontological one whereby actual or "historical" biblical personages stand apart from and observe the doings of human virtues and faculties of mind. In the *Ordo virtutum*, the Old Testament Patriarchs and Prophets, who are markedly male and "historical" personages, comment in the play's very first line, really in the dramatic role of collective *prologus*, upon the numinous (or indeed nebulous) feminine energies: "Qui sunt hi, qui ut nubes?"[9] The "cloudlike" Virtues proclaim themselves to be the illuminational source of Christ himself, as the building blocks of their heavenly groom's very limbs ("Verbum dei clarescit in forma hominis, / et ideo fulgemus cum illo, / edificantes membra sui pulcri corporis" 160). And in so doing, they initiate the series of antiphonal responses, or self-proclamations, of each Virtue. This personification thus serves as a kind of actional first link in a programmatic chain delineating the qualities of the individual human body (*forma hominis*) and the *cor-*

pus mysticum of Christ. That Anima, focal personification in so many of the cosmic allegories of the later Middle Ages (such as Bernardus Silvestris's contemporary *Cosmographia*), must be at first signally *felix* underscores the normative state of affairs that this particular *female* property—for personifications in Hildegard's poetics must perforce be female (more about which below)—celebrates that most proper of emotional states belonging to the well-regulated woman in patriarchal culture.

Felix Anima:
O dulcis divinitas, et o suavis vita,
in qua perferam vestem preclaram,
illud accipiens quod perdidi
in prima apparitione,
ad te suspiro, et omnes Virtutes invoco. (160)

[Oh sweet divinity, oh gentle life,
in which I shall wear a radiant robe,
receiving that which I lost
in my first manifestation—
I sigh for you, and invoke all the Virtues.]

The opening invocation programs the actions or prayers of all the subsequent Virtues: each will in turn proclaim herself as a Platonic embodiment at the thematic level. But Happy Soul or Felix Anima fails to ascend to the Virtues, with whom she has been communicating through song, once she realizes her embodied nature and receives the beguiling jibes of Diabolus. Only the testimony of each Virtue or human faculty can brace her for reunion with them, and the sole transformation sequence, placed in the context of the unidimensional Virtues, has involved Soul from her joyful state to *infelix*, and back, at the play's conclusion, to purity and reintegration with the community of Virtues.

Although the ethical picture afforded by the play marks a static and robust simplicity, the semiotic mechanism of "characterization" also grounds itself as a kind of germinal and reductive effect. While in their own spoken discourses the cloudlike or airy figures ("ut nubes") employ ecphonesis or apostrophe ("*O dulcis divinitas*"), following Felix Anima's most programmatic of self-ascriptions regarding action (she sighs regularly, "Ad te suspiro"), they may in a sense *be* airy or breathy entities. They are not not just Platonic spirits at the thematic level but the linguistic pulsions of air that mark or initiate a semiotic prosopopeia or personification. It may be of structural importance that apostrophe, which Jonathan Culler has described as the corollary of prosopopeia (personification)—that trope being, of course, the mechanism whereby allegorical fictions embody abstractions as human and sentient persons—recurs so frequently in the speeches and songs of Hildegard's Virtues. The "O" of apostrophe Culler has interpreted as the signature of pure *vox*, the marginal property of language itself (largely in Romantic poetics) and the image of human *spiritus* or *pneuma*.[10] Comprising the succeeding itinerary of singing and praising personifications—a sequence that includes recognizable figures including Scientia Dei, Humilitas, Caritas, Timor Dei, Obedientia, Fides, Spes, Castitas, Innocentia, Contemptus Mundi, Amor Caelestis, Disciplina, Verecundia, Misericordia, and Victoria—are lyrical effusions, mostly epideictic, though now and then condemnatory (and, against Diabolus, entirely so). The personifications thereby function minimally, both as thematic props and as semiotic engines built around the pneum(at)ic force of sentience, voice, linguistic address. They are effusions of air or cloud that undergo discursive conversion to lyrical outbursts of joy or praise or respect or derision; and so, we can understand the semiotic and psychodynamic operation of the minimalistic dramatical *sententiae* that comprise a lengthy prayer cast as a *ludus*, a play.

Back on the thematic level of the play's ethical structure, Felix Anima, Timor Dei (Fear of God), and Amor Caelestis (Love of Heaven) might be taken as the emotional regulators controlling the tone and psychic bearing of Hildegard's divine and dramatic hymn.[11] These normative emotions of real women (joy or happiness, fear or respect, and love) guide the action, or program the very being, of all the personified Virtues; correspondingly, prosopopeia stands as the most effective and apparently stable trope for expressing salutary human emotions best configured as feminine psychic or social attributions. On the semiotic plane of rhetoric's generative structure, the ecphonetic or apostrophic "O" mimics the psychic dynamics of the simple and sanctioned emotions—joy, fear and obedience, hope, contempt of the world, shamefastness, mercy, and victory—that largely constitute the play's Virtue community. Their social values as well mark suitably symbolic psychic posturing of the female in a male, patriarchal society.

Diabolus, however, embodies something markedly masculine and epistemologically alien to the conditions and self-ascriptions of the Virtues. If the female personifications extol joy, love, and fear (of God) as their most programmatic registers, Diabolus assaults these emotional registers directly:

> *Virtutes*:
> O Timor, valde utilis es nobis:
> habemus enim perfectum studium
>   numquam a te separari.
> *Diabolus*:
> Euge! euge! quis est tantus timor? et quis est tantus amor? Ubi est
>   pugnator, et ubi est remunerator? Vos nescitis quid colitis. (166)

> [*Virtues*:
> Fear, you can help us greatly:
> we are filled with the longing
>   never to part from you.
> *Diabolus*:
> Bravo! Bravo! What is this great fear, and this great love? Where is
>   the champion? Where the prize-giver? You don't even know
>   what you are worshipping!]

This line of attack carried out by Diabolus, one of an epistemological nature since it concerns the knowledge domain of the personified Virtues, picks up momentum later on, even after the Virtues rebuff his initial insults. Toward the finale of the play and following the Virtues' steadfast adherence to their ethical moorings, Diabolus shrieks at Castitas or Chastity in particular:

> Tu nescis quid colis, quia venter tuus vacuus est pulcra forma de viro
> sumpta—ubi transis preceptum quod deus in suavi copula precepit;
> unde nescis quid sis! (178)

> [You don't know what you are nurturing, for your belly is devoid of
> the beautiful form that woman receives from man; in this you transgress the command that God enjoined in the sweet act of love; so you
> don't even know what you are!]

Diabolus impugns Chastity, as an icon for all human womanhood, for not bringing forth children. On the theologically and typologically charged thematic level, Chastity had invited Diabolus's taunts by proclaiming herself to be an abstract type for Mary, so designating herself via one of Hildegard's most famous formulations—"in virginea forma dulce miraculum colui" (178; in a virgin form I nurtured a sweet miracle)—rejecting the combative language and thinking of Diabolus.

But the strange invective furthers the self-reflexive language of rhetoric's programmatic tropes conceived as generative semiotic engines again, said tropes enabling Hildegard's fiction in the first place. Indeed, the phrase *suavi copula*, which might warrant a more vulgar English rendering ("sweet or soft fucking"), as well invokes the grammatical purview of the term *copula*, an expression that was itself overdetermined grammatically and ethically in medieval thought. The concept marks the verbal "is" of grammatical predication (X is Y) and of ontological being itself. Diabolus ironically concludes with an allusion to a kind of knowledge he might enjoy while the personification Chastity or Castitas might not: *unde nescis quid sis*—"you don't know what you *are*"—that is, "you are a rhetorical personification or embodied abstraction"! This rhetorically or poetically self-reflexive innuendo conflicts with the intuitively obvious meaning of the phrase: "You are supposed to be a sexually and reproductively endowed woman who, through being chaste, misses her reason for being."

The logic governing my conclusion here is complex in that it programs too the semiotics of medieval rhetoric's tropes. I have already asserted that apostrophe, as evinced in the telltale "O" which signifies pure vocal exhalation, stands as the corollary of prosopopeia. Every apostrophized abstraction or nonhuman thing implies that that thing is conscious, personified. And the personification of numinous or airy entities enables Hildegard's minimalistic narrative or dramatic poetics in the first place. Moreover, it can be said that the starkly plosive gust initiating the programmatic and symbolic (of prosopopeia) ecphonesis or apostrophe fits in with the normative and simple emotions (joy, fear, and the like) characteristic of female consciousness and personhood in a patriarchal universe, local or cosmic. But the textual "presence" of a personified agent, fully realized as a dramatic personage on a play stage, represents in semiotic terms the actions of the grammatical and ontological copula that determines a whole spectrum of rhetorical tropes. This further set of values once again turns the *Ordo virtutum* into a symbolic staging or dramatization of rhetoric's deep structure and not just of theology and ethics.

The grammatical copula is the "is" of any syntactical predication: "X is a human." It thus serves, according to Aristotle, as the grammatical determinant in the most prominent and aesthetically pleasing of the master tropes, metaphor. And so the long-standing example of a metaphor, the trope that violates a received ontology: Achilles *is* a lion.[12] The example shows how a grammatical relationship consequently underwrites or programs an ontological—and a corporeal—relationship at what we might think of as the "meta-metaphorical" or metafigural level, since the rhetorical and grammatical dimensions of metaphorical and syntactical copulas find analogy in the copulating human body.[13] Aristotle first distinguished simile from metaphor by alluding to the (metafigural) imagery of the human phallus as the engine of bodily copulation or sexual union. According to Aristotle, simile was "equal to metaphor in all but its copula," which caused simile to be less beautiful or attractive and thus aesthetically inferior. This distinction among the gendered qualities of the tropes and figures, which is redolent of biological pronouncements about masculine and feminine animal bodies in *De generatione* and *De metaphysica*, programs Aristotle's thinking about aesthetic and ontological superiority or inferiority in the *Rhetoric*.[14] Female is to simile as male is to metaphor. More precisely, simile "is a metaphor differing only by the addition of a word [*metafora diapherousa prosthesei*], wherefore it is less pleasant because it is longer."[15] We might be struck by the ironic fact that the phallus, a superadded or excrescent corporeal limb, surpasses metafigurally the graphic or phonic "prosthesis" of simile, a prosthesis that isomorphically indicates the figure's ontological and epistemological inferiority, its lack or hole. The whole system of thought, however, merely underpins what Jan Ziolkowski has so convincingly shown: grammar and rhetoric, with all the latter's attendant tropes and the system's insistence on punning on *copula*'s simultaneously sexual and merely grammatical values, would inescapably get represented through sexual terminology in works of literature. If grammar was a subset of ethics, Hildegard's similarly sexualized allegory of rhetoric upholds her ethical imperatives as did the pronouncements of Alan of Lille.[16]

As Shirley Sharon-Zisser has well documented, theories of phallic power, ontological presence, and rhetorical *energia* depend on this philosophical resolution.[17] Paramount are the findings of Georges Bataille and of course Jacques Lacan. In his own monumental study on the philosophical agency of metaphor entitled "The Solar Anus," Bataille emphasizes that "the *copula* of [grammatical or syntactical] terms is no less irritating than the *copulation* of bodies," a condition that urges him to conclude with his most lurid and volatile of aphorisms about poetic metaphor: "And when I scream I AM THE SUN an integral erection results, because the verb *to be* is the vehicle of amorous frenzy."[18] Metaphor rules as master trope over the inferior figure simile; simile expresses itself on the metafigural level as metaphor manqué since it lacks metaphor's phallic status and more efficacious, aesthetically compact copulative power.

The sexualization of grammatical and ontological as well as lexical relations in the philosophical systems of Aristotle and then Bataille organizes Lacan's claim that the verb "to be" and the logical or dialectical copula "is" has phallic resonance, functioning as the signifier of a woman's "own desire in the body of him to whom she addresses her demand for love."[19] For Lacan, the phallic signifier serves as "the most tangible element in the real of sexual copulation, and also the most symbolic in the literal (typographical) sense of the term, since it is equivalent ... to the (logical) copula."[20] In the structuralist scheme begun by Bataille and resolved by Lacan, we see the ontological, epistemological, and phenomenological statuses of the master tropes simile and metaphor as contingent upon metafigural images of sexualized bodies.

Personification in turn joins the structural spectrum comprising metaphor and simile as Aristotle, Bataille, and Lacan have defined them. Metaphor and simile, in short, have undergone a process of binarization in the aforementioned structural economy. The binarism records the oppositionality of gender and biological embodiment (male/female), an opposition correlative to the staging of (phallic) presence itself. Its further corollary might lie in the rhetorical distinction between "primary" and "secondary" personification. As theorists of medieval rhetoric and poetics including Morton Bloomfield, William Strange, David Lawton, Lavinia Griffiths, and myself have argued, readers of personification allegory need to distinguish between the so-called "simple animate metaphors" that inhabit the narratological level of *narrative discourse* in a text and the true or "full" personified characters that inhabit the narratological level of *narrative story* and that can thereby interact and dialogue with, in moment-by-moment real time, human characters beside them.[21] Once again, a grammatico-ontological copula distinguishes the ontic plenitude separating full-scale narrative personification—the kind that can be further enhanced by dramatic presentation itself—from local or ornamental discursive personification. Proof comes in a cryptic scene, for instance, toward the conclusion of the B text of *Piers Plowman*: the actual "presence" of the personification character Elde (Old Age) depends upon whether we read a programmatic zeugma about Will the narrator's sex life, as he has claimed that his own phallic power ceases once his "lyme" has been "forbeten" by "Elde and heo" (that is, Old Age and his wife, Kit) after many years of marriage.²² Do we take "old age" as a local animate metaphor that has taken Will's own penile power? Or do we take Old Age as an interloper in Will's nuptial bed who has worn down the protagonist's masculine member? The rhetorical and ontological distinction between narratologically different kinds of personification hangs upon the imagined image of a bodily copulation enabled by phallic *energia*. Personification apprehended as local animate metaphor, as mere ornament, has always enjoyed the efficacy of no more than simile; but narrative personification fabulation seizes the *is-ness* of metaphor, transcoding the figural *as* the literal.

This excursus into the philosophy of rhetoric through a sketch of its erotic and psychic mechanisms provides a platform upon which to build a new apparatus for understanding how Hildegard's female-gendered personifications lack or gain ontological and epistemological plenitude; and it imparts through this apparatus ways of reseeing Hildegard's male Diabolus, holder of privileged knowledge in relation to the necessarily gendered female personifications of the *Ordo virtutum*.

To summarize quickly, we have seen how, drawing on Lacanian theory, we can rewrite the textual generation of personification characters as the building up, and the disposition in a structural spectrum, of related tropes each determined by the status of a grammatico-ontological copula. Metaphor holds prime place in the Aristotelian economy of presence and agency owing to the phallic "is" of its copula. Simile's place is secondary, owing to its semiotic role analogous to the phallus manqué, to its "lack" of aesthetic superiority as represented in the "is like" of its copula. Personification understood as real character invention corresponds to the ontic plenitude of metaphor, while personification understood as simple animate metaphor suffers from ontic lack. Whereas metaphor and simile admit a grammatical copula that stands in for an ontological one, personification—its first, superior variety always serving as a literalized version of the more figural, second variety anyway—further literalizes the image of a copulating body in order to make the semiotic distinction between its narrative and its merely discursive variety. That "old age" can be taken as Old Age at the conclusion of *Piers Plowman* B depends on an imagined bodily copulation.

In a correspondingly overladen moment concerning the semiotics of the text's master tropes, *Ordo virtutum* foregrounds the imagery of copulating bodies in order to question the ontological and epistemological status of Hildegard's personified Virtues *qua personifications*. Diabolus charges: "you transgress the command that God enjoined in the sweet act of love [*suavi copula*]; so you don't even know what you are [*unde nescis quid sis*]!" The expression, used vulgarly in the devil's carnivalesque discourse, carries a fully grammatical and ontological capacity. What the succeeding claim, "you know not *what* you are," implies, to repeat, is not so much that the Virtues lack the knowledge that, as sentient beings, they should have been engendered, and should engender, via sexual commerce; rather, it implies that they should have self-conscious knowledge of themselves as personifications, as only linguistically generated entities. The phrase is one of the few starkly direct examples in allegory of a reference to a personification's ontological status: "you know not that you are a personified abstraction." Such self-reflexive moments, in which the rhetorical machinery of personification allegory becomes a topical issue within a character's speech, are rare in Western literature. Indeed, an historically climactic example comes in the sacred *autos* of Calderón de la Barca five centuries after Hildegard when we witness the personification of Allegory herself in a similarly strange dramatic episode.[23] In Hildegard's play, Diabolus seems to enjoy an epistemologically select position which can name the state of the personifications' nonknowledge as textual entities; he moreover attaches that knowledge to an image of literal copulation, the bodily instantiation of the grammatical or ontological copula that the philosophy of rhetoric can find inhering in the semiotic structures of the master tropes.

In Bakhtinian terms, Diabolus embodies a spectrum of linguistic forms ranging from the vulgar and carnivalesque (he speaks in prose while he rants at and insults the Virtues) to the philosophically privileged or hieratic. The Virtues occupy a discursive place amounting to a semantic ground-zero, or degree-zero, as they offer their own monological utterances of praise or blame.[24] Hildegard's dramatically reductive schema represents the gendered status quo of this system; and it would be instructive for us to look further into the self-reflexive quality of female personification figuration in terms of the history of rhetoric in large and of Hildegard's poetics in particular. In short, it is important to account for Hildegard's dramatic personification in light of the fact that early personification characters from classical and medieval allegory were necessarily women. Much has been done to explain this effect using grammatical formalism[25]—that is, the traditional rationale that personified characters must be female because the gender of abstract nouns, especially in Latin, were always feminine.

Although nothing could seem more fundamental than grammatical correspondence (if feminine gender, then female embodiment), the rhetorical dissemination of energies that enables and empowers the tropes and figures makes for an explanatory scheme in which femininity, embodiment, and figuration seem even more inescapably tied together at deep structural levels. In classical rhetorical theory, particularly of the Roman stamp as exhibited in the authoritative pronouncements of Quintilian, persuasive discourse often amounted to the sheer inventory of figures that exemplified the binarism of inside/outside in order to convey the notion of deformation, deviation, or deception regarding truth claims.[26] Since this process involved concealment, masking, or translating an interior into an exterior, rhetoric as a duplicitous action would be automatically associated with any kind of embodiment to begin with, and subsequently with an embodiment involving sartorial or cosmetic dressing up, mantling, and seduction. Quintilian had conceived of the rhetorical terms *forma* and *figura* as applied "to any form in which thought is expressed, just as it is to bodies [*sicut in corporibus*] which, whatever their composition, must have some shape [*utique habitus est aliquis*]" (9.1.10).[27] The *habitus* ("shape" or "state of dress") more often than not acquired a feminine quality in the excessive public rhetoric of the empire, as Quintilian had early on complained in the *Institutes*:

> For we have come to regard direct and natural speech as incompatible with genius, while all that is in any way abnormal is admired as exquisite. Similarly we see that some people place a higher value on figures which are in any way monstrous or distorted [*prodigiosis corporibus*] than they do on those who have not lost any of the advantages of the normal form of man [*habitu boni*]. There are even some who are captivated by the shams of artifice and think that there is more beauty in those who pluck out superfluous hair or use depilatories, who dress their locks by scorching them with the curling iron. (2.5.11–12)

In this jeremiad, Quintilian begins by discussing "natural speech," that is, the controlled use of figures and tropes in persuasion, but goes on to confuse rhetorical figures with actual bodies (*corpora*). The central point is that public rhetoric has seen a universal and programmatic shift from masculine comportment in speech, iconized in the "normal form of man" (*habitus* [*vir*] *bonus*), to that which is sexually hybrid, perhaps monstrous, though definitely feminine as the cosmetic tally indicates. Rhetorical troping itself thus comes to be identified with the phenomenology of the female human body.

The realization, one central to the probative ideology of Roman public life, of course involves an ontological blunder, a cognitive misprision, in its own right. But once late classical or early medieval ideological and rhetorical systems could proclaim figuration to be interchangeable with femininity, they could make a further cognitive error in linking femininity with personification because that trope in particular could be identified with figuration or tropological masking more than any of the other tropes and figures. The classical name of the trope bears this out perforce: prosopopeia comes from *prosopon poiein*, "to make a face or mask." Masks, faces, facades involve the same semiotic economy that programs the classical notion of figure and of femininity—an economy comprising the binarisms inside/outside, substrate/surface, invisible/visible, primary/secondary, true self/false self. To personify the concept of personification, rhetoric's self-reflexive trope par excellence, would by necessity demand the deployment of female forms or bodies in an actual narrative.

Diabolus's remarks therefore resonate with this ideologically charged and historically determined (in the way that mere grammatical formalism cannot adduce historical force) state of affairs. The male Diabolus reflects an epistemologically privileged subject position which stands outside the tropological association of femininity and personificational status. This is ironic, of course, since Diabolus lacks the moral primacy enjoyed by the personified Virtues, a condition that places him outside the moral economy established by God for the Virtues that constitute human consciousness and life. But as one might expect in the sort of poststructural rhetorical analysis I have sketched in this essay, moral systems are often at odds with tropological systems; the privileging factors in the two systems place signal "characters" such as Diabolus—who are in semiotic terms sign functions to begin with—under deconstruction (Diabolus as morally excluded agent versus Diabolus as epistemologically privileged agent).

This resolution shows how postmodern allegorical models of the sort crafted by Paul de Man can reconfigure even the most monumental and dramatically reductive of personification allegories from the Middle Ages. If Christian ethics of the liberatory sort envisioned by Hildegard of Bingen could empower women and elevate the female form along with female feelings as a legitimate human register, the tropological or metafigural systems used to generate the requisite dramatic personifications could reinstall the pre-Christian ideological status of rhetoric in which masculinity was equated to the privileged subject position lacked in the feminine.

This sexual or gender "dimorphism" existing at purely imaginary or symbolic levels "inside" rhetoric's deep structure determines as well the sets of distinctions that stand between phallic metaphor and similaic "lack," two tropes interrelated in terms of their ontological copulas. The *Ordo virtutum* may present female or human feelings in deific dimensions; but its deep structural elements *capture* its female protagonists in a kind of rhetorical or semiotic determinism.[28]

Hildegard's *Ordo virtutum* therefore stands as one of the final, dramatically reductive allegorical set pieces that "narrate" the semiotic armature of personification allegory through a cast of entirely female personification characters prior to the mixing up of male and female personifications in the allegories of the later Middle Ages—prior to allegories best exemplified in a composition such as de Lorris and de Meun's *Roman de la rose* or Langland's *Piers Plowman*. As a programmatic set piece conveying Christian metaphysical and moral truths, it provides an occulted counternarrative about the ideological value of the master trope prosopopeia and the social coding of female feeling and form in the patriarchal culture of the Middle Ages. If feminist criticism treats Hildegard's amplification of the potential role and powers of women in the intellectual world of the twelfth century, her play strangely compromises that benefit. And just as I have only hinted at the structural importance of Hildegard's "full-scale" personifications in a dramatic medium, so I would have to further theorize, were time and space plentiful enough at this conclusion, how Hildegard transforms and projects herself into the stripped-down rhetorical universe of her personification *ordo*. Some thoughts from Joan Ferrante help in this final formulation: "Hildegard . . . presents the contrast between what she says of herself in the first person and what she says to those she is addressing. Sometimes, of course, she claims to be speaking with the voice of God, which, if not a fictional character, is surely the equivalent of the allegorical women in Hrotsvit's plays and Christine's narratives."[29] In league with her theological, ethical, and mystical projects is Hildegard's poetic devotion to the deep structures of rhetoric and grammar. Such devotion feels both self-conscious and unconscious at times. As the most innovative woman writer and thinker of the twelfth century, as one invested in the transformation of women regarding spiritual and perhaps earthly power, Hildegard of Bingen dispenses literature's master tropes with the self-conscious aplomb of her contemporary allegorists Alan of Lille and Bernardus Silvestris.

Notes

1. For antimetabole's customary definition, see Richard A. Lanham, *A Handlist of Rhetorical Terms*, 2nd ed. (Berkeley and Los Angeles: University of California Press, 1991), 14; see Jeanne Fahnestock, *Rhetorical Figures in Science* (New York and Oxford: Oxford University Press, 1999), 122–55, for antimetabole's power to organize whole fields of thought (modern physics especially) as a cognitive mode; and on the "supplemental" or disseminatory powers of rhetorical tropes based in the binary oppositions that tropes transcend or overpower, see Jacques Derrida, *Dissemination*, trans. and intro. Barbara E. Johnson, (Chicago: University of Chicago Press, 1981), 25.

2. The reification or locating of emotions in women's bodily organs was widespread in the Galenic medical thought of the Middle Ages; the conceit has its corollary as well in the likening of body parts or powers to components of the state. See Carole Rawcliffe, *Sources for the History of Medicine in Medieval England* (Kalamazoo, Mich.: Medieval Institute Publications, 1995), 11.

3. Prudentius, vol. 1, trans. H. J. Thomson, Loeb Classical Library (Cambridge, Mass.: Harvard University Press, 1949): "hanc procul Ira tumens, spumanti fervida rictu, / sanguinea intorquens subfuso lumina felle" (lines 113–15); *The Pilgrimage of the Lyf of the Manhode, from the French of Guillaume de Deguileville*, ed. William Aldis Wright (1869; New York: AMS Press, 1975), 133: "Thilke olde was disgysee For with poyntes she was armed al aboute as an irchoun Bi a baudrike she hadde a sithe and in hire handes she hadde twey calliowns greye And as me thoughte fyre com out of hem bi hire visage And wel j telle yow al were it that with oute woodshipe she was it seemede not soo In hire mouth she hadde a sawe but what to doone there with j ne wiste if firt j ne askede hire"; see too *The Pilgrimage of the Life of Man, Englisht by John Lydgate, A.D. 1426*, ed. F. J. Furnivall, EETS e.s. 77, 83, 92 (London: Kegan Paul, Trench, Trübner, 1899–1904), 418–19, lines 15543–58:

Thanne off me, thus yt be-fyl.
As I wente toward an hyl,
With on I mette, hydous and wykke,
And al *hys* body Armyd thykke
With hallys that wer sharp and kene:
And as I koude deme and sene,
Lyk a skyn off an yrchown
He was arrayed vp and doun,
Ygyrt with a brood fawchon;
In euery hand a callyoun,
Out off wyche (yt ys no doute)
The rede fyr gan sparklyn oute;
And yt sempte by hys vysage
That he was ffalyn in A rage;

And in hys mouth A sawe off stel
he bar.

For a good comparison of Deguileville's female Anger to Langland's male Wrath in *Piers Plowman*, see Lawrence M. Clopper, "Langland and Allegory: A Proposition," *Yearbook of Langland Studies* 15 (2001), 35–46.

4. See William Langland, *Piers Plowman: The B Version*, ed. George Kane and E. Talbot Donaldson (London: Athlone Press, 1975), 14.216–17, for the depiction of a male Pride who had earlier appeared in female form; see 15.10–15 for a male Soul who had at first been depicted as a woman.

5. For discussion of Diabolus's nonmusical and masculine role, see Margot Fassler, "Composer and Dramatist: 'Melodious Singing and the Freshness of Remorse,'" in *Voice of the Living Light: Hildegard of Bingen and Her World*, ed. Barbara Newman (Berkeley and Los Angeles: University of California Press, 1998), 149–75 (reference at 173), and Patricia Demers, "*In virginea forma*: The Salvific Feminine in the Plays of Hrotsvitha of Gandersheim and Hildegard of Bingen," in *Reimagining Women: Representations of Women in Culture*, ed. Shirley Neuman and Glennis Stephenson (Toronto: University of Toronto Press, 1993), 45–60 (reference at 55).

6. For de Man, prosopopeia, the trope wherein human sentience and form are given to that which is nonhuman, enacts not only an "enfacement" but a "defacement" owing to errant tropological forces within rhetoric. Programmatic and apodictic personification fables seem to simplify knowledge about human emotions, virtues, and vices; they would thus depend on static, robust, graspable actions. But the deManian theory of personified action in allegory, it is now widely known, contends that such ethical or ontological crystallizations or simplifications undermine their efforts through rhetoric's chaotic force. For the fullest statement on prosopopeia so understood, see de Man's "Autobiography as Defacement," in *The Rhetoric of Romanticism* (New York: Columbia University Press, 1984), 267–81.

7. The strongest biographical readings of Hildegard's compositions can be found in Peter Dronke, *Women Writers from the Middle Ages: A Critical Study of Texts from Perpetua (†203) to Marguerite Porete (†1310)* (Cambridge and New York: Cambridge University Press, 1984), 144–201. Recent essays in the fine collection edited by Maud Burnett McInerney, *Hildegard of Bingen: A Book of Essays* (New York: Garland, 1998), continue this kind of critical work.

8. Fassler, "Composer and Dramatist," 174. Aside from the tempting analogy stated by Fassler between Volmar and Diabolus, virtually nothing has been theorized about the validity of the analogy. See Bruce W. Holsinger, *Music, Body, and Desire in Medieval Culture: Hildegard of Bingen to Chaucer* (Stanford: Stanford University Press, 1999), 94, who merely concurs with Fassler's points on the masculinity and nonmusicality of Hildegard's Diabolus.

9. Citations to *Ordo virtutum* are from Peter Dronke, ed. and trans., *Nine Medieval Latin Plays* (Cambridge: Cambridge University Press, 1994), 147–84.

10. Jonathan Culler, *The Pursuit of Signs: Semiotics, Literature, Deconstruction* (Ithaca: Cornell University Press, 1981), 241.

11. Note especially the regulatory property of the customarily negative emotion fear in Timor Dei's speech: "Ego, Timor Dei, vos felicissimas filias preparo / ut inspiciatis in deum vivum et non pereatis" (I, Fear of God, can prepare you, blissful daughters, to gaze upon the living God and not die of it).

12. Following Shirley Sharon-Zisser, I have tried to articulate the structure of the grammatico-ontological copula in the master tropes metaphor, simile, personification, and metalepsis, and then to use that articulation toward better understanding the imagery of copulating allegorical bodies in *Piers Plowman*. See my "Inventing the Subject and the Personification of Will in *Piers Plowman*: Rhetorical, Erotic, and Ideological Origins and Limits in Langland's Allegorical Poetics," in *William Langland's Piers Plowman: A Book of Essays*, ed. Kathleen Hewett-Smith (New York and London: Routledge, 2001), 195–231 (reference at 215–18).

13. For Sharon-Zisser's Lacanian reading of the metaphoric and similaic copulas as perceived in Aristotle, see "Re(De)- Erecting Collatine: Castrative *Collatio* in *The Rape of Lucrece*," *Rhetoric Society Quarterly* 29 (1999), 55–70 (reference at 56), and "'Similes Hollow'd with Sighs': The Transferential Erotics of the Similaic Copula in Shakespeare's 'A Lover's Complaint,'" *Exemplaria* 11 (1999), 206–10.

14. Regarding animal bodies and sexual dimorphism in the *Metaphysics*, see Richard McKeon, ed. and intro., *The Basic Works of Aristotle* (New York: Random House, 1947), 1055b. For Aristotle's thoughts on generation and sexual differentiation, see *Generation of Animals*, 730b (p. 678): "the development of the embryo takes place in the female; neither the male himself nor the female emits semen into the male, but the female receives within herself the share contributed by both, because in the female is the material from which is made the resulting product. . . . Nature uses the semen as a tool and as possessing motion in actuality, just as tools are used in the products of any art, for in them lies in a certain sense the motion of the art."

15. Aristotle, *"Art" of Rhetoric*, trans. J. H. Freese, Loeb Classical Library (Cambridge, Mass.: Harvard University Press, 1975), *Rhetoric* 3.10.3 (1410b): "For the simile (*eikon*), as we have said, is a metaphor differing only by the addition of a word, wherefore it is less pleasant because it is longer (*makroteros*); it does not say this *is* that, so that the mind does not even examine this. Of necessity, therefore, all style and enthymemes that give us rapid information are smart" (396–97).

16. See Jan Ziolkowski, *Alan of Lille's Grammar of Sex: The Meaning of Grammar to a Twelfth-Century Intellectual* (Cambridge, Mass.: Medieval Academy of America, 1985), 69–70, 98.

17. See Shirley Sharon-Zisser, "'Illustrer notre langue maternelle': Illustrative Similes and Failed Phallic Economy in Early Modern Rhetoric," *Exemplaria* 9 (1997): 393–419. Sharon-Zisser, 401, shows further how Aristotle "transcoded" the inferior or defective female of the biological treatises with the inferiority or "gynecologization" of simile in *Rhetoric*.

18. Georges Bataille, *Visions of Excess: Selected Writings, 1927–1939*, trans. Allan Stoekl with Carl R. Lovitt and Donald M. Leslie Jr., ed. and intro. Allan Stoekl (Minneapolis: University of Minnesota Press, 1985), 5.

19. Jacques Lacan, *Écrits: A Selection*, trans. Alan Sheridan (New York: W. W. Norton, 1977), 290.

20. Ibid., 287.

21. See James J. Paxson, *The Poetics of Personification* (Cambridge: Cambridge University Press, 1994), 41–42, for discussion of personifications that are narratologically distinguishable in terms of their operation on level of discourse or level of story.

22. James J. Paxson, "Gender Personified, Personification Gendered, and the Body Figuralized in *Piers Plowman*," *Yearbook of Langland Studies* 12 (1998), 65–96 (reference at 89–92).

23. See Barbara E. Kurtz, *The Play of Allegory in the Autos Sacramentales of Pedro Calderón de la Barca* (Washington, D.C.: Catholic University of America Press, 1991), 52–56, for discussion of the self-proclaimed "docta Alegoría, tropo retórico" [learned Allegory, rhetorical trope] who appears in the prologue to *El sacro Parnaso* of 1659.

24. E.g., the effect marks an *apparent* degree-zero from which rhetorical and poetical complexities would seem to unfold along a spectrum or biaxial Cartesian graph. For structuralism's debt to this graphic or pictorial metafigure in the critical discourse treating the modern novel, see Roland Barthes, *Writing Degree Zero*, trans. Annette Lavers and Colin Smith (New York: Hill and Wang, 1968), 9–18. Roughly analogous to Barthesian semic degree-zero is the structural principle of Bakhtinian monologism; two or more disparate or different monologisms in contact and in mutual exchange constitute dialogism or dialogic status in Bakhtin's poetics. For general definitions of these ubiquitous terms, see M. M. Bakhtin, *The Dialogic Imagination*, ed. Michael Holquist, trans. Caryl Emerson and Michael Holquist (Austin: University of Texas Press, 1981), 263–75; the segment appears in the important essay "Discourse in the Novel" (259–422). Thomas J. Farrell, "Introduction: Bakhtin, Liminality, and Medieval Literature," in his edited volume *Bakhtin and Medieval Voices* (Gainesville: University Press of Florida, 1995), 1–14, provides what I take to be the best general introduction concerning the application of Bakhtin's theories to medieval Latin didactic literature and drama.

25. I summarize the arguments of grammatical formalism or "grammatical identity" in "Personification's Gender," *Rhetorica* 16 (1998), 149–79 (reference at 159–62). Chief proponents of the grammatical-identity theory have been Joseph Addison, "Dialogues upon the Usefulness of Ancient Medals," *Miscellaneous Works*, ed. A. C. Guthkelch (London: G. Bell and Sons, 1914), 2:298; E. H. Gombrich, *Studies in the Art of the Renaissance*, vol. 2, *Symbolic Images* (Chicago: University of Chicago Press, 1972), 125; and most recently Maureen Quilligan, *The Allegory of Female Authority: Christine de Pizan's "Cité des Dames"* (Ithaca: Cornell University Press, 1991), 24–25. In *Piers Plowman* criticism, the regular distinction between fully

actional personification characterization and local ornamental personification has characterized such work as Morton W. Bloomfield, "A Grammatical Approach to Personification Allegory," *Modern Philology* 60 (1963), 161–71 (reference at 164); William C. Strange, "The Willful Trope: Some Notes on Personification with Illustrations from *Piers* (A)," *Annuale Medievale* 9 (1968): 26–39; Lavinia Griffiths, *Personification in "Piers Plowman"* (Cambridge: D. S. Brewer, 1985), 4; and David Lawton, "The Subject of *Piers Plowman*," *Yearbook of Langland Studies* 1 (1987), 1–30 (reference at 9–10). Also, see note 19.

26. Tzvetan Todorov, *Theories of the Symbol*, trans. Catherine Porter (Ithaca: Cornell University Press, 1982), 73.

27. Quintilian citations are from *The Institutio Oratoria of Quintilian*, trans. H. E. Butler, Loeb Classical Library (Cambridge, Mass.: Harvard University Press, 1920).

28. I emphasize the concept of "allegorical capture"—the taking of conceptual or historical materials violently for allegorical purposes within a textual or performative universe—in homage to the term's coinage and development in one of the best recent theoretical books in allegory theory: see Gordon Teskey, *Allegory and Violence* (Ithaca: Cornell University Press, 1996), 5.

29. Joan Ferrante, "Public Postures and Private Maneuvers: Roles Medieval Women Play," in *Women and Power in the Middle Ages*, ed. Mary Erler and Maryanne Kowaleski (Athens: University of Georgia Press, 1988), 213–29 (reference at 221).

3

The Spiritual Role of the Emotions in Mechthild of Magdeburg, Angela of Foligno, and Teresa of Avila

Elena Carrera

One of the questions that modern readers may ask themselves when reading the often deeply emotional accounts written or dictated by women in medieval and early modern Europe is why they were considered of sufficient interest to have been preserved throughout the centuries. A related question might be whether the women who left personal testimonies were aware of the existence of other women's accounts and, if so, to what extent this contributed to their self-perception as writers or as people who had a message to pass on. The three women chosen for this study can be grouped together as part of the long tradition of Christian mysticism, which encouraged introspection and description of personal experiences.[1] They also have in common the fact that they used the vernacular in their accounts. The German beguine Mechthild of Magdeburg (ca. 1207–1282) wrote in Low German *Das fliessende Licht der Gottheit*, a book of poems interspersed with pieces of rhythmic narrative about her visions, at the request of her Dominican confessor Heinrich of Halle, who edited it.[2] Angela of Foligno, a Franciscan Tertiary (ca. 1248–1309), dictated detailed accounts of her visions in Umbrian dialect to her confessor and relative Fra Arnaldo, who simultaneously translated them into a simple and often syntactically flawed Latin.[3] The Spanish Carmelite reformer and mystic Teresa of Avila (1515–1582) wrote in Spanish two autobiographical accounts, *The Book of Her Life* (1562–65) and *The Book of Foundations* (1573), as well as three other books of prayer based on her experience.[4]

It is unlikely that Angela and Mechthild had even heard of one another, but Teresa had probably heard of the *Book of Angela of Foligno*, which had circulated in manuscript copies in Belgium, Spain, France, and parts of Italy until it was finally published in Spain in 1505 (in Latin version) and 1510 (in Spanish) in the printing house set up by the Franciscan reformer Cardinal Cisneros. Even if she had not known Angela's *Book* directly, she had read books on meditative prayer by Franciscan writers who were certainly familiar with the work of the Italian Tertiary.[5] The publication of Angela's personal testimony in Spain had been intended as a means of promoting spiritual fervor among religious and laity alike. As a first-person account in the tradition of St. Augustine's *Confessions*, it offered the general population a more accessible model of spirituality than the existing third-person devotional treatises and hagiographies. Sixteenth-century Spanish nuns and lay people, who lacked theological training, found in Angela's descriptions a model of self-examination and meditation that was based not on learning but on emotional experiences. Evidence of the popularity of the Spanish version of Angela's book in the 1520s and 1530s is the fact it was used to justify the activities of some of the female leaders of the spiritual movement of *alumbrados*, a group of predominantly lay people who claimed to be directly inspired by God and questioned the authority of theologians.[6]

For modern readers, Mechthild's, Angela's, and Teresa's accounts are invaluable documents of the patterns for self-interpretation and self-expression that prevailed in each of their historical contexts. But they also show, as I will seek to demonstrate, how medieval paradigms of self-interpretation that engaged the emotions in the contemplation of Christ's life were transferred from one context to another, and survived well into the early modern period. Mechthild, Angela, and Teresa, like other religious writers before them, interpreted their emotions in terms of the Christian pattern of salvation. They followed a traditional method of prayer that began with vocal prayer, mortification, and examination of conscience (*via purgativa*), progressed to meditation on the Christian mysteries (*via illuminativa*), and led to a transforming union with God through mental prayer (*via unitiva*).[7] They used similar visual images, but they also drew on specific cultural practices—courtly love poetry, passion drama, meditation on images of the suffering Christ—to produce very articulate and idiosyncratic accounts of their personal experiences. Describing their emotions, sensations, and sensuous visions, they not only were able to gain a sense of self but also held up a mirror in which readers could see and recognize themselves.

One of the differences between Teresa's texts and the earlier accounts is that she makes more explicit references to readers. The fact that she read some of the existing spiritual testimonies can explain her greater self-consciousness as a writer. And, as we shall see, it can also account for her greater ability to understand her emotions rather than simply respond to cultural expectations and inherited prejudices.

The Value of Women's Testimonies in the Context of Affective Spirituality

It is commonly believed that medieval women's experiences of their body and of language were radically different from those of men. This belief is supported by frequent claims of the kind made by Elizabeth Petroff in *Body and Soul*, that "medieval mystical texts by women will not fit into a traditional Western notion of literature, because they derive from a different experience of the body, a different epistemology, and a different relationship to language."[8] When we look at accounts by medieval women, we find deep-rooted cultural conditioning, marked by gender prejudices drawing on the Aristotelian view that women were guided by their passions rather than by stable judgements, or on the Patristic belief that spirit was to flesh as male was to female.[9] However, tempting as it may be to explore the cultural context of those writings in terms of the prevailing associations of maleness with reason and spirit, and femaleness with emotion and the body, this parameter of analysis would prove too simplistic. It would not account, for instance, for traditional Christian practices, taught by Cistercian monks in the twelfth century and by Franciscan friars well into the seventeenth century, that stimulated the emotions of shame and sorrow during meditation. It would also be difficult to find gender patterns in the early Christian practice of confession, a highly dramatized, visual, and emotional public enactment of repentance and chastisement recorded by Tertullian (ca. 160–230) in his *Treatises on Penance* and by St. Jerome in the *Epistles*.[10] This public form of confession, referred to as *exomologesis*, was practiced by men and women alike until the mid-sixteenth century, when it was ruled out by the Council of Trent (1545–63).

It could also be argued that gender was no more divisive than class as far as education was concerned, and that part of the problem we face when trying to establish gendered patterns of behavior is that we are forced to draw conclusions from a very restricted textual legacy which represents only the views of a (predominantly male) elite. The women whose testimonies have been preserved are generally seen as having had a limited access to formal education in Latin, rhetoric, or theology.[11] But this is seen as a limitation only in comparison with the few men who did have access to education, rather than in relation to the rest of their contemporaries.

Women who, like Mechthild and Angela and Teresa, left spiritual accounts in the vernacular had learned to reflect on the life of Christ and on their own lives through exposure to orally delivered poetry, dramatizations, and sermons, which were concerned with private emotions. Angela's education seems to have been heavily dependent on sermons and conversations with her confessor, as well as on popular religious imagery, while Mechthild had been acquainted with courtly love poetry (*Minnesang*) as a beguine and had probably read St. Augustine, St. Gregory, Bernard of Clairvaux, and Hugh of St. Victor when she later lived at the Abbey of Helfta.[12] Teresa had been a keen reader of chivalric romances in her youth and later read St. Augustine's *Confessions,* as well as a number of devotional treatises by Franciscans and *devotio moderna* writers.[13] All three women had sufficient time and leisure to reflect on and communicate their own emotional experiences in terms of the motifs, allegories, and patterns of self-expression made available to them. Rather than assume that they drew on "gendered" epistemological tools, I will explore how their experiences were filtered through the language they inherited—the language of poetry and sermons—and the public discourse in which they sought to participate by offering their testimony.

We have little biographical information on Mechthild and Angela, and, since their books were rearranged by their confessors, we cannot know whether these are chronological accounts of their spiritual evolution. We do know that Mechthild started her religious life as a beguine in Magdeburg around 1230, that she began to write after some twenty years, and that she wrote her last extant accounts (the seventh part of *Das fliessende Licht*) after 1270, the year in which she joined the Abbey of Helfta, becoming a Dominican Tertiary to escape her persecutors. She justified her writing as arising from her need to share the graces obtained from God.

Of Angela we know, for instance, that she dictated her visions to Fra Arnaldo between 1292 and 1296, primarily as a preventative measure, since he feared that she might be a case of demonic delusion. His concern was related to an embarrassing episode in 1291 when he had found her lying on the pavement at the threshold of the Basilica of St. Francis in Assisi, shrieking with all her might in great despair, attracting the attention of many friars who knew them both (2.4; T168–70). This bizarre incident allegedly took place five years after Angela's experience of "conversion," the first of the thirty steps of the spiritual progression she recounts in her book. It had all begun with a sudden acknowledgement of her sins, which had made her weep bitterly, feeling not so much love as pain, shame, and fear of hell, and urged her to look for a priest who could hear her general confession (1.1–2; T132). She recounts that later she experienced love of God as a great fire that made her scream with joy on hearing anyone speak about God, and that she would not have been able to restrain herself even if people had tried to stop her with an axe (1.18; T152, L131). The fact that she could not stop screaming despite feeling ashamed ("verecundabar valde") led others to believe that she was sick and possessed ("infirma et indaemoniata") (T152).

During a deeply emotional experience in which she was "set afire" by the "perception of the meaning of the cross," Angela pledged perpetual chastity despite the fact that she was married (1.8; T138, L126). In the ninth step, she saw in a vision that the Way of the Cross meant that she had to divest herself of all her clothes and possessions and walk toward the cross naked (1.9; T138). Soon she became able to practice greater detachment with the subsequent death of her mother, husband and eight children, all within three years. But rather than recording the grief or sorrow expected of a widow, she recounts that she had prayed to God for all this to happen and thus felt a great consolation (1.9). We do not know whether these were her real feelings or simply a retrospective teleological interpretation, subordinated to the aims of her testimony. It is conceivable that her experience at the time was already mediated by her wish to conform to the role of a holy woman, which led her to live as a penitent and resulted in her admittance into the Franciscan third order in 1291.

In contrast with the limited information we have on Angela's and Mechthild's lives, Teresa's is extensively documented, even though much of what was recorded by her early biographers followed hagiographical conventions.[14] We know that she took the veil at a Carmelite convent in 1536 at the age of twenty-one. Two years later she began to depart from her convent's practice of vocal prayer by following the Franciscan method of meditative prayer on her own.[15] At thirty-nine she began to have visions and, consequently, to seek the advice of experienced confessors, who were convinced that she was a victim of demonic delusion. Her life and prayer were further examined when, four years later, she came to the idea of founding a small reformed convent that would be more conducive to prayer than the one in which she had taken her vows (*Life* 32.9–10). Like Angela and Mechthild, she began to recount her visions in great detail for confessors who examined and censored them, and she eventually obtained their approval. After a series of written confessions (of which only one from 1560 is now extant) she was asked to write an extended account of her life, which became her famous autobiography (*Life*).

Women who, like Mechthild and Angela and Teresa, had mystic visions were asked to recount their personal experiences, not only as a measure to prevent demonic delusion, but primarily because they were seen as recipients of a direct knowledge of God that could not be attained through study. Their experiential knowledge of God, through the will and the emotions, was an essential part of the Judeo-Christian tradition. In the Old Testament, for instance, we find examples of this experiential approach, based on a nonverbal form of communication often associated with the feminine, or with the affective experience of sucking at the breast (Isa. 66:10–13). The idea that religious experience offered consolation, and demanded the individual's involvement through the emotions of joy and love rather than through the use of the intellect, was a recurrent one in both the Old and the New Testament.

For the Church Fathers, the intellectual approach to biblical exegesis was not sufficient, since the text of Scripture needed to be "lived" in order to be understood. St. Gregory, for instance, emphasizes that love is the best way of approaching spiritual matters and knowing them.[16] St. Basil also endorses this "affective" approach when he reminds his readers that the desire for God has purifying and strengthening effects on the soul (*Epistles* 2.4).[17] In their writings we find a hermeneutic approach to the text of Scripture and to the self that began with self-interpretation and aimed at self-transformation in the experience of mystical union with God. This tradition, which can be accurately named "affective hermeneutics," was revived in the twelfth century with the discovery of St. Gregory's texts by the Cistercian writers William of St. Thierry (1085–1148) and St. Bernard of Clairvaux (1090/91–1153), who were also inspired by the mystical writings of Dionysius the Areopagite (Syrian monk, probably fifth century).[18] Bernard, for instance, draws on the authority of Scripture (Matt. 5:8) to teach, like Gregory, that the best way for people to know God is by cultivating love.[19] In Mechthild's writing, the path of love appears to be almost incompatible with intellectual learning: "many a man who excels in learnedness and natural intelligence will not dare subject himself to the power of naked love. Only to the simple and pure who bear God in mind in all their actions will God lower himself naturally" (2.23).[20]

The idea that people needed to open their heart to the effect of God's love, which would transform their lives, was promoted in the earliest Christian texts. This opening up was stimulated by communal devotional practices such as chanting or prayer, as is described in St. Augustine's *Confessions*: "How I wept during your hymns and songs! I was deeply moved by the music of the sweet chants of your Church. The sounds flowed into my ears and the truth was distilled into my heart. This caused the feelings of devotion to overflow. Tears ran, and it was good for me to have that experience."[21] The experience of feeling "moved" and being flooded with tears transcended the private sphere on three accounts: it was encouraged by an external source, was regulated by the Christian pattern of devotion, and was offered to readers as an example of how they too could be emotionally involved in and transformed by the Christian faith. We begin to see how emotions and the communication of emotional experiences played a crucial role in this hermeneutic approach to spirituality.

Texts like the *Confessions*, which address all readers, seem to blur gender distinctions. There are, nonetheless, qualitative and quantitative differences between references to emotions by male writers like Augustine and the degree of visual display and theatricality shown by the spiritual testimonies left by women in later centuries, following his example and, more particularly, that of Mary Magdalene. Augustine's description of how he experienced conversion by feeling moved and by quietly shedding tears clearly contrasts with the scriptural and hagiographical accounts of Mary Magdalene's abundant tears bathing Christ's feet as she knelt to ask for forgiveness (Luke 7:36–50; *Legenda aurea*).

The example of Mary Magdalene might have inspired Angela's public displays of sorrow mentioned above. It might also have acted as an authoritative model in Mechthild's visual descriptions of how she would fall onto the ground shaking with fear ("eisende") and asking for mercy, every time she considered her faults and the prospect of purgatory, even though she knew that she had been granted the gift of "bekantû minne" [discerning love] (5.33). Taken in isolation, Angela's and Mechthild's testimonies would seem to reinforce to some extent the old prejudice that associated women with emotion, even though Mechthild's emphasis on discerning love also counteracts the traditional view that emotion was inferior and irreconcilably opposed to the intellect.[22] Nonetheless, if we look at the spiritual context in which those testimonies were written, we see that while the emotions were feared or warned against by theologians like Peter Lombard, they also played an important role within spiritual practices adopted by men and women alike. St. Francis, for instance, would cultivate shame through public acts of self-humiliation, such as revealing his past sins in his sermons, or begging his brethren to reproach him and to drag him, stripped of his outer garments, through the public square.[23] Mechthild's text also gives some indication of the spiritual function of emotions among men, as when the Lord is reported saying that he loved the Dominican Order for their "powerful sighing, heartfelt weeping, vivid desire, severe discipline, distressing desolation, loyal humility, joyous love" (3.21).[24] To know God's love, individuals had to involve their emotions rather than their intellect. As Mechthild argues, "no one can know consolation, pain, or longing, unless he has been touched by them himself" (5.8).[25]

It could thus be argued that emotional experiences linked with such devotional practices were in principle genderless, but that when it came to speaking about their knowledge of God, women lacked the intellectual training of writers like Augustine or Bernard. They also had little opportunity to express themselves in public, given the well-known warnings of St. Paul against women's active participation in the Church (1 Cor. 14:34;1 Tim. 2:9–15). The fact that women did not have the right to speak in public can partly explain the emphasis they placed on the emotions as means of self-expression. This cultural prejudice was clearly a source of tension for Teresa, who at one point in her *Life* refers with certain envy to those who have "the learning, talents, and freedom to preach and confess," complaining that her own experience was limited to "a taste of what it is to be unable to do anything in the service of the Lord" (30.21). She defends her right to speak by invoking God's authority and the love of God, arguing that He wants her to speak (31.21). Nevertheless, her knowledge could not be made public without being checked against the truth of Scripture by expert theologians. Her *Life* was kept in custody by her confessor Domingo Báñez, and she was encouraged to write *The Way of Perfection* (1565) for the nuns in her newly founded convent. In this second book she makes a number of overt complaints about the fact that women can follow the models of Mary or Mary Magdalene in weeping to express their love for the Lord, but they cannot act as spiritual teachers. For instance, in a passage crossed out by her censor, she protests that women are expected to weep and lament in secret over spiritual truths they cannot discuss in the public sphere.[26]

Through her practice of meditation and her dealing with confessors, she became increasingly confident in her affective approach to prayer, which led her to argue in her next book, *Meditations on the Song of Songs* (1566), that her nuns should not be excluded from it: "I hold it as certain that we do not offend Him when we find delight and consolation in His words and works." Her argument was that women should be able to pursue an experiential, affective knowledge of God, but if they wanted to make this public, they would need the approval of learned men: "nor must we make women stand so far away from enjoyment of the Lord's riches. If they argue and teach and think they are right without showing their writings to learned men; yes, that would be wrong" (1.8).[27] Teresa thus appears to have accepted the limitations imposed on women by educated men, who judged them to be more emotional and less able intellectually than themselves. But she was also aware that women's greater emotionality placed them in a privileged position to make contact with Christ's humanity during prayer. If they had nothing to say, they could at least weep and also enjoy their experience of God. The fact that this did not require special intellectual ability or training was an advantage emphasized by Teresa in her next book, *Foundations* (1573), when she tried to persuade her nuns to practice meditation: "you will realize that not all imaginations have the required ability to pursue this, but all souls are able to love" (5.2).[28] Thus love not only was a concept used to explain Incarnation and the Christian pattern of salvation but was also seen as a powerful tool that helped Christians come in contact with God.

Via purgativa: *Repentance as a Form of Self-Knowledge and Self-Expression*

The Christian pattern of salvation served to explain people's behavior, thoughts, and aspirations in terms of the paradigm of sin, repentance, and divine grace. But repentance was also a means for ordinary people to express themselves in public through emotional displays, in imitation of the scriptural role model of Mary Magdalene. Angela pays great attention to repentance, in both its public and private dimensions. She thus recounts how she experienced God's mercy but this served only to increase her lamentations and pain ("plus plangit et dolet quam prius") and her desire to do severe mortifications (1.4; T134, L125). She then began to cultivate self-knowledge ("cognitio sui") and to weep bitterly every time she acknowledged her limitations, feeling that those tears were given to her. Her ability to weep gave her some consolation, but it was a bitter one (1.4).[29] She claims that in the sixth step she had an illumination through which she gained a deeper awareness of her sins, but also of her need for forgiveness: "I asked all the creatures whom I felt I had offended not to accuse me" (1.6; T136, L125). This was the first of the three traditional ascending ways toward mystical union with God, the *via purgativa*.

The tension we find in Angela between the love and grace that God grants freely and the weakness and limitations that prevent mankind from paying him back with the same currency is a recurrent theme in Christian writing. It is also one on which medieval mystics tended to draw repeatedly, giving detailed testimony of how this situation of conflict affected them personally. Mechthild, for instance, describes her experience of letting herself be dominated by feelings such as gloom and darkness, bitterness ("sûrekeit"), or impatience, and finding that the only thing she can do is express her powerful feeling of longing by crying and lamenting miserably (5.33; N193). She then feels pushed to confess humbly her lack of virtue and receives "the grace to be allowed to creep into the kitchen like a beaten dog" (5.33).

Mechthild's account is to some extent validated by the authority of Augustine's *Confessions*, which abounds in self-debasing formulae such as "wretch that I am" (2.7), "poor thing that I was" (3.4), and "how vile I was, how twisted and filthy, covered in sores and ulcers" (8.16). These phrases were intended to provide an edifying testimony of how one can benefit from God's grace when one gathers sufficient humility to recognize and accept one's weaknesses. They also served to stress how human creatures are powerless without God's help, an idea that clearly shapes Mechthild's self-perception. She thus recounts how, when considering her faults, she is overcome by a fear of God ("gœtlich vorhte"), which makes her "creep like a little worm into the earth" and sit yelling to heaven, asking for mercy (7.6; N262). In such instances Mechthild is doing more than adopting the "fixed" position of a repentant sinner, or consenting to the attitude of self-humiliation recommended for Christians. She is constructing a sense of self through emotions that, whether internalized or recognized, she experiences as hers.

Moreover, Mechthild's self-debasement becomes most meaningful when it is integrated in the cultural practices of *imitatio Christi* that she has inherited. Since God proved his love for humankind through the poverty, suffering, and contempt endured by the incarnated Christ, Mechthild can now ask for love and forgiveness by showing repentance and the willingness to identify with Christ's suffering and humility: "that I may grieve for Your great humiliation and my sinful wretchedness" (6.37; N246, G203). Her emotions are regulated by prevailing cultural patterns, but they are also tools that enable her to participate in the Christian public discourse as an individual.

The path of love that Mechthild is instructed to follow involves detachment not only on a material level but also on a spiritual level, namely, by shedding all emotions and tendencies that may be incompatible with love: "You should love nothingness, you should flee anything" (1.35).[30] In prayer, she visualizes herself and her emotions using figurative, visual "props" to represent abstract concepts, thus making them easier to grasp.[31] She describes how she would adorn herself with her own "ignobleness" [unedelkeit] and "dress with the filth that I am myself"; then she would shoe herself with the precious time she had wasted and gird herself with the pain she deserved; she would put on the "coat of wickedness" of which she was full, and place on her head the "crown of shameful secret sins" [crone der heimlichen schemede] that she had committed (6.1; N205). She then stresses how, by practicing prayer, she came to accept her limitations and her suffering, and to prefer these clothes to all earthly goods (6.1). It is important to note how humility plays a crucial role in Mechthild's prayer, helping her to detach herself from external pursuits such as deceptive status symbols and beautiful clothes and to move on to a deeper and more worthwhile form of yearning. Only after this preparation can she seek union with the divinity: "thus adorned I seek Jesus, my sweet Lord, but cannot find Him quickly. Everything is heavy and clumsy. One should step before Him with a strong yearning, a shame of sin, a flowing love and a humble fear" (6.1; G171).[32]

Mechthild insists that her attitude of humility is not an end in itself but a first step toward transformation through love: "then all the filth of sin will disappear before the eyes of Our Lord, and He begins to shine lovingly on the soul as she overflows with heartfelt love" (6.1; N205, G170–71). Opposing true love to sinful "false" tendencies, she is able to counteract age-old misogynistic prejudices which had presented women as temptresses. For instance, while St. Jerome and other Church Fathers had interpreted the Old Testament stories of Samson, David, Solomon, and Ammon as a warning against the influence of women, Mechthild implicitly exculpates her sex by clarifying that those biblical men had simply "fallen prey to false love" [do vielen si in die valschen minne] (2.24; N61).[33]

In Angela's testimony, by contrast, the theme of deceptiveness is integrated into a discourse of humility that blurs gender boundaries. At the beginning of her *Instructions*, she recounts how she followed an ascetic pattern of behavior, but she then confesses that she sought to conform to the image of the holy woman (by affecting outward poverty, hardship, and discipline) in order to gain other people's recognition, while her inner feelings did not really comply with what was expected of her (T404–6, L219–20).[34] In the course of the *Instructions* she quite often appears as a sort of oracle who, when consulted, provides the "right" answers to some of the most controversial theological questions of her time. Her preaching had gained her the reputation of being a *magistra theologorum*.[35] But her position of authority had also given rise to envy and suspicion, which led her to internalize the accusations she received and to confess to having been a fraud (by feigning sanctity) and to have misled others: "I am responsible for the death of many souls, including my own" (T406, L220). Angela's claims were perhaps no more than an act of self-humiliation, intended to counteract her fame as a holy woman and a spiritual teacher: "'Here's the woman whose entire life was one big lie!' And men and women around would say: 'Look at the great miracle God has done! He has made this woman disclose the iniquities, malice, hypocrisies and sins which she had concealed so well all her life!' But all this outcry against me would still not satisfy my soul" (T406, L220). This bizarre confession appears to be related to the tradition of *exomologesis* mentioned above, though it can also be read as the manifestation of a conflict within her between gender expectations about women preaching by example (in imitation of Mary or Mary Magdalene) and her increasingly recognized public role as a preacher. On the one hand, by responding to pressure from her followers in such an emotional way, she may have reinforced general prejudices about women's weakness. On the other hand, by adopting the (genderless) position of the repentant sinner, she was able to invoke God's grace as a means to overcome her personal limitations.

Via meditativa: *Engaging with Christ's Suffering
or with Christ's Love?*

The power of God's grace is emphasized in Angela's account of how she progressed from the *via purgativa* to the *via meditativa*: during the seventh step she suddenly received "the grace of beginning to look at the cross" (1.7; T136, L125) and was enabled to pray with "the great fire of love" (1.18; T152, L131). In the tenth step, she had numerous visions of the crucified Christ asking her to do something to pay back what he had done for her. He persuaded her by showing her very graphic evidence of his love: "he even showed me how his beard, eyebrows, and hair had been plucked out and enumerated each and every of the blows of the whip that he had received. And he said: 'I have endured all these things for you'" (1.10; T140, L127). We are told that she first responded to Christ's Passion with her guilt and extreme sadness, feeling how her tears burned her flesh (T141), but we cannot know whether she already had these emotions within her and simply channeled them by projecting them onto her relationship with Christ, or whether her emotions and sensations were encouraged by her method of meditation.

The emphasis that Angela placed on the Passion as a source of meditation through visualization and empathy was part of a devotional trend that gained importance throughout Europe under the influence of Franciscans in the thirteenth century and reached its peak in sixteenth-century Spain.[36] This form of meditation became a popular practice because it was easier for people to connect emotionally with the mystery of the Passion by invoking their own feelings of suffering, sadness, or shame than it was to try to engage intellectually with other Christian mysteries such as that of the Trinity. Moreover, as we see in Angela's text, thinking of the Passion as the ultimate act of love gave Christians the opportunity to understand and accept their own suffering as a means of expressing their love and gratitude to God.

During the fourteenth step Angela was called by Christ to place her mouth on the wound in his side and had an almost physical experience of being purified by the blood flowing from it (1.14; T142–44, L128). This is a recurrent theme in thirteenth- and fourteenth-century women's visions, which has been interpreted as an affirmation of the religious significance of emotionality and physicality among women.[37] Even though emotionality was not exclusive to women, it was not uncommon for the bodies and the health of women mystics to be affected by their meditation on the Passion.[38] Angela offers ample testimony of such occurrences, as when she began to swoon in front of images of the Passion and to become feverish and ill (1.18; T152, L131), or when, on one occasion, she realized that she could feel such intense delight ("maior consolatio quam unquam fuissem experta") in contemplating both the humanity and the divinity of Christ that she spent most of the day standing in her cell and was eventually found lying on the floor, speechless and seemingly dead (1.19; T153–55, L131). Later, during the twentieth step, she was practicing meditation on the Passion, focusing on highly visual elements from the Crucifixion such as the impact of the nails on Christ's flesh, and wishing to receive a vision of how small bits of his hands and feet had been driven into the wood, when she had a very physical experience of sorrow: "such was my sorrow over the pain that Christ had endured that I could no longer stand on my feet. I bent over and sat down; I stretched out my arms on the ground and inclined my head on them" (3.5; T192–94, L145–46). This led to a vision of Christ's throat and arms, which created in her a new, intense feeling of joy ("tantam laetitiam, nova laetitia ab aliis laetitis"), displacing all other feelings and sensations (T194, L146).

While Angela presents her meditation on the Passion as a gift from God which made her surrender completely, Teresa emphasizes how she actively strove to represent within her the scenes of the Passion, and how she chose those in which Christ was alone and afflicted because she was convinced that if he was "in need" he would "accept" her more readily (*Life* 9.4). She particularly liked the scene of Christ's prayer in the garden, in which she visualized his sweat and agony and "desired to wipe away the sweat He so painfully experienced" (9.4). Like Angela, she sees meditation on the Passion as a stage beyond self-examination, but she is more explicit than her precursor in recommending this practice to readers as a means of drawing God's tenderness ("ternura") to themselves by considering "His Passion with such heavy sorrows, His life so afflicted, and by delighting in the sight of His works, His grandeur, how He loves us" (*Life* 10.2).[39]

In contrast with Teresa's proactive approach, Angela's and Mechthild's accounts appear to be underpinned by the idea that when God bestows his grace, the soul has no other choice than to respond. Angela, for instance, stresses how she felt forced to respond to Christ's love by pledging chastity, even though she herself was not ready to commit herself: "and I asked him to make me maintain this chastity with all my limbs and all my feelings, since on the one hand I was afraid of making this promise and on the other hand the above-mentioned fire compelled me to make it and I could not do otherwise" (1.8).[40] Similarly, in Mechthild's text we find a declaration by Lady Love that does not leave much room for the soul to choose: "pursuing you was my desire; catching you was my pleasure; binding you was my joy; in wounding you I united you with me; . . . I have forced the

Almighty God from the heavens, have taken His human life, and have returned Him gloriously to His father. How dare you, worthless worm, wish to cure yourself of me?" (1.3).[41] Although this passage reflects a certain tension, Mechthild emphasizes how her soul was forcefully persuaded to participate in the Christian pattern of redemption. This was presented not only as an act of love but also as an illness (the *mal d'amour* of courtly love) from which she was not allowed to recover, or convalesce.

While Mechthild and Angela describe their love primarily as a response to God's love, Teresa suggests to her nuns in *The Way of Perfection* that they already have a great capacity for love and that this places them in a privileged position to strive for spiritual perfection, since their way of loving can be transformed into a purer, more disinterested form of love through the imitation of Christ (11.4). All they need to do is analyze their feelings and use them to make contact with the humanity of Christ during meditation:

> If you are joyful, look at Him as risen. Just imagining how He rose from the tomb will bring you joy. . . . If you are experiencing trials or are sad, behold Him on the way to the garden: what great affliction He bore in His soul; for having become suffering itself, He tells us about it and complains of it. Or behold Him bound to the column, filled with pain, with all His flesh torn in pieces for the great love He bears you; . . . He will look at you with those eyes so beautiful and compassionate, filled with tears; He will forget His sorrows so as to console you in yours, merely because you yourselves go to Him to be consoled, and you turn your head to look at Him. (26.4–5)[42]

Teresa's approach to meditation here bears resemblances to Ignatius's suggestion that when starting to practice meditation one should give one's emotions play: thus, when thinking of the Resurrection, one should ask for the grace of participating in the ineffable joy of the glorious Christ and, when meditating on the Passion, one should ask for pain and tears, suffering with him.[43] But Teresa takes such suggestions further by encouraging the nuns to make the most of the moods and emotions they are already feeling, and to expect that Christ will adapt to their needs. She stresses how, as Christ's "brides," they are free from the obligations of married women: "they say that for a woman to be a good wife toward her husband she must be sad when he is sad, and joyful when he is joyful, even though she may not be so. (See what subjection you have been freed from, Sisters!) The Lord, without deception, truly acts in such a way with us. He is the one who submits, and He wants you to be the lady with authority to rule; He submits to your will" (26.4).[44] In a context in which women were seen as emotional creatures who needed to be controlled by their husbands' (or confessors') intellect, Teresa emphasizes how women can value and benefit from their emotions by turning them to a spiritual purpose.

Via unitiva: *The Ineffable Experience of Union*

Meditation on Christ's life and Passion was seen, not as an end in itself, but as a way of making contact with Christ's humanity which could lead to the experience of union with his divinity (*via unitiva*). Angela describes how she experienced her first mystical union with God in the twenty-fourth step, when she took Communion, savored its very beautiful but unfamiliar meatlike taste, and began to languish of excessive love of God (7.3).[45] But this experience was preceded by a series of acts in which she demonstrated her love for Christ in a seemingly outrageous way, as when she drank the water with which she had washed lepers' wounds and, choking with the scabs, she found them as sweet as Communion (5.3). Hers is an account of progression and regression between the most sublime visions and the greatest suffering and despair. Every time her mystical union with God was over, her soul entered the "dark night" described in Dionysius' mystical treatises.

This approach to mystical prayer was radically different from that of Mechthild, who rarely referred to Christ's Passion, but explored instead the boundaries of courtly love poetry in depicting her soul in dialogue with Lady Love ("minne"), a female personification of God. This so-called *Minnemystiek*, shared by her contemporaries Hadewijch of Antwerp (d. 1310) and Marguerite Porete (ca. 1250–1310), was based on St. Bernard's use of courtly love conventions to interpret the erotic language of the Song of Songs as representing the love between Christ and the soul as his bride.[46] Mechthild, however, does not provide an *explication de texte* in Bernard's style, but offers direct accounts of her visions as theatrical dialogues in which the soul takes the ready-made persona of the *Minnesang* lover: "Be silent, Lady Love: do not say any more. / All creatures and I bow before You, loveliest maiden of them all. / Please tell my love that His bed is ready, / And I lovingly long for Him. / If this letter is too long, the reason is this: / I was at matins, when I bound countless flowers. / It is a sweet lamentation: those who die from love / Shall be buried in God" (1.3; N10,

G9). Her depiction of the meeting between the soul and God is thus filtered through the language and themes of the Song of Songs—the bed, the flowers—and shaped through the prevailing courtly love conventions, such as lovesickness ("das ich minnesiech nach im si") (1.3), or the rich imagery of courtly splendor (1.4). Personified as a young woman, the soul surrenders to her divine love, who is even more lovesick for her than she is for him (1.4). God's infinite love, in turn, imposes itself not only over the soul but also over all the emotions and tendencies that rule it, which, being incompatible with the divine love, are perceived as sins: "but the dust of sin, which falls upon us against our will, will be destroyed by the fire of love, as the eyes of our soul are touched by the Divinity with the pitiful, sighing sweet longing which no creature can withstand" (6.1; G170).[47] Here, as in Angela's text, the soul is represented as powerless and passive, unable to withstand sin or divine grace. But, in contrast to Angela's account of progression and regression between sin, repentance, and grace, Mechthild's text stresses how divine grace, manifested as longing, rules supreme. All that is needed for perfect love to occur is for the individual to engage his or her own will in responding to God's longing: "I longed for you before the beginning of the world. I long for you and you long for me. Where two burning desires meet, there love is perfect" (7.16).[48]

Before reaching this stage, however, the soul must "overcome the distress of repentance, the pain of confession, the toil of penance, the love of the world, the devil's temptation, the excessiveness of the flesh, and the cursed self-will" (1.44).[49] The soul of Mechthild's text moves through the path of love ("Minnewege") by taking a number of steps described in very visual terms: in the shape of a very pure maid, the soul appears dressed up "in the shirt of gentle humility" and wearing also "a white dress of pure chastity, so pure that she cannot tolerate thoughts, words, or contacts that might soil her" (1.44; G22). In contrast to Angela's description of how she felt forced to pledge chastity, Mechthild appears to have simply received it, or had it imposed on her as one is given a dress to wear. Mechthild's dialogue then turns into a theatrical performance, in which her soul adopts a passive role, following close stage directions: "I cannot dance, Lord; You are distracting me. / If You wish me to leap, / Then You must lead me with Your singing. / Then I will leap into recognition, / From recognition into practice, / From practice over all human senses. / There will I stay and still crawl onward" (1.44; N28–29, G23). Her good performance is then rewarded with the promise of union with Christ: "Maiden, you did this dance of praise very well. . . . you are now inwardly tired. Come at midday to the shade of the well into the bed of love; there you shall be refreshed with Him" (1.44; G23).

When she reaches the "secret chambers of the innocent Divinity," Mechthild's soul finds "love's bed and love's dress, prepared for God and man," and is asked to let go of some of her emotions: "therefore you must shed both your fear and shame [vorhte und schame], as well as all outward virtues. Instead, you shall want to experience eternally those virtues which you bear within yourself by nature. That is your noble longing [begerunge] and your fathomless desire [girheit], which I shall fill eternally with My endless generosity" (1.44; N31, G25). Instead of the more external emotions of fear and shame, traditionally associated with feminine behavior, Mechthild is encouraged to cultivate yearning and desire, which she is expected to find inside her and which will move her deeper within herself. Among these deeper emotions seven types of love can be discerned: "gleeful" [vro^{e}liche], "fearful" [vo^{e}rhtende], "strong" [starke], "affectionate" [minnende minne], "wise" [wise], "free" [vrie], and "mighty" [gewaltige] (2.11; N47, G39). Love is the most important emotion, since it can transform the soul, as Gregory, Ambrose, and Bernard emphasized. As Mechthild further emphasizes, the practice of affective prayer brings many benefits, and transforms negative emotions such as sadness or fear into their positive counterparts: "it renders a sour heart sweet, a sad heart glad, a poor heart rich, a stupid heart wise, a timid heart fearless, a sick heart strong, a blind heart clear-sighted, a cold heart ardent" (5.13; G140).[50]

The description of prayer as the love encounter between Christ and the soul as his bride (based on Bernard's exegesis of the *Cantica canticorum*) is also the focus of Teresa's *Meditations on the Song of Songs*. She begins this book by claiming that the sisters do not have to limit themselves to the thoughts and feelings about the Passion contained in Scripture, but can also add their own: "the Lord gives us license—from what I think—just as He does when we think of the Passion and consider many more things about the anguish and torments the Lord must have suffered than the Evangelists record" (*Meditations*, 1.8). Stressing the powerful effect of the scriptural words on herself and others—"what endearing words! What sweetness! One of these words would have been enough for us to be dissolved in You" (3.14)—she also suggests that some souls will be moved so deeply that they will be transformed through their union with Christ as Bridegroom:

but when this most wealthy Bridegroom desires to enrich and favor the soul more, He changes it into Himself to such a point that, just as a person is caused to swoon from great pleasure and happiness, it seems to the soul it is left suspended in those divine arms, leaning on that sacred side and those divine breasts. It doesn't know how to do anything more than rejoice, sustained by the divine milk with which its Spouse is nourishing it and making it better so that He might favor it. (4.4)

It appears that in this advanced stage of prayer (*via unitiva*) individuals do not have the kind of freedom and control over their feelings that Teresa suggested they had in earlier stages. But the bliss they are able to feel now is the culmination of their perseverance in practicing prayer. It acts as a reward, replacing the emotions of fear, shame, and sadness which had helped them to identify first with Christ's humanity and then with the deep joy of union with his divinity. Using the Song's words "He brought me into the wine cellar" to refer to this deeper stage of prayer, Teresa suggests that individuals still have some choice in deciding to what extent to participate in that union: "He brings her into the wine cellar so that she may come out more abundantly enriched. It doesn't seem the King wants to keep anything from her. He wants her to drink in conformity with her desire and become wholly inebriated" (6.3). But she also exhorts her readers to let go of themselves and of their attachment to their body in order to gain greater pleasure and a greater understanding of God (6.3). The range of positive, rewarding emotions that the nuns can expect to feel during unitive prayer is as broad as they wish: "O souls that practice prayer, taste all these words! How many ways there are of thinking about our God. How many different kinds of food we can make from Him! He is manna, for the taste we get from Him conforms to the taste we prefer" (5.2). Through this scriptural allusion to the taste of prayer (Wisdom 16:20), she offers her readers the opportunity to adapt their practice of prayer to their emotional needs.

A Reevaluation of Teresa's Self-Reflectiveness

Teresa's writing is considerably more self-conscious and self-reflective than that of the medieval women mystics discussed in this essay. One of the reasons for her greater self-consciousness as a writer lies in the fact, noted in the essay's introduction, that she and her confessors were exposed to a longer tradition of testimonial writing, and were aware of the impact of books such as Augustine's *Confessions* or Angela of Foligno's *Book* in encouraging spiritual fervor among their readers. Teresa had also inherited a more developed vernacular language, which included a multiplicity of figurative ways of describing mystical prayer.[51] But the principal factor contributing to the self-reflectiveness that pervades Teresa's writing was her regular practice of confession, which was more frequent and structured than it had been for her predecessors. Since 1554 she had been under the spiritual direction of the Jesuits, who heard her confessions fortnightly, as recommended by the Council of Trent guidelines (1551).[52] Through this regular practice she was able to look at her experiences of prayer while questioning the inherited patterns of self-examination. Thus when she came to writing her *Life* in 1562, she was used to reflecting on her weaknesses and obtaining feedback from confessors.

Furthermore, Teresa had the opportunity to create a supportive environment in which women could practice mental prayer, founding fifteen small convents between 1562 and 1582 as part of her reform of the Carmelite Order. She then used her writing as a way of providing adequate instruction for her nuns, presenting it as a continuation of her private conversations with them. Given the success of her reform, it is hardly surprising that she employed emotionally charged terms to describe her frustration in not being able to speak in public of her experience of union with God: "to be silent and conceal this great impulse of happiness, when experiencing it, is no small pain" (*Interior Castle* 6.6.11).

Teresa's position was not very different from that of the majority of men, who also lacked the necessary status and education to speak in public. But her advantage over unlearned men was that her unusual experiences during prayer gave her the opportunity to write about her feelings and the tensions within herself: "in the midst of these experiences that are both painful and delightful together, our Lord sometimes gives the soul feelings of jubilation and a strange prayer it doesn't understand" (*Interior Castle* 6.6.10). Like Mechthild and Angela, she wrote of her pain, her joy, and her delight during prayer, but she went further than them in reflecting on the cultural tensions that prevented her from behaving and speaking otherwise, and in explicitly addressing her readers to encourage them to follow her example in practicing affective prayer: "I am writing about this favor here so that if He grants it to you, you may give Him much praise and know what is taking place. . . . What I'm saying seems like gibberish, but certainly the experience takes place in this way, for the joy is so excessive the soul wouldn't want to enjoy it alone but wants to tell everyone about it so that they might help this soul praise our Lord. . . . Oh, how many festivals and demonstrations the soul would organize, if it could, that all might know its joy!" (6.6.10). She was clearly aware that in reflecting on her own emotions, she was also providing guidance to readers on how they could best deal with them by opening up to God's love and grace.

Regrettably, her idiosyncratic, emotional approach to spirituality was seen as potentially dangerous, since it did not require theological training and thus might lead to heretical ideas. In 1580 she was forced by her Dominican confessor Diego de Yanguas to burn her manuscript of *Meditations* as a measure to prevent the nuns and the population at large from following her method of prayer and believing that they could rely less on dogma and on the advice of theologians than on direct experience of God. The book survived only because one of her nuns kept an unauthorized copy. Teresa's efforts to promote among ordinary people the affective prayer she had learned from books and developed though her practice were further obliterated by the arguments of the learned theologians who, during her canonization process (1590–1622), emphasized that she was a saint inspired by God, rather than a woman who reflected on and understood her emotions.

In spiritual testimonies like Mechthild's, Angela's, or Teresa's, "private" emotions became part of a public discourse, that of medieval Christian devotion, which recommended certain emotional behaviors, such as weeping and self-belittlement, and discouraged others, such as anger or hatred. Their accounts were mediated by devotional practices such as meditation on the suffering Christ, repentance, and confession, which served to some extent to regulate people's behavior (a form of social control), but which also offered individuals, independent of their gender or level of education, an opportunity to look at themselves (their aspirations and emotions) in relation to the pattern of salvation. These women's testimonies of how they practiced self-examination, and how they involved their imagination and their emotions in meditation, are examples of how unlettered people could strive and persevere on the experiential path to knowledge of God.

This experiential path was not exclusively followed by women, even though it was the only option for those women who wished to attain spiritual knowledge. Angela, Mechthild, and Teresa did not have the same access to education as some of their male contemporaries, but they turned this limitation into an advantage by seeking for themselves the knowledge of God that theologians would seek through the study of Scripture and

Tradition. In their accounts, Angela and Mechthild show how they opened themselves up to the effect of God's grace by becoming repentant and how they responded to it by moving on from emotions such as fear, shame, and sorrow to feelings of compassion and love. Teresa followed Angela's example but also took a step further by using her testimony to challenge readers to look at their own emotions. While Angela and Mechthild described the complex and changing emotional states through which they responded to God's grace, Teresa adopted a more proactive approach, demonstrating how people could simply become aware of their own moods and feelings and give them a spiritual purpose. She showed the way from lament to laughter, much to the confusion of theologians who had expected women to be able to do little more than weep and repent.

Notes

1. For an overview of the "experiential mysticism" that developed particularly in the thirteenth and fourteenth centuries, see Bernard McGinn, *The Flowering of Mysticism: Men and Women in the New Mysticism (1200–1350)* (New York: Crossroad, 1998), esp. 24–30; 141–52 on Angela; 222–44 on Mechthild.

2. I will refer to the oldest extant version of Mechthild's work, the mid-fourteenth-century Einsiedler manuscript, in the Alemannic dialect of Middle High German, following the most recent critical edition: Mechthild von Magdeburg, *Das fliessende Licht der Gottheit*, ed. Hans Neumann (Munich: Artemis, 1990–93). In some cases, particularly in passages describing emotions, I will provide my own translations in the text and quote the original in a note. Whenever possible, I will refer to the English translation *Flowing Light of the Divinity*, trans. Christiane Mesch Galvani, ed. and intro. Susan Clark (New York: Garland, 1991). I will give book and chapter numbers, as well as the page numbers in Neumann's edition (hereafter cited as N) and Galvani's translation (G).

3. These accounts have been preserved to date as a book in two parts: a *Memorial*, or personal testimony, and a collection of letters to her disciples, known as *Instructions*. References to the *Memorial* part will include chapter and, when applicable, section numbers. All quotations of the original are from the critical edition by Ludger Thier and Abele Calufetti, *Il libro della Beata da Foligno* (Grottaferrata: Editiones Collegii S. Bonaventurae ad Claras Aquas, 1985), hereafter cited as T, based on the most authoritative Latin manuscript. Translations will be either mine or taken from the most recent English version: Angela of Foligno, *Complete Works*, trans. and intro. Paul Laplanche (New York: Paulist Press, 1993), cited as L.

4. The first version of *Life* (1562) has not been preserved, but it is generally thought that chapters 11–22 and 32–40, which focus on her prayer and visions, were added in the extant version of 1565. The other books are cited below. Given the

numerous editions of Teresa's works, I will use chapter and section numbers in my references. Unless otherwise stated, I will quote from the U.S. English translation, *The Collected Works of St. Teresa of Avila*, trans. Otilio Rodríguez and Kieran Kavanaugh (Washington, D.C.: Institute of Carmelite Studies, 1980), which includes her principal texts with the exception of *Foundations*. Quotations of original words describing emotions will be taken from *Obras completas de Santa Teresa*, ed. Efrén de la Madre de Dios and Otger Steggink (Madrid: BAC, 1986).

5. Among the Franciscan books from which Teresa learned her method of prayer was that of the lay brother Bernardino de Laredo, which clearly drew on Angela's book; see his *Subida del Monte Sión* (1538), in *Místicos Franciscanos Españoles*, ed. Juan Bautista Gomis, 3 vols. (Madrid: BAC, 1948), 2:13–442.

6. See Melquíades Andrés Martín, *La teología española en el siglo XVI*, 2 vols. (Madrid: BAC, 1976), 2:255. For an overview of the *alumbrado* movement, see Alastair Hamilton, *Heresy and Mysticism in Sixteenth-century Spain: The "Alumbrados"* (Cambridge: James Clarke, 1992).

7. This distinction between levels of prayer, drawn by Dionysius the Areopagite, was also used by authors like Richard of St. Victor in the twelfth century and Bernardino de Laredo in the sixteenth.

8. Elizabeth A. Petroff, *Body and Soul: Essays on Medieval Women and Mysticism* (New York: Oxford University Press, 1994), ix. See also Gerda Lerner's seminal feminist studies, *The Creation of Patriarchy* (New York: Oxford University Press, 1986), and *The Creation of Feminist Consciousness: From the Middle Ages to Eighteen-seventy* (Oxford: Oxford University Press, 1990).

9. For an overview of gender prejudices within the Judeo-Christian tradition, see Kari Elisabeth Børresen, *Subordination and Equivalence: The Nature and Role of Women in Augustine and Thomas Aquinas*, trans. Charles H. Talbot (Washington, D.C.: University Press of America, 1981); Rosemary Radford Ruether, *Women and Redemption: A Theological History* (London: SCM Press, 1998).

10. The reference to Tertullian is provided in Michel Foucault, "Technologies of the Self," in *Technologies of the Self: A Seminar with Michel Foucault*, ed. Luther H. Martin, Huck Gutman, and Patrick H. Hutton (London: Tavistock, 1988), 16–49, at 41.

11. Hildegard of Bingen (1098–1179), Mechthild of Hackeborn (1241–1299), and Gertrud of Helfta (1256–1302) are among the most educated nuns who left written testimonies in Latin.

12. Beguines, found especially in northern France, the Low Countries, Switzerland, and the Rhineland in the thirteenth century, were laywomen who sought spiritual perfection on their own, usually under the direction of Dominican confessors. They were probably the first "women's movement" in Western history. For an overview of Mechthild's life and work in English, see Elizabeth A. Andersen, *The Voices of Mechthild of Magdeburg* (Oxford: Peter Lang, 2000). See also John Howard, "The German Mystic: Mechthild of Magdeburg," in *Medieval Women Writers*, ed. Katharina Wilson (Manchester: Manchester University Press, 1984), 153–63.

13. We find references to her reading not only in the *Book of Her Life* but also in her *Constitutions*. The *devotio moderna*, a fifteenth-century movement of spiritual reform from Lower Germany, provides a link between the beguine movement to which Mechthild belonged and the Franciscan spirituality that inspired Angela and Teresa; see "Devotio Moderna" in the *Dictionnaire de spiritualité ascétique et mystique*, ed. Marcel Viller et al., 17 vols. (Paris: Beauchesne, 1932–95), 3: cols. 727–47; Albert Hyma, *The Christian Renaissance: A History of the "Devotio Moderna,"* 2nd ed. (Hamden, Conn.: Archon, 1965); John Engen's introduction to *Devotio Moderna: Basic Writings* (New York: Paulist Press, 1988), esp. 8–27.

14. See for instance Francisco de Ribera, *La vida de la Madre Teresa de Jesús* (Salamanca: Pedro Lasso, 1590); Fray Luis de León, "De la vida, muerte y virtudes y milagros de la Santa Madre Teresa de Jesús," in *Obras completas castellanas*, 1:921–941.

15. She was influenced by Francisco de Osuna's *Third Spiritual Alphabet* (1527), which she saw as her "only master" between 1538 and 1559 (*Life* 4.7).

16. St. Gregory, *Homiliae in Evangelia*, ed. Raymond Étaix (Turnhout: Brepols, 1999), 14.4, 99.

17. See *Dictionnaire de spiritualité*, 9: cols. 473–75.

18. For a study of the affective language used by St. Bernard and other Cistercian writers from the period, see Caroline Walker Bynum, *Jesus as Mother: Studies in the Spirituality of the High Middle Ages* (Berkeley and Los Angeles: University of California Press, 1982).

19. "The Steps of Humility," in *Treatises* (Kalamazoo, Mich.: Cistercian Publications, 1980), 25–90, at 34.

20. Translation mine; "Owe, das tuᵒt menig man nit, der wise ist von lere und von natúrlichen sinnen, das er sich iht getoᵉrre legen in die gewalt der nakkenden minne. Mere die einvaltigen reinen, die got in allem irem tuᵒnde luterlich meinent, zuᵒ den muᵒs sich got natúrlich neigen" (N57).

21. *Confessions*, trans. Henry Chadwick (Oxford: Oxford University Press, 1991), 9.6–7, 164–65.

22. The standard view was, as Peter Lombard (ca. 1100–ca. 1160) put it in his *Sentences*, that the serpent "tempted woman because he knew in her lesser intellectual vigour than in man"; see *Sententiarum textus* (Basel: Ludovicus Hornken, 1513), bk. 2, chap. 1, fol. 84v. See also St. John Chrysostom's warnings against women, cited by Heinrich Kramer and James Sprenger in their famous *Malleus Maleficarum* (1487), trans. and ed. Montague Summers (New York: Dover, 1971), 43.

23. St. Bonaventure, "Ad sorores," *The Works of Bonaventure*, trans. José de Vinck, 5 vols. (Paterson, N.J.: St. Anthony Guild Press, 1960–70), 1:207–55, at 216.

24. Translation mine; "crefteklichen súfzen, herzeklichen weinen, lebendige gerunge, herte twang, kumberlich ellende, getrúwú demuᵉtekeit, vrœlichú minne" (N137).

25. Translation mine; "nieman weis, was trost oder pine oder gerunge ist, er werde selber e geru^eret mit disen drin" (N161).
26. The cautious censor was her Dominican confessor García de Toledo. Kavanaugh's English translation of *The Way of Perfection* is based on the second (revised) version, which Teresa wrote in 1569. The twenty lines erased from the original manuscript have been reconstructed partly in *Obras completas* and partly in Tomás de la Cruz, *Camino de perfección*, facs. ed., 2 vols. (Rome: Teresianum, 1965), 1:67*–68*; see my "Writing Rearguard Action, Fighting Ideological Selves: Teresa of Avila's Reinterpretation of Gender Stereotypes in *Camino de perfección*," *Bulletin of Hispanic Studies*, 79.3 (2002), 299–308.
27. "Tengo por cierto no le pesa que nos consolemos y deleitemos en sus palabras y obras. . . . Que tampoco no hemos de quedar las mujeres tan fuera de gozar las riquezas del Señor; de disputarlas y enseñarlas, pareciéndoles aciertan, sin que se lo muestren a letrados, esto sí" (*Obras* 426).
28. My translation, from *Libro de las fundaciones*, in *Obras*, 671–815, at 688. Teresa's firsthand experience of God during meditation was seen as very valuable to some of her confessors, who encouraged her to write another book about her method of prayer, *Interior Castle* (1577).
29. ". . . quamvis aliqualis consolatio mihi esset quod poteram plangere in quolibet passu; sed erat una consolatio amera" (1.4; T134).
30. Translation mine; "du solt minnen das niht, / du solt vliehen das iht" (N24; cf. G20).
31. On Mechthild's use of visual symbols, see Margot Schmidt, "Elemente der Schau bei Mechthild von Magdeburg und Mechthild von Hackeborn: Zur Bedeutung der geistliche Sinne," in *Frauenmystik im Mittelalter*, ed. Peter Dinzelbacher and Dieter R. Bauer (Ostfildern bei Stuttgart: Schwabenverlag, 1985), 123–51.
32. "Alsus gezieret su^oche ich Jhesum, minen su^essen herren, und ich vinde in mit keinen dingen also schiere, alleine si sint ungevo^ege und swere. Man sol rehte vro^emelich hin tretten mit creftiger gerunge und mit schuldiger schemunge und mit vliessender liebi und mit demu^etiger vorhte" (N205).
33. See Jerome's letter to Eustochium [sic], daughter of Paula, on the preservation of virginity (lett. 22), in *The Principal Works of St. Jerome*, trans. W. H. Fremantle (Oxford: James Parker, 1893), 26.
34. Angela of Foligno, *Complete Works*, 219–20.
35. Angela's reputation as a teacher of theology is mentioned by Romana Guarnieri in her preface to Angela of Foligno's *Complete Works*, 9.
36. See Jacques Hourlier and André Rayez, "Humanité du Christ," *Dictionnaire de spiritualité*, vol. 7, cols. 1053–96. McGinn uses the terms "affectus" and "fiery love" as synonyms, and attributes the development of this emphatic approach to the passion to St. Bonaventure; see *The Flowering of Mysticism*, 151–52.
37. See Caroline Walker Bynum, *Fragmentation and Redemption: Essays on*

Gender and the Human Body in Medieval Religion (New York: Zone, 1991), 134. The fact that this emotionality was not exclusive to women, though it was often expressed in a feminine language, was demonstrated by Bynum in her earlier seminal work *Jesus as Mother* (see note 18).

38. The physiological impact of some Christian devotional practices on medieval women was the subject matter of two seminal studies: Rudolph M. Bell, *Holy Anorexia* (Chicago: University of Chicago Press, 1985); Caroline Walker Bynum, *Holy Feast and Holy Fast: The Religious Significance of Food to Medieval Women* (Berkeley and Los Angeles: University of California Press, 1987).

39. "[S]u Pasión con tan graves dolores, su vida tan afligida; en deleitarnos de ver sus obras, su grandeza, lo que nos ama," *Obras*, 66–67. On "passion mysticism," see Richard Kieckhefer, *Unquiet Souls: Fourteenth-Century Saints and Their Religious Milieu* (Chicago: University of Chicago Press, 1984), 107.

40. Translation mine; "et rogabam eum quod ipse me faceret istud praedictum observare, scilicet istam castitatem omnium membrorum et sensuum; quia ex una parte timebam promittere et ex alia parte ignis praedictus cogebat me promittere praedicta, et no poteram facere aliud" (T136; cf. L126). I translate *sensuum* as "feelings," but *sensus* had other meanings—sensation, emotion, affection.

41. Translation mine; "das ich dich jagete, des luste mich; das ich dich vieng, des gerte ich; das ich dich bant, des fro^ewete ich mich; do ich dich wundote, do wurde du mit mir vereinet; . . . Ich han den almehtigen got von dem himelrich getriben und han ime benomen sin mo^enschlich leben und han in mit eren sinem vatter wider gegeben, wie wenest du sno^eder wurm mo^egen vor mir genesen?" (N9–10; cf. G8).

42. "Si estáis alegre, miralde resucitado; que sólo imaginar cómo salió del sepulcro os alegrará. . . . Si estáis con trabajos u triste, miralde camino del Huerto. ¡Qué aflición tan grande llevava en su alma!; pues con ser el mesmo sufrimiento la dice y se queja de ella; u miralde atado a la Columna lleno de dolores, todas sus carnes hechas pedazos por lo mucho que os ama: . . . miraros ha Él con unos ojos tan hermosos y piadosos, llenos de lágrimas, y olvidará sus dolores por consolar los vuestros, sólo por que os vais vos con Él a consolar y volváis la cabeza a mirarle" (Valladolid ms., *Obras* 342).

43. Ignatius of Loyola, *Spiritual Exercises*, no. 48, first week.

44. "Ansí como dicen ha de hacer la mujer, para ser bien casada, con su marido: que si está triste, se ha de mostrar ella triste, y si está alegre, aunque nunca lo esté, alegre. Mirad de qué sujeción os havéis librado, hermanas. Esto con verdad, sin fingimiento, hace el Señor con nosotros: que Él se hace el sujeto, y quiere seáis vos la señora y andar Él a vuestra voluntad" (Valladolid ms., *Obras* 342).

45. "habet saporem carnis, sed alterius saporis sapidissimi, et nescio eum similare alicui rei de mundo"; "iacebam langues pro isto excessivo amore" (T310).

46. Bernard's interpretation offered a more personal and intimate alternative to the traditional interpretation, proposed by Origen, of the Song as portraying the love between Christ and his Church. For an overview of the various exegetical tra-

ditions, see E. Ann Matter, *The Voice of My Beloved: "The Song of Songs" in Western Medieval Christianity* (Philadelphia: University of Pennsylvania Press, 1990).

47. "Aber der sto^{v}b der súnden der uf úns vallet alsemere als ane únsern dank der wirt von der minne fúr also drate ze nihte als únser seleno^{v}gen wank der gotheit geru^{e}ret mit der ellendiger, súfzendiger su^{e}ssen gerunge, der kein creature mag widerstan" (N204).

48. McGinn's translation, in *The Flowering of Mysticism*, 236; "Ich habe din begert e der welte beginne. Ich gere din und du begerest min. Wa zwo^{e}i heisse begerunge zesamen koment, da ist die minne vollekomen" (N268; cf. G221).

49. Translation mine; "also du kumest über die not der rúwe und über die pine der bihte und über die arbeit der bu^{o}sse und über die liebin der welte und über die bekorunge dez túvels und über die überflússekeit des vleisches und über den verwassenen eigenen willen" (N27; cf. G22).

50. "Es machet ein sur herze su^{e}sse, ein trurig herze vro, ein arm herze rich, ein tump herze wise, ein blo^{e}de herze ku^{e}ne, ein krank herze stark, ein blint herze sehende, ein kalte sele brinnende" (N166).

51. Spanish had begun to develop as a mystical language through works such as *Carro de dos vidas* (1500) and García de Cisneros's *Exercitatorio espiritual* (1500), which included numerous translations from Latin mystical works.

52. On its session of November 25, 1551, the Council of Trent increased the annual obligation established by the fourth Lateran Council and made confession available as often as fortnightly, as a measure to prevent the spread of heresy; see Henry Charles Lea, *A History of Auricular Confession and Indulgences in the Latin Church*, 3 vols. (Philadelphia: Lea, 1896).

4

"Us for to wepe no man may lett"
Resistant Female Grief in the Medieval English Lazarus Plays

Katharine Goodland

In the N-Town cycle's *Raising of Lazarus,* as soon as Lazarus is interred, Mary Magdalene declares to her sister Martha, "Lete us sytt down here by þe grave / or we go hens wepe all oure fylle" (167–68).[1] Martha joins her, proclaiming, "Us for to wepe no man may lett" (169). Their exchange suggests that they expect their weeping to provoke opposition, and it does. Four male consolers, outraged by the sisters' conduct, take turns chastising them, denouncing their behavior as shameful and offensive: "Arys for shame ȝe do not ryght / streyth from þis grave ȝe xul go hens / þus for to grugge ageyns godys myght / Aȝens hyȝ god ȝe do offens" (173–76). The consolers seem unduly scandalized. How can women's tears offend one so powerful as God? But Martha explicitly poses the sisters' mourning at the grave as a form of resistance to male control, and the consolers respond in kind. They view the sisters' mourning as potent, a dangerous affront that must be curtailed. The public nature of this confrontation—in the open, at the gravesite—implies that the sisters' laments have a rhetorical appeal that the consolers find threatening to their position as the self-appointed spokesmen of "godys myght."

This gendered conflict between the discourse of female lament and the discourse of male control, so clearly delineated in the N-Town cycle, manifests itself, albeit more subtly and in different ways, in all of the extant manuscripts of the medieval English Lazarus plays. What is at stake is not simply a contest between female emotion and male control. In its deep structure it is an encounter between two different constructions of death and mourning: the dominant Christian belief that faith in God brings eternal life, and therefore one should not grieve over the dead; and the residual practice of lament for the dead, an oral tradition usually led by women in which "eternal life"—living on in the memory of the community—depends upon repetitive performances of mourning.[2] As a social practice presided over by women, ritual lament poses resistance to male social authority and the tenets of the dominant Christian ideology.

In his poetically astute reading of the Corpus Christi Passion plays Peter Dronke argues that the characterization of the mourning Virgin Mary, the *Planctus Mariae,* draws upon this tradition of residual lament: "the *nature* of the texts we have suggests . . . that the lament of Mary was not primarily a learned invention at all. On the contrary, when these laments surface in the learned world, they still bear all the marks of a non-theological genre and lyric impulse, the marks of a traditional type of woman's lament."[3] Dronke perceives several prominent features of female lament in his analysis of the medieval *Planctus*: Mary's love for life expressed in her laments for the decay of Christ's physical beauty; the frequent use of direct address, a key rhetorical feature of lament; and Mary's "unredeemable grief" which prevails over the Christian promise of salvation. He points to the dissonance of Mary's bitter tone in the Christian context of the Passion plays. Instead of affirming the "truth of the Redemption," Mary's "sorrowing remains unabated to the end." Dronke observes that Mary's "unredeemable grief" is evidence of "a particularly forceful resurgence of the ancient non-theological traditions of women's laments."

As Dronke's observations indicate, the genre of female lamentation encompasses the idea that grief, or mourning, is an obligatory performance with clear rhetorical features.[4] An ancient practice, reaching back beyond the historical records of archaic Greece, lamentation for the dead continues even today in parts of eastern Europe, Africa, and the Mediterranean.[5] A public performance that is usually led by the close female relatives of the deceased, its purpose is to articulate and therefore also contain the impending chaos that can accompany the intense emotions and altered social structure of a community that attends the death of one of its members.[6] The lamenters' narratives about the deceased, punctuated by shrieks and wails, honor and appease the spirit of the dead, assisting the soul in its journey through the afterlife. The stages of the body's passage, first in the home immediately after death, then in the burial procession, and finally at the grave where it is incorporated into the earth, mirror the condition of the bereaved community. Distinct rhetorical figures and gestures perform the emotions of rage, helplessness, and fear attendant upon death. Through direct address, interrogative apostrophes, incantations, wails, and shrieks the female lamenters are believed to commune with the spirit of the dead at the same time that they articulate the emotions and anxieties of their respective communities. Gestures of self-mutilation—tearing the hair and rending the face—align the mourners with the dead: just as death disfigures the body, so the mourners disfigure themselves. Lamenters wish for death and sit on the ground near the grave, denying separation and participating in the state of the dead. Their performance articulates social disorder and physical decay as a precondition for social regeneration and renewal. Because lamentation is an oral, performative genre, its efficacy depends upon repetition to sustain the presence of the deceased in the cultural memory: the essence of ritual lamentation is therefore expressed in its most common motif, unforgettable or inconsolable grief.

The persistence of ritual lament, or "wailing the dead" as it was known in England, is demonstrated by depictions of mourning and death in literature and widely scattered denunciations of the practice into the early years of the seventeenth century.[7] Denunciations of weeping over the dead are especially prevalent in sermons and treatises in the first decades of the Reformation. The early Protestant tirades against lament show that it coexisted with Catholic practices. Protestant prelates refer to the customs as both "popish" and "heathen." Matthew Parker, the future archbishop of Canterbury, used his 1551 funeral sermon for Martin Bucer as an occasion to exhort his parishioners to reform their mourning customs: "It agreeth not with the rules of faith, for a christian man to bewalye the dead. For who can deny that to be against faith, which is flatly forbidden by the scriptures." He admonishes his English audience to refrain from "wommanish wayling, and childish infirmitie . . . for it is both unseemly and wicked to use any howling or blubbering for him, unlesse we desire to be accounted creatures rather beastly in nature than furnished with the use of reason."[8] Hugh Latimer in his fifth Lincolnshire sermon in 1553 proclaims, "In the time of popery, before the gospel came amongst us, we went to buriales, with wepyng and wailing, as thoughe there were no god."[9] Similarly, Thomas Becon's dying man in *The Sicke mannes Salve* asserts, "Let the infideles mourne for their dead: the Christian ought to reioyse, whan anye of the faithfull be called from this vale of misery unto the glorious kingdom of God."[10] An anonymous treatise from the middle of the sixteenth century admonishes the English, "We muste not lamente and mourne of ungodlynesse and superstycion, as the unfaythefull heathen do whiche beleve not the resurrecyon of the dead."[11]

An ecclesiastical record from 1590 documents a mourning ritual in

Lancashire that bears a striking resemblance to that of the N-Town *Lazarus* and other medieval accounts of mourning the dead. The record refers to "enormities and abuses" and "superstition used in the burial of the dead" by the local community: "And when the corpse is ready to be put into the grave, some by kissing the dead corpse, others by wailing the dead with more than heathenish outcries, others with open invocations for the dead, and another sort with jangling the bells, so disturb the whole action, that the minister is oft compelled to let pass that part of the service and to withdraw himself from their tumultuous assembly."[12] In the N-Town *Lazarus* Martha and Mary wail loudly as their brother is interred, and Mary kisses his grave before she departs. The play is also structured around the four phases of residual lament: lament in the home, during the procession to the grave, at the grave, and following the burial. In the Digby *Mary Magdalene*, Mary refers to the custom of carrying the corpse to the grave accompanied by weepers, a practice resembling the final burial scene in the *Alliterative Morthe Arthure*.[13] Numerous references in sermons, consolatory letters, and literature throughout the sixteenth century indicate that "wailing the dead" was a deeply ingrained if residual mourning practice that was partially acculturated to Catholicism, continuing in parts of England for a generation or more after the Reformation.[14]

Two defining features of ritual lament are in tension with the central tenets of Christian eschatology. Inconsolable grief seems to subvert the Christian promise of redemption and eternal life, and the belief that women's cries could commune with the dead challenges the Christian belief in Jesus as the mediator between the human and heavenly realms. The medieval English Lazarus plays, even more than the Passion plays, reveal ambivalence in attempting to reconcile these opposed systems of value. In the Passion plays Mary's laments for Christ, despite the resistant sentiments noted by Dronke, align themselves with the religious pedagogy that construed weeping for Christ as a sign of compunction for sin.[15] While the *Planctus* is nonbiblical, the doctrine of Mary's Compassion—her share in Christ's suffering through her mourning—assimilated this resistant mode to Christian eschatology.[16] Such a rapprochement between grief and faith is less tenable and more complex in the Lazarus plays.[17]

All of the Lazarus plays modify the narrative emphasis of John's gospel, an alteration that reveals their ideological preoccupation.[18] They shift the focus of the plot away from the miracle that reveals Jesus's divine nature to the problem of mourning the natural death of a family member. The gospel's narrative climax is Jesus's command "Lazarus, come forth" (John

11:43), a moment that, as Rosemary Woolf notes, is presented perfunctorily in the medieval plays. In contrast, the four Corpus Christi Lazarus plays and the Lazarus episode of the Digby *Mary Magdalene* all focus on the problem of death and the propriety of the sisters' mourning. The scriptural story of Jesus's divine power over death becomes, in medieval drama, the story of the death of a family member and how the two surviving sisters should grieve. The discursive tension in these plays seems aimed at transforming, or at least controlling, the social construction of mourning: turning the grief-stricken away from the practice of lament led by women and toward the rituals of the Church controlled by men. The sisters' central role in the plots of the Lazarus plays indicates the lingering authority of women over matters of death and mourning in medieval England.

The plays' ideological work is complicated by the fact that in scripture Jesus weeps with Mary Magdalene and her fellow mourners just before he raises Lazarus from the dead: "When Jesus saw her [Mary] weeping, and the Jews who came with her also weeping, he was deeply moved in spirit and troubled; and he said, 'Where have you laid him?' They said to him, 'Lord, come and see.' Jesus wept" (John 11:33–36). This moment gave rise to two opposing interpretive traditions: one that framed Jesus's display of sorrow as an endorsement of women's tears, and another that discredited this perspective. The moment was variously interpreted as indicating Jesus's emotional restraint in the face of death, or his spiritual exertion while performing the miracle, or his pity for nonbelievers.

Christine de Pizan uses the scriptural passage to argue against "those who attack women for their habit of weeping." She points out that Jesus was moved to compassion "when he saw Mary Magdalene and her sister Martha weep for their dead brother" and asserts that their sorrow moved Jesus to resurrect Lazarus: "What special favors has God bestowed on women because of their tears!"[19] Her defense of female grief draws on a tradition of Christian thought that sees tears as expressions of compunction for sin.[20] Women were considered to be naturally more compassionate than men, and therefore more easily moved to Christian compunction and piety.[21]

An opposing homiletic tradition censures female grief and mourning for the dead.[22] These texts interpret Jesus's weeping as a gesture that signifies disapproval rather than empathy. Basil of Seleucia argues that Jesus wept in order to limit mourning by setting an example of restraint: "He wept, He did not lament, or wail, or moan, or rend His garments, or tear His hair." In contrasting Jesus's simple weeping with ritual lamentation, the bishop seeks to reform the mourning practices of his audience. Like the consolers of the N-Town *Lazarus* who echo him, he argues that excessive weeping implies a lack of faith and offends God: "Do not offend the One who has experienced the Resurrection by weeping immoderately." He asserts that Jesus wept, not out of pity for Mary Magdalene or Lazarus, but out of mercy for the "misguided views" of the Jews.[23] A late Middle English sermon dated sometime after 1490, like Basil of Seleucia's homily, shifts the meaning of Jesus's tears from sorrow to censure, stating that Jesus wept "to make us undirstond how hard it is for anny man to ryse ageyn from synne when that he is fallen ther-in."[24] These interpretations efface the gospel's description of the sisters' grief, indicating that female mourning practices were a significant source of social friction.

The discursive maneuvers of the medieval English Lazarus plays, like those of the homiletic tradition, manifest cultural anxiety over the performance of female grief. All of the Lazarus plays differ in their portrayals of mourning women, variations that are consistent with each cycle's central theological idea.[25] David Mills notes the Chester's emphasis "upon the fulfillment of divine purpose," the N-Town's "concentration upon grace," the York's illumination of "human foible," and the Towneley's exploration of "vital sin."[26] These distinct thematic emphases help to account for the differing ways each play treats the sisters' grief. The Chester *Lazarus* assimilates the sisters' ritual tears to prayer. Paradoxically, their feminine helplessness endows them with spiritual power: because they cry out for Jesus, he hears and answers their tears.

The sisters' faith in Jesus drives the plot of the Chester play: when he responds to their prayerful laments, Jesus fulfills his divine purpose. In contrast, the N-Town, York, and Towneley versions depict the sisters' sorrow as excessive, contrary to faith, and offensive to God. In the N-Town, the male consolers praise Jesus's miracle as a gift of grace that Mary Magdalene, in her resistant and excessive mourning, never acknowledges. The York *Lazarus* casts mourning for the dead as the result of limited human perception, and therefore reveals the human foible of incorrectly interpreting the meaning of a dead body. The Towneley's stern focus upon sin is consistent with its negative portrayal of female grief. In this version Jesus reprimands Mary Magdalene for her spiritual weakness. Finally, the Digby play presents a stoic Magdalene whose manly self-control marks her as a uniquely devout and heroic woman. This portrayal is in keeping with the genre of the play and the aristocratic ethos embodied by its heroine. Lawrence Clopper observes that "the playwright wishes to present

Mary as an apostle in her own right."[27] This may help to explain why she does not grieve. Because she is meant to be an exemplum of unwavering faith following her conversion, it is incumbent upon her to refrain from mourning the death of her only brother.[28]

As in the homiletic tradition, the scriptural moment in which Jesus weeps appears to have presented a dilemma for the compilers of the medieval Lazarus plays. Each of them uses a different strategy to distance Jesus from female grief and any association with mourning for the dead. These divergent representations reflect Christ's different overall function in each cycle, which Alexandra Johnston succinctly identifies: "In York he teaches; in Chester he acts; in Towneley he suffers; in N-Town he forgives."[29] Even given these thematic differences, however, it is significant that when the plays are viewed synoptically, Jesus's tears emerge as a source of tension. In the York *Lazarus*, Jesus teaches Martha and her sister that grieving is sinful, and therefore refrains from weeping himself. In the Chester, he actively responds to their tears, and the moment at which he purportedly weeps is ambiguous. Two Jews, who are portrayed as evil and unreliable witnesses, comment upon his weeping, but there is no other indication from Jesus's words or the stage directions that he actually weeps. In the Towneley, Jesus weeps as he prays, implying that his tears are the result of his spiritual exertion. Here Jesus weeps, not in empathy with Mary Magdalene's sorrow, but instead because of the immense effort required to lift Lazarus out of his sinful state. In the N-Town, like the Chester, the moment is ambiguous. Jesus says that the weeping of Mary Magdalene and the Jews who are with her causes him to weep, but the Latin rubric before line 373 has an odd distancing effect. It says "hic ihesus fingit se lacrimari" [here Jesus pretends to weep]. Does the rubric mean to suggest that the real Jesus only pretended to weep, or that the person portraying Jesus is supposed to enact Jesus weeping? The second possibility is inconsistent with the text, for presumably the other characters in the play are also "pretending" to weep, yet there is no rubric designating this. The first possibility is even more strange. Why would the real Jesus only pretend to weep? Does this mean to imply that because he is God and he knows there is no cause for sorrow, he cannot actually feel it, yet as a human he feels compelled to display compassion? The uneasiness again manifests the play's ambivalence toward female grief. In the N-Town *Lazarus*, Mary Magdalene's grief is at once necessary and sinful: her tears impel Lazarus's resurrection, but Jesus's response to her (pretended or otherwise) denotes forgiveness rather than empathy.

The thematic differences among the cycles and the varying depictions of Christ's tears are no doubt also related to the regional historical development of each cycle, a question that merits further investigation. For my purposes, it is noteworthy that all of the extant Lazarus plays deviate markedly from John's gospel in ways that indicate considerable anxiety over the control of female mourning for the dead. Moreover, all of the plays are predicated upon the view that grieving is a gendered activity, and that mourning women are potentially helpless, immoderate, and in need of containment through prayer, privacy, and, perhaps above all, masculine control. Nevertheless, in all of them female grief is integral to the unfolding dramatic action. The sisters' mourning, however denounced and curtailed and eventually supplanted by Christ's divine power, is a precondition for the performance of the miracle.

The N-Town *Lazarus*

The N-Town *Raising of Lazarus* enacts a gendered confrontation between the Christian doctrine espoused by four male consolers and the mourning ritual articulated by Martha and Mary Magdalene. Mary Magdalene's sorrow is characterized as excessive and troublesome, yet dramatically essential to Lazarus's resurrection. Her psychological and spiritual alignment with her brother drives the developing action, which unfolds in four episodes before Jesus arrives: Lazarus's death and the moments immediately following his demise; the funeral procession and burial; lamentation at the grave; and continued mourning after the interment. These four phases precisely correspond to the phases of mourning in the practice of ritual lament, a structure that also emphasizes the central conflict of the play.[30] Each episode involves a dispute between Lazarus's sisters and four male "consolers" over the propriety of grief. During each stage Martha and Mary Magdalene mourn violently in vivid gestures that evoke ritual lament: they tear their hair, wish for death, and throw themselves on the ground. Their exhibitions of sorrow draw sharp criticism from the male consolers. The men repeatedly attempt to curtail the sisters' laments, telling them that their weeping is pointless because death is both natural and unavoidable. The sisters respond by insisting upon their natural right and inherent obligation to grieve for their brother. Jesus's arrival moderates the discord between the consolers and the sisters, but because Mary Magdalene never acknowledges Jesus's power over death, the conflict is never completely resolved. This lack of resolution reinforces the gendered assumptions upon which the drama is based.

Throughout the play Mary Magdalene's entire being is aligned with Lazarus's condition. Just before he dies, she intuits his impending demise: "Alas Alas what eylight me / myne herte for wo is wundyr grete" (55–56). Premonition is a characteristic feature of lamentation. Prophetic utterances embody the belief that the woman's psyche is intimately connected to the life cycle of the universe. Women's cries were believed to influence this cycle, so it was considered bad luck to mourn before death occurred. In a compelling rendering of this idea, Lazarus dies only a few lines after Mary Magdalene's exclamation of woe. This moment registers the threatening power of female mourning, for whether the Magdalen's grief intuits or accelerates her brother's demise, her sorrow is intimately tied to his destiny.

Immediately upon his death, the two sisters wail fervently, using gestures and motifs customary of lament. Mary Magdalene tears her hair: "Alas ffor wo myn here I rende / Myn owyn dere brothyr lyth here now ded" (109–10). Martha's heart, like the body of her brother and the earth that is its destiny, is "colde as clay" (115). Mary Magdalene wishes to "ly down by hym and dey" (124), for "all joye is turnyd to woo" (128). These are familiar conceits from the genre of lamentation. Her desire for death elicits words of Christian consolation from the First Consoler: "Be of good comforte and thank god of al / Ffor deth is dew to every man" (129–30). Martha defends their laments, observing that mourning, like death, is natural and necessary: "We all xul dye þat is sertan / but ȝit þe blood of kynde nature / Whan deth þe brothyr Awey hath tan / must nedys murne þat sepulture" (133–36). The Second Consoler admonishes them, urging them to proceed with the burial: "holde ȝour pes / All ȝour wepynge may not amende itt / of ȝour sorwynge þer fore now ses / And helpe he were buryed in a cley pitt" (137–40). This exchange clearly indicates the contrasting perspectives which are delineated by gender: the women articulate the residual view that their cries are both obligatory and necessary, while the men represent the Christian view that they are useless and therefore excessive.

The group processes to the grave, the men carrying the body and the women following behind "with carefull herte" (152). The women lament throughout the procession and the burial. Mary Magdalene then attempts to remain at the grave to mourn after Lazarus is interred. From the viewpoint of ritual lament, the sisters' continual lamenting would have been efficacious, for their voices would have assisted the soul's journey, while providing cathartic relief for the community. From the Christian perspective, however, their voices are both excessive and offensive because, as the consolers repeatedly tell them, their cries accomplish nothing, show doubt about the resurrection, and therefore offend God. The women's public display of grief elicits the most intense rebuke from the consolers. Mary Magdalene utters two more lines of lament before the consolers manage to remove her from her brother's tomb. As they do so, she declares: "my brotherys graue lete me fyrst kys / Alas no whith may helpe my mon / Ffare wel my brothyr fare wel my blys" (178–80). In the genre of lament the mourner would bid farewell by kissing the corpse. Though she kisses the grave rather than the corpse, Mary Magdalene's gesture of farewell echoes this custom. The displacement of her kiss from the corpse to the grave suggests angst over portraying the actual gesture, which, as indicated by the ecclesiastical record from Lancashire, prevailed into the late sixteenth century. Her lyric good-bye elicits further censure from the Third Consoler: "In dede ȝe do ryght sore amys / so sore to wepe as þe do here" (183–84). The sisters' behavior at Lazarus's tomb moves the consolers to their most severe reproofs. The consolers seem to object most to the ritualistic implications of the sisters' public performance of grief, for they tell the sisters to return to the privacy of their home to mourn, and agree to stay and comfort them.

In her home Mary Magdalene denies social interaction in a characteristic gesture of continued mourning and communion with the dead. When Jesus arrives she says that he has come too late, rejecting the consolers' admonishments to cease her mourning. Martha turns to Jesus, expressing her faith in him, but Mary Magdalene remains disconsolate: "Alas my mowth is bytter as galle / grett sorwyn my herte on tweyn hath scorn / Now þat my brothyr from syth is lorn / þer may no myrth my care releve / Alas þe tyme þat I was born / þe swerde of sorwe myn hert doth cleve" (323–28). Her use of the motif of the "sword of sorrow" alludes to the sorrow of the Virgin Mary. In fulfillment of Simeon's prophecy in Luke 2:34–35, Mary experiences piercing agony during Christ's Passion. However, this analogy between Mary's grief and Mary Magdalene's seems precarious, because the play strongly suggests that Mary Magdalene's mourning puts her in a state of sin.

The play extends this unstable analogy between Mary Magdalene and the Virgin. In the N-Town *Passion,* the Virgin's mourning and Christ's suffering are intertwined. After Christ's burial, Mary weeps in the temple, and as she does, Christ harrows hell and then rises again. This simultaneous staging invests Mary's tears with dramatic agency, showing her full participation—through her mourning—in the salvation of the world.[31] Similarly, in the N-Town *Lazarus*, Mary Magdalene's choices seem to drive her brother's destiny. Her return to the community from the isolation of her grief prefigures Lazarus's return from the grave: a poetic echo indicates this connection between Mary Magdalene's dolor and recovery and Lazarus's death and resurrection. When Jesus asks for Mary Magdalene, Martha calls to her: "Sustyr magdalen com out of halle" (337). Jesus echoes this come-out call when he invokes Lazarus to rise: "Ffrom þat depe pitt come out a-non" (422). The word "halle," while designating the living space of medieval homes, also sounds very much like the word "hell." The implication of this echo is reinforced by Jesus's call to Lazarus to come out of the "depe pitt," a common epithet for hell. In other words, Mary Magdalene must first emerge from the sin of her mourning before Lazarus can be raised by Jesus from the hell of death. Again and again in this play, Mary Magdalene's sorrow and Lazarus's destiny are intertwined. The play expands upon the gospel account in order to emphasize the excessive nature of Mary Magdalene's mourning even as that excess compels the action.

Moreover, the play intensifies the focus upon Mary Magdalene's grief by dilating simple narrative references in John into moments of high drama. In scripture, John simply states: "When the Jews who were with her in the house, consoling her, saw Mary rise quickly and go out, they followed her, supposing that she was going to the tomb to weep there" (John 11:31). In the N-Town play, the Third and Fourth Consolers exchange excited comments on her behavior. The Third Consoler exclaims, "Herke gode ffrendys I ʒow pray / Aftyr þis woman in hast we wende / I am a-ferde ryght in good fay / here-self for sorwe þat she wyl shende" (345–48). The Fourth Consoler agrees, "Here brothyr so sore is in hire mende / She may not ete drynke nor slepe / streyte to his grave she goth on ende / As a mad woman þer for to wepe" (349–52). Another telling augmentation of the gospel is the moment of Jesus's arrival, which in the N-town becomes another opportunity for portraying Mary Magdalene's grief as excessive and troublesome. Whereas in John she goes to Jesus as soon as Martha calls her, in the N-town play she responds bitterly to her sister's summons (341) and goes to him reluctantly: "me thynkyth longe or I come thedyr" (344). She greets Jesus with the familiar biblical line that he could have prevented Lazarus's death if only he had been present (353–56).[32] However, her ensuing lament seems to challenge his healing power, because she asserts that nothing can conquer death: "Ageyn deth is no resystens / Alas myn hert is woundyrly wo / Whan þat I thynke of his Absens / þat ȝe ȝour-self in herte lovyd so" (357–60). These embellishments of scripture characterize Mary Magdalene as excessive in her sorrow and deepen the implication that her grief is sinful, but they also make her mourning central to the play's architecture.

Jesus's arrival reconciles the opposition between the consolers and the sisters, creating a community of mourners for the first time in the play. In his presence, the consolers express their sorrow. The First Consoler confesses that "þe losse of hym doth marre oure mood" (364). The Second Consoler echoes him in a lilting lyric: "now he is gon, gon is oure frende" (368). This chorus of grief compels Jesus to weep: "I can not me for wo restreyn / but I must wepe lyke as ȝe do" (371–72). Jesus's expression of sorrow, however, does not sanction Mary Magdalene's mourning, and the tension between her role as mourner and Jesus's role as redeemer is never resolved. Mary Magdalene, whose grief forms the dramatic premise for Jesus's miracle, never acknowledges Jesus's power over death, even after Lazarus rises from the tomb. At the end of the play the consolers join in a choric refrain that noticeably excludes the voices of the women. Together the consolers proclaim their faith in Jesus as the conqueror over death: "O sovereyn lord of most excellens / helpe vs of ȝour grace whan þat we go hens / Ffor aȝens deth us helpyht not to stryve / but aȝen ȝoure myght is no resistens / oure deth ȝe may A-slake and kepe vs stylle on lyve" (444–48). This echo of Mary Magdalene's earlier words, "Ageyn deth is no resystens" (357) emphasizes her marked absence from the concluding hymn of praise. The characterization of her sorrow as excessive and sinful thus reinforces the gendered assumption that women are more prone to grief than men, and therefore in need of masculine guidance and control in times of sorrow.

Despite the consolers' protestations, the sisters, and especially Mary Magdalene, manage to perform virtually all the stages and gestures of ritual lament before Jesus arrives. The evidence from the Lancashire record describing the coexistence of Catholic burial and ritual lament indicates that the portrayal of mourning and burial in the N-Town *Lazarus* corresponded fairly accurately to actual practice. Anthropologists have long observed that when it comes to matters of burial, cultural beliefs and practices are extremely conservative and resistant to change. As the N-Town *Lazarus* demonstrates, the denounced and excessive female lamenter performs important cultural work. She ensures that the dead are mourned, commemorated, and remembered in the community, even as she is ostracized for doing so.

The York *Lazarus*

Whereas in the N-Town *Lazarus* the mourning by Mary Magdalene is dramatically necessary and yet resistant to the play's teleology, the York *Lazarus* achieves closure through the Magdalen's dramatic repudiation of her inconsolable grief. The play uses a commonplace of women's lament— the mourner's cry of anguish as she gazes upon the dead body—to demonstrate that Christ's miracle alters human perception even as it heals unforgettable grief. The drama defines Lazarus's dead body as signifier, enacting a ritual transformation of its meaning. First interpreted by Maria (as the York play calls the Magdalen) as an emblem of unending pain, Lazarus's body accrues new meaning for those who see and believe in Jesus's miracle.

Early in the play Jesus declares to his apostles that he will go to Bethany to cure the sisters of their sorrow, explicitly linking the necessity of his miracle to their mourning behavior: "His sisteres praye with bowsom beede / And for comforte þei call and craue, / Therfore go we togedir / To make þere myrthis more" (141–44). Jesus describes the sisters' mourning as a form of prayer, but their cries have no Christian sentiments: they are grounded in the ethos of inconsolable grief and the motifs of lament. Jesus's reference to the rosaries the sisters presumably hold as they wail shows once again how ritual lament seems to have coexisted with Christian practices. But the juxtaposition of lament with prayer creates a dissonance that the action of the play attempts to resolve. As the plot unfolds, it enacts the displacement of the ethos of unforgettable sorrow with the Christian promise of eternal life.

The action develops in a sequence of rhetorical forms that impart the play's discursive design: the sisters' laments are superseded first by Jesus's prayer, then Lazarus's exhortation, and finally Jesus's blessing as the sanctioned interpretations of the meaning of Lazarus's body. The act of seeing, a reference both to the character's perception of the corpse and the audience's experience of the action onstage, forms the premise of each character's address. The sisters' profound sorrow drives the plot of the play as Maria cries out in despair and Martha searches for Jesus to help them.

Maria's lament articulates her ritual perception of Lazarus's body as a lifeless corpse, a gaze that embodies unending pain: "Allas, owtane Goddis will allone, / Þat I schulld sitte to see þis sight / For I may morne and make my mone, / So wo in worlde was neuere wight. / Þat I loued most is fro me gone, / My dere brothir þat Lazar hight / And I durst saye I wolde be slone / For nowe me fayles both mynde and myght" (147–54). She ends her lament, transfixed by Lazarus's dead body, insisting upon her inconsolable grief and desire to join him: "My welthe is wente for euere, / No medycyne mende me may. / A, dede, þou do thy deuer / And haue me hense away" (155–58). Apart from being a beautiful alliterative lyric, this twelve-line lament possesses many of the characteristics of ritual lament. The opening of the lyric, with the words "to see þis sight," establishes the importance of the mourner's gaze on the body: her lament will interpret and articulate the meaning of death. She establishes her right to mourn by announcing that she weeps for her brother, Lazarus. She proclaims her grief as unending and more severe than anyone's. Finally, she wishes to die in order to preclude separation from her brother. Despite what Jesus says, Maria does not pray; she mourns. Moreover, with her opening line, "Allas, owtane Goddis will allone," she directly cries out against God's will that her only brother should die. The resistant stance of her lament heightens the emotional drama of these lyric exchanges. In ritual lament, the mourner addresses the corpse, asking the deceased why he has abandoned the mourner. In the play, this rhetorical gesture is transferred from the corpse to God as Maria cries out in the extremity of her grief. This shift suggests, as in the book of Job, that God hears and answers those who cry out to him, even when they do so in anger.

Like Maria, who denies that she will ever be cured of her sorrow, Martha begins with ritual lament, expressing inconsolable grief and a desire for death: "Allas, for ruthe now may I raue / And febilly fare by frith and felde, / Wolde God þat I wer grathed in graue, / Þat dede hadde tane me vndir telde. / For hele in harte mon I neuere haue" (159–63). However, at the midpoint of her lament she turns away from her brother's dead body, looking to Jesus for comfort: "But if he helpe þat all may welde, / Of Crist I will som comforte craue / For he may be my bote and belde" (164–66). She resolves not to cease looking "Tille I my souereyne see" (168), thus shifting her gaze from her brother's lifeless body to her lord's incarnate one. Martha's change prefigures her sister's. Unfortunately, the precise details of Maria's exchange with Jesus are a mystery, because nearly four complete stanzas are missing from the manuscript at this point. The missing elements are Jesus's arrival at Bethany and his exchanges with each sister. The manuscript resumes with the removal of the stone from Lazarus's grave and Jesus's supplication to God.

When Jesus prays to God, asking him to return Lazarus to life, he echoes Maria's cry of agony, calling attention to the new meaning his miracle bestows upon the dead body. Maria's wail has directed the audience to experience the grief and disorder of death through her suffering gaze: "þat I schulld sitte to see þis sight" (148). In contrast, Christ avows that those who see his miracle, "Þat standis and bidis to se þat sight" (180), will know that God has sent him. Similarly, when Lazarus emerges from the tomb, he designates his body as a sign, not of death, as in Maria's vision, but of God's power. The event, he declares, "þus hast schewed þi myght in me" (188). In yet another reference to vision and perception, Lazarus urges the audience to see that Christ's miracle denotes his incarnate deity and bestows salvation upon the faithful. Those who believe will not see a corpse, but instead a vision of eternal life: "By certayne singnes here may men see / How þat þou art Goddis sone verray. / All þo þat trulye trastis in þe / Schall neuere dye, þis dar I saye" (190–93). This sequence of speeches redefines the meaning of death, replacing the imprint of inconsolable grief with the Christian belief in redemption and eternal life.

Even as it displaces Maria's sorrowing gaze with Christ's spectacle of joy, however, the York *Lazarus* pays tribute to the authorial voice of women's laments. For just as Maria's gaze initially guides the audience to see Lazarus's death as torment, the play's closure depends upon her affirmation to redirect the audience's sight to Christ: "Here may men fynde a faythfull frende / Þat þus has couered vs of oure care" (198–99). In a final echo of the "sight" of her opening lament, Jesus, empowered by Maria's transformation, reminds the audience, "ȝe þat haue sene þis sight / My blissyng with ȝo be" (208–9).

Supplanting Maria's ritual lament by Jesus's raising of the dead, the York play reinscribes the ethos of inconsolable grief as a sign of disbelief and excessive sorrow. Those who trust in Christ will not see a corpse when they look upon the dead; they will see the promise of Christ's blessing: redemption and eternal life. Yet, because the sisters' laments drive the action, the play's dramatic closure rests upon a paradox. Jesus's blessing upon the audience in lines 208–9 for "seeing" raises the question of what exactly they have just seen. They have witnessed not only the miraculous raising of Lazarus but also the insistent grief of mourning women, grief with the power to beckon the Son of God himself.

The Chester *Lazarus*

Whereas the York play rewrites the ethos of mourning through the poetic repetition and transformation of a conventional ritual motif of lament, the Chester *Lazarus* assimilates the sisters' mourning ritual to prayer. As in the N-Town and York cycles, the sisters' grief structures the action of the Chester play, which begins with the sisters' cries of woe and ends with their lyrics of joy. This framing of the play by the sisters' sorrow and subsequent joy demonstrates how essential their voices are to the legitimacy of its ideological message. For, as in the York *Lazarus*, the Chester's dramatic closure depends upon Martha's and Maria's concluding testimonials to Jesus's power. As in the N-Town *Lazarus*, the sisters mourn at Lazarus's tomb, a clear departure from John's gospel account that reveals the play's concern with the propriety of female grief. Yet, in contrast to the N-town and the York versions, which oppose mourning to Christian faith, the Chester play aligns them. In this version the sisters do not need to be taught the meaning of eternal life, as in the gospel account and in the other cycles; they already know and believe. Their ritual at Lazarus's tomb becomes an ideal act of Christian piety: they are not mourning for their dead brother but are supplicating Jesus with their prayerful tears.

The play opens with Maria crying for Jesus: "A lord Jesu, that me is woo / to wytt my brother syckly soo! / In feeble tyme Christ yoode me froo" (301–3). While punctuated with the traditional sighs of "A" and "Alas," the Chester sisters' cries denote Christian helplessness and faith rather than rites of lament. Following Maria's opening lament, the play departs from scripture, as Martha herself seeks out Jesus instead of sending a messenger: "Yea sister, abowt I will goe / and seeke Jesu too and froo" (305–6). Placing the women firmly at the center of the dramatic action, this alteration also creates the opportunity for an exchange between Martha and Jesus in which he tells her that he is God's son and "that sickenes is not deadly" (314). Martha seems to understand Jesus's elliptical language. When she returns home, she finds Maria in the throes of grief: "A, Martha, sister, alas, alas! / My brother ys dead syth thou heere was. / Had Jesus my lord binne in this, / this case had not befalne" (317–20). Martha has returned home to find an apparent contradiction: Jesus promised that her brother's illness was not fatal. Yet she already knows that he can raise the dead: "Yea, sister, neare is Godes grace. / Manye a man hee holpen hasse. / Yett may hee doe for us in this case / and him to life call" (321–24). The two sisters decide to mourn at their brother's tomb as a means of invoking Jesus's aid.

As in the N-Town, the scene at Lazarus's burial site vividly evokes residual lament as the sisters enact a tearful vigil. They sit on the ground in postures of extreme grief, their language indicating the ritualized nature of their sorrow. Maria declares, "Here will I sitt and mourninge make / tyll that Jesu my sorrowe slake. / My teene to harte, lord, thou take, / and leech mee of my woe" (325–28). Maria does not simply feel sorrow, she "makes" mourning. Similarly, Martha declares: "In sorrowe and woe here wyll I wake, / and lament for Lazar my brothers sake. / Though I for coulde and pennance quake, / heathen will I not goe" (329–32). The sisters are not merely expressing feelings, they are performing a ritual, for they declare they will remain at the tomb, despite personal discomfort, until they achieve clearly articulated ends: Maria will mourn until Jesus comes to cure her, and Martha will "wake" for her brother's benefit. Their ritual objectives show that they believe their cries will be heard and answered by Jesus.

The scene's staging reinforces the implicit power of their cries, for the Latin rubric before line 333 suggests that the sisters' ritual weeping and Jesus's decision to go to them occur simultaneously: "Tunc pariter juxta sepulchrum sedebunt plorantes, et Jesus procul sit" [Then they, the weepers, sit together near the tomb and Jesus is at a distance]. Although they were understood to be separated by several days' travel, the stage direction indicates that the sisters and Jesus are onstage at the same time. The visual telescoping of space and time indicates that the sisters' mourning ritual has invoked divine will: Jesus seems to have been mysteriously beckoned by their tears when he declares to his disciples: "Brethren, Goe we to Judye" (333).

Because Martha already knows that Jesus has the power to raise the dead, the sisters' ritual at their brother's grave is aligned with Christian teleology. Their wails are depicted as fervent supplications heard and answered by Christ rather than as ritual laments with the power to awaken the dead. Moreover, as in the N-Town *Lazarus*, the iconography of the sisters' lamenting at a sepulchre creates a typological association with the laments of the three Maries in the Resurrection sequence. Echoing Christine de Pizan's defense of female woe, the Chester play consecrates the ability of women's helpless tears to commune with God.

Jesus hears and answers their laments. When he arrives at their home in Bethany, each sister lyrically addresses him in turn. Their respective dialogues with Jesus follow scripture, which develops the theological concept that resurrection and grace depend upon faith in God. Although they do not fully perceive the extent of Jesus's power, they have complete faith in his teachings, which each dutifully recites at his bidding. Martha tells him that she steadfastly believes that he is God's son and asks him to have mercy on her and her sister (394–400). When Maria enters, she simultaneously professes sorrow and steadfast belief: "A, lord Jesu, haddest thou binne here, / Lazarre my brother, thy owne deare / had not binne dead in this manere. / Mych sorrowe is me upon" (418–21). At the point where Jesus purportedly weeps, the rubric refers to the entrance of two Jews, mentioning nothing about Jesus's tears.[33] In the absence of a rubric or clear stage direction, the only indication that Jesus weeps comes from the bitter words of the First Jew as Jesus approaches Lazarus's tomb: "See fellowe, for cockes soule, / this freake beginneth to reeme and yowle / and make great dowle for gowle / that hee loved well before" (426–29). The First Jew's remark differs markedly in tone and purpose from the scriptural account: "So the Jews said, 'See how he loved him!'" (John 11:36). Because the Chester play aligns weeping and prayer, the exaggerated response of the Jews may indicate their stereotypical association with hearts of stone. In this case the Chester seems to defend weeping for the dead, as long as that weeping occurs within the framework of faith. The auditors are encouraged to turn to Jesus in their sorrow, like the sisters in the play. Jesus's characterization affirms moderate grief, which is here defined as mourning that is submissive to the masculine control of the Church.

When Lazarus emerges from the tomb at Jesus's command, he presents to the audience the allegorical meaning of the miracle. He praises his lord for freeing him from sin and death: "Lord, when I hard the voyce of thee, / all hell fayled of there postie, / so fast from them my soule can flee; / all divells were afrayd" (454–57). In scripture Lazarus goes silently on his way (John 11:44). The Chester play, in contrast, shifts the dramatic focus back to the two sisters. They affirm Jesus's power with hymns of joy, drawing attention to the fact that their grief has compelled the play's dramatic movement. Martha sings a hymn of praise, emphasizing that Jesus has saved them "from mych woe" (460). Maria's hymn is twice as long. She begins by echoing her sister's sentiment that Jesus has cured them of grief:

"for nowe my harte is glad and light / to see my brother ryse in my sight" (467–68). In the second stanza she assumes the traditional role of the lament poet; her personal testimony inscribes the meaning of the miracle onto the communal memory: "By verey signe nowe men maye see / that thou arte Godes Sonne" (476–77). The Chester *Lazarus* thus constructs female grief as powerful when it is perfectly aligned with Christian faith. Because the sisters never doubt Jesus's power, he responds to their tearful prayers and fulfills his destiny. This version of the Lazarus miracle thus reconciles ritual lament with Christian doctrine by assimilating the ritual of grief to the exertions of prayer.

The Chester play demonstrates how residual lament and Catholic doctrine coexisted. There is a compelling analogy here between the sisters' belief that their tears are spiritually efficacious and Margery Kempe's gift of tears. During the Easter vigil Margery would weep for hours on end for the souls in purgatory, believing that her tears helped to release them from their suffering.[34] Since the ultimate message of the Chester *Raising of Lazarus* is that faith in Jesus leads to salvation and triumph over death, the agency of the sisters' tears is assimilated to and contained within Christian eschatology. But the centrality of the sisters' grief to the dramatic structure of the play resists this accommodation.

The Towneley *Lazarus*

The Towneley *Lazarus* differs significantly from the N-Town, York, and Chester in subject matter and theme. Whereas the other three plays stress Jesus's love and pity for suffering humankind, the Towneley play emphasizes God's exacting judgment, the need for unwavering faith, and personal accountability. It highlights the importance of spiritual autonomy over reciprocal communal empathy.

The Chester play opens with Martha's and Maria's cries, and in the York and N-Town, Jesus specifically links his decision to go to Bethany to the sisters' laments. The Towneley play passes over this connection. Instead, it emphasizes Jesus's supernatural knowledge by opening with his announcement to the disciples that he knows Lazarus has died. The play also departs from scripture in characterizing Maria's grief as a sign of weakness bordering on sinful despair. This depiction is in keeping with the play's stark mood and dramatic theme: "that God releases the faithful from bondage."[35] The play insists that the only secure means of salvation is through faith in Christ. In the stern homily Lazarus delivers from the edge of his tomb, he cautions the audience against reliance upon the goodwill of others to save them from the torments of hell. While diminishing the roles of the sisters relative to the other plays, the Towneley play nevertheless associates Maria's grief with Lazarus's death and resurrection. Like the N-Town play, the Towneley *Lazarus* casts Maria's grief as a form of confinement from which she must be released, just as Lazarus must be freed from the captivity of death. In the N-Town, however, Maria's choice to emerge from her mourning invests her with agency—it is her will that is a precondition for Lazarus's resurrection. In the Towneley *Lazarus*, Jesus must free the Magdalen from her sorrow before he frees Lazarus from the bondage of sin and death.

Even though the Towneley play minimizes the agency of female grief, it still links Maria's emotional state with Lazarus. Lazarus's exhortation on death reinforces the message that mourning for the dead is sinful. Echoing Luke's parable of Lazarus and the rich man, it aligns his return from the grave with Christ's Harrowing of Hell and the call of God's trumpet on the day of the Last Judgment. When Martha tells Maria that Jesus has come, her words suggest that Maria's mourning is a form of bondage: "Sister, lefe this sorowful bande" (63),[36] whereas in John's account Martha simply says, "The Teacher is here and is calling for you" (11:28). Moreover, in the scriptural account the Magdalen runs to Jesus without hesitation: "And when she heard it, she rose quickly and went to him" (11:29). The Towneley play presents her emotional state in a more negative light. Here Maria exclaims, "A, for godys luf let me go!" (66), as if she is struggling to extricate herself from unseen chains. A repetition of "bande" makes explicit the association of Maria's release from grief and Lazarus's release from death: after Jesus commands, "Com furth, lazare, and stand vs by" (97), he directs, "Take and lawse hym foote and hande, / And from his throte take the bande" (99–100). It is not clear whom he addresses with the instructions to strip Lazarus of his grave clothes. Presumably it is the sisters, for they are the only others onstage.

By stressing that the Magdalen's sorrow, like death itself, is a form of bondage from which only faith in Jesus can free her, the Towneley *Lazarus* suggests that her grief is sinful. Jesus reinforces this meaning in his unbiblically austere response to her anguish. Twice the Towneley Jesus deviates from scripture and implies that Maria's feelings show spiritual frailty. The first time occurs when Maria greets Jesus with a description of her sorrow drawn from a familiar motif of ritual lament: "mekill sorow may men se / Of my sister here and me: / We are heuy as any lede, / ffor our broder that thus is dede" (69–72). Her melancholy elicits a stern warning from Jesus, who cautions her: "Bot loke no fayntyse ne no slawth / Bryng you oute of stedfast trawthe" (77–78).[37] Maria's sorrow elicits not compassion, as in John, but censure; Jesus implies that her emotion borders on despair. Prior to this moment Jesus has used the word "fayn" twice: first in assuring Martha that she "may be fayn [joyful]" (43) because her "brothere shall rise and lif agayn" (44), and next because he (Jesus) has come to help them: "Go tell thi sister mawdlayn / That I com, ye may be fayn" (61–62). The repetition of the word and its etymological antonym indicates that Maria's behavior directly opposes the appropriate Christian response, both to Jesus's arrival and to Lazarus's death.

The Towneley version also subtly emends the biblical account of Jesus's weeping, just enough to eliminate any affinity between Maria's and Jesus's tears. The Towneley rubric "Et lacrimatus est Jhesus, dicens" comes just before Jesus utters the words "ffader, I pray the that thou rase / lazare that was thi hyne, / And bryng hym oute of his mysese / And oute of hell pyne" (89–92).[38] This conflation of weeping with prayer signifies, as Seth Riemer argues, the intensity of Jesus's supplication rather than empathy for the bereaved sisters.[39]

Upon emerging from the tomb, Lazarus addresses the audience with a memento-mori sermon. Throughout the address, Jesus and Martha and Maria remain on the stage. As Barbara Gusick points out, this presence is "an uncomfortable fit".[40] The exhortation's stark and frightening message conflicts with a biblical story that originally encompassed both communal empathy and the need for personal faith. The Towneley Jesus is directive and stern rather than loving and compassionate. Given the presence of his sisters onstage next to Jesus, Lazarus's warning to the audience that the family's "sorow" will "slake" (157) is especially discordant. Maria did not cease sorrowing: Jesus made her stop. The Towneley *Lazarus* thus condemns female mourning to such an extent that it subverts its own dramatic and theological coherence. Dramatically, as Gusick's remark indicates, this condemnation is incongruous with the staging of the play. Theologically, the play's message contradicts that of John's gospel, which presents a compassionate and forgiving Jesus who moderates rather than denounces grief.

The Digby *Mary Magdelene*

Although the Lazarus episode in the Digby *Mary Magdalene* differs markedly from the Towneley in its characterization of the Magdalen, it embodies similar disapproval toward mourning for the dead. Lazarus's death is one among many episodes in this saint's play that follows the life of Mary Magdalene from her worldly aristocratic adolescence in her father's kingdom (Jerusalem, Bethany, and the castle of Magdala), through her waywardness and sin, to her ultimate sanctification and saintly performance of miracles. Significantly, early in the play when her father Cyrus dies, it is Mary Magdalene's inordinate mourning for his death that makes her vulnerable to lechery, the first of the seven deadly sins to overtake her.[41] Thus her stoic response to her brother's death later in the play demonstrates her transformation and newfound elevated spirituality. Both sisters in the Digby play are less passionate in their grief than in the cycle plays. This stoicism reflects their social status; as aristocrats, they can afford to hire mourners rather than engage in the dirty work of mourning themselves. Mary is depicted as even less emotional than Martha. When her brother dies, she expresses unwavering faith rather than grief: "Jhesu, my Lord, be yower sokowre, / And he mott be yower gostys welth!" (824–25). Martha, referring to their obligation to bury their brother rather than to mourn him as in the cycle plays, responds: "We must nedys ower devyrs doo, / To þe erth to bryng wythowt delay" (832–33). Unlike the sisters of the other plays, these sisters waste no time with waking and wailing. All business, they immediately arrange for Lazarus's burial. These conspicuously aristocratic and dispassionate ladies contrast sharply with the mourning women of the cycle plays. Mary Magdalene refrains from weeping herself, but nevertheless honors "custom" by ordering her knights to hire black-clad weepers for her brother's funeral: "As þe vse is now, and hath byn aye, / Wyth wepers to þe erth yow hym bryng. / Alle þis must be donne as I yow saye, / Clad in blake, wythowtyn lesyng" (834–37). This particular line is more evidence of residual social practice, for we find the heroine of the play telling us that it is the "custom" to have "weepers" accompany funeral processions. Mary Magdalene's self-conscious appeal to "custom" as justification for her brother's funeral rite also points to an inherent dichotomy between her personal adherence to Christian doctrine and her public accommodation of residual practice, further implying a hierarchy of values. For her stoic response underwrites her heroism and sustains the hagiographic integrity of the play. This impassive Lady Magdalene displaces her grief onto the emblematically somber procession that carries her brother's corpse to the grave, foreshadowing post-Reformation England's aesthetic enshrinement of female mourning.[42]

Conclusion

The medieval English Lazarus plays resolve the perceived opposition between the residual practice of lament and the dominant Christian eschatology, redirecting and containing the potentially subversive ethos of this construction of female grief. The N-Town and Towneley plays construct mourning as a form of confinement, akin to sin, from which Christian faith provides release. The York play similarly acknowledges the centrality of the sisters' mourning, even as it reinscribes their grief as excessive and contrary to faith. In contrast, the Chester version characterizes the sisters as models of Christian humility, whose helplessness paradoxically endows them with the power to summon the Son of God himself. Perhaps the most ambivalent representation of female grief, however, is in the characterization of the heroine of the Digby *Mary Magdalene* as tearless and firm in the face of her only brother's death. As an aristocratic heroine, this stoic lady claims her superior social and spiritual status by not weeping. Instead, she acquiesces to the custom of hiring weepers to carry Lazarus to the grave, a practice that she places herself above.

As the plays attempt to assimilate residual mourning practices to Christian eschatology, they also perform resistance to that teleology. The intensity of Martha's and Mary's grief for their brother must have resonated with medieval audiences who faced so many deaths of loved ones during their brief lives. On the one hand the cultural work done by these plays reinforces the gendered assumption that women are naturally more prone to excessive sorrow than men, and that grief itself is an excessive, feminine emotion. On the other hand, they acknowledge the resistant power of female grief, constructing it upon the underlying paradox that women's tears are not only excessive and subversive but also necessary and efficacious.

Notes

An earlier version of this essay appeared in *Early Theatre*. I am grateful to Lisa Perfetti and the anonymous readers at University Press of Florida for their insightful comments. Jennifer Vaught made helpful editorial comments on an early draft.

Lisa Carp assisted with research and proofing. Finally, I am thankful for the Medieval Mondays group at Purdue University, and especially Ann Astell who encouraged me to present this argument as a paper at their gathering.

1. Citations of the N-Town cycle are from *Ludus Coventriae or The Play Called Corpus Christi*, ed. K. S. Block, Early English Text Society (Oxford: Oxford University Press, 1922; repr. 1974). Citations from the York cycle are from *The York Plays*, ed. Richard Beadle (London: Edward Arnold, 1982). Citations of the Chester cycle are from *The Chester Mystery Cycle*, ed. R. M. Lumiansky and David Mills, Early English Text Society (Oxford: Oxford University Press, 1974). All references to the commentary or glossary of the Chester cycle are from *The Chester Mystery Cycle*, vol. 2, *Commentary and Glossary*, ed. R. M. Lumiansky and David Mills, Early English Text Society (Oxford: Oxford University Press, 1986). Citations of the Towneley cycle are from *The Towneley Plays*, ed. George England and Alfred Pollard, Early English Text Society (London: Kegan Paul, Trench, Trubner and Company, 1897). Citations of the Digby *Saint Mary Magdalen* are from *The Late Medieval Religious Plays of Bodleian MSS Digby 133 and Museo 160*, ed. Donald Baker, John Murphy, and Louis Hall, Early English Text Society (Oxford: Oxford University Press, 1982), 24–95.

2. Margaret Alexiou, *The Ritual Lament in Greek Tradition* (Cambridge: Cambridge University Press, 1974); Mary Agnes Doyle, *Games of Lamentation: The Irish Wake Performance Tradition* (Ann Arbor, Mich.: University Microfilms, 1988); Gail Holst-Warhoft, *Dangerous Voices: Women's Laments and Greek Literature* (London: Routledge, 1992), 103–4.

3. Peter Dronke, "Laments of the Maries: From the Beginnings to the Mystery Plays," in *Idee, Gestalt, Geschichte: Festschrift für Klaus von See; Studien zur europäischen Kulturtradition*, ed. Gerd Wolfgang Weber (Odense: Odense University Press, 1988), 89–116, at 103–104. Subsequent citations of Dronke refer to this article, p. 116.

4. In referring to women's laments for the dead as a "genre," I am drawing on the distinctions made by Adena Rosmarin in *The Power of Genre* (Minneapolis: University of Minnesota Press, 1985), 50. Rosmarin identifies two major categories of genre, critical and ethnic. The critical genre is "prescriptive, but what it prescribes is not [always] literary, but critical practice"; the ethnic genre, in contrast, represents an attempt "to describe, and perhaps define, the attitudes of a given body of people to their literature." Identification of an ethnic genre requires the "testimony of members of the society" as well as "metataxonomic discourse in a culture's literature." My argument relies upon both approaches to genre. The extant research on ritual lamentation establishes the characteristics of a critical genre. I use this critical genre to illuminate traces of the cultural practice of female lament in medieval and Renaissance drama. I also demonstrate that the English tradition provides independent confirmation of the presence of women's laments for the dead as an ethnic genre, or cultural practice, through the testimony of censorship and the discursive practices embodied in its literature.

5. See Nikolai Kaufman, "Laments from Four Continents: Europe, Asia, Africa, and America," *International Folklore Review* 7 (1990): 22–29; Tauno F. Mustanoja, "*Beowulf* and the Tradition of Ritual Lamentation," *Neuphilologische Mitteilungen* 67 (1967): 2–27.

6. See Alexiou, *Ritual Lament*; Doyle, *Games of Lamentation*, 6, 138; Angela Bourke, "More in Anger than in Sorrow: Irish Women's Lament Poetry," in *Feminist Messages: Coding in Women's Folk Culture*, ed. Joan N. Radner (Urbana: University of Illinois Press, 1993), 160–82; Angela Bourke, "The Irish Traditional Lament and the Grieving Process," *Women's Studies International Forum* 11 (1988): 287; Tauno F. Mustanoja, "The Unnamed Woman's Song of Mourning Over Beowulf and the Tradition of Ritual Lamentation," *Neuphilolgische Mitteilungen* 68 (1967), 21–22; Gail Holst-Warhoft, *Dangerous Voices*; Sharon T. Strocchia, *Death and Ritual in Renaissance Florence* (Baltimore: Johns Hopkins University Press, 1992); Bade Ajuwon, "Lament for the Dead as a Universal Folk Tradition," *Fabula* 22 (1981): 272–80; Nikolai Kaufman, "Laments from Four Continents"; Nancy Sultan, "Private Speech, Public Pain: The Power of Women's Laments in Ancient Greek Poetry and Tragedy," in *Rediscovering the Muses: Women's Musical Traditions*, ed. Kimberly Marshall (Boston: Northeastern University Press, 1993), 92–110; Gary A. Anderson, *A Time to Mourn, A Time to Dance: The Expression of Grief and Joy in Israelite Religion* (University Park: Pennsylvania State University Press, 1991); Rosmarin, *The Power of Genre*.

7. For a study of laments for the dead in medieval English literature, see Velma Bourgeois Richmond, *Laments for the Dead in Medieval Narrative* (Pittsburgh: Duquesne University Press, 1966) and Renate Hass, "The Laments for the Dead," in *The Alliterative Morte Arthure: A Reassessment of the Poem*, ed. Karl Heinz Goller (London: D. S. Brewer, 1981), 117–91. Hass shows that "Within [the poem's] 4346 lines it includes ten such laments, and of its last five hundred verses well over one third of them are devoted to dramatic lamentations which convey the poem's complex message" (117). Richmond observes that 125 extant English Romance narratives composed between 1225 and 1535 contain five hundred passages of laments for the dead. In these narratives the men lament as well, but it is important to note that they do so only in the absence of women—usually when they are on the battlefield. Roland, of course, from the *Chanson de Roland* is the best-known example of this. The women in this literature are depicted as manipulative when they lament. The secular literature, like the medieval religious drama, embodies gendering and ambivalence over lamentation, albeit in a different manner. The Geatish woman's song at the end of *Beowulf* is another literary example of women performing the work of mourning the dead for the community.

8. Matthew Parker, *A Funerall Sermon . . . Preached at S. Maries in Cambridge, Anno 1551, at the buriall of . . . Martin Bucer*, trans. Thomas Newton (London, 1587). Cited in G. W. Pigman, *Grief and the English Renaissance Elegy* (Cambridge: Cambridge University Press, 1985), 30.

9. Pigman, *Grief*, 32.

10. Cited in Pigman, *Grief*, 31.

11. *The Preparacyon to the Crosse with the Preparacyon to deeth* (London: Thomas Petyte, n.d., ca. 1545), N5v, cited in Patricia Phillippy, "The Sisters of Magdalen: Mourning and Female Community in Post-Reformation England." I am grateful to Professor Phillippy for sharing an early draft of her paper with me, which is now in her book *Women, Death, and Literature in Post-Reformation England* (Cambridge: Cambridge University Press, 2002), 5.

12. F. R. Raines, ed., *A Description of the State, Civil and Ecclesiastical, of the County of Lancaster about the Year 1590* (Manchester: Chetham Society, 1875), 5–7. Cited in David Cressy, *Birth, Marriage, and Death: Ritual, Religion and the Life-Cycle in Tudor and Stuart England* (Oxford: Oxford University Press, 1997), 400.

13. *The Alliterative Morte Arthure: A Critical Edition*, ed. Valerie Krishna (New York: Burt Franklin, 1976), lines 4328–41 (emphasis added): "The baronage of Bretayne thane, bechopes and othire, / Graythes them to Glasthenbery with gloppynnande [sorrowing] hertes, / To bery thare the bolde kynge and bryng to þe erthe, / With all wirchipe and welthe þat any wy scholde. / Throly belles thay rynge and *Requiem* syngys, / Dosse messes and matyns with mournande notes: / Relygeous reueste in theire riche copes, / Pontyficalles and prelates in precyouse wedys, / Dukes and dusszeperis in theire dule-cotes, / *Cowntasses knelande and claspande theire handes,* / *Ladys languessande [pining, sorrowing] and lowrande [mournful, forlorn] to schewe;* / All was buskede in blake, birdes and othire, / That schewede at the sepulture, with sylande teris—/ Whas neuer so sorowfull a syghte seen in theire tym."

14. In early modern drama there are several references to the practice of "wailing the dead" in Webster's and Shakespeare's plays in particular. In *Richard III*, Buckingham and Richard fear that their unlawful execution of Hastings will be protested by the citizens "wailing" for him. The women characters in the play successfully use lament as a form of resistance to male control and ultimately undermine Richard's will to power. See my "'Obsequious Laments': Mourning and Communal Memory in Shakespeare's *Richard III*," *Journal of Religion and the Arts* 7.5 (2003): 31–64. In Webster's *The White Devil* Cornelia stages a lament over her dead son. Finally, as late as 1612 Anthony Stafford in his *Meditations and Resolutions* griped, "It is a wonder to see the childish whining we now-adayes use at the funeralls of our friends. If we could houl them back again, our Lamentations were to some purpose; but as they are, they are vaine and in vain"; cited in *Shakespeare's England*, 2 vols. (Oxford: Clarendon Press, 1916), 2:151.

15. For an explication of this pedagogy, see George R. Keiser, "The Middle English *Planctus Mariae* and the Rhetoric of Pathos," in *The Popular Literature of Medieval England*, ed. Thomas J. Heffernan (Knoxville: University of Tennessee Press, 1985), and Eamon Duffy, *The Stripping of the Altars: Traditional Religion in England, 1400–1580* (New Haven: Yale University Press, 1992), 38–39, 260–61. For other analyses of the Virgin's Lament in the Middle Ages, see Sarah Stanbury, "The Virgin's Gaze: Spectacle and Transgression in Middle English Lyrics of the Passion,"

PMLA 106.5 (1991): 1083–93; Donna Spivey Ellington, "Impassioned Mother or Passive Icon: The Virgin's Role in Late Medieval and Early Modern Passion Sermons," *Renaissance Quarterly* 48 (1995): 227–62; Alexandra E. Johnston, "Acting Mary: The Emotional Realism of the Mature Virgin in the N-Town Plays," in *From Page to Performance: Essays in Early English Drama*, ed. John A. Alford (East Lansing: Michigan State University Press, 1995), 85–98.

16. For an elucidation of this doctrine and the Counter-Reformation reconsideration of it, see Harvey E. Hamburgh, "The Problem of *Lo Spasimo* of the Virgin in *Cinquecento* Paintings of the *Descent from the Cross*," *Sixteenth Century Journal* 12 (1981): 45–74.

17. Medieval English drama, as Claire Sponsler observes in *Drama and Resistance: Bodies, Goods, and Theatricality in Late Medieval England* (Minneapolis: University of Minnesota Press, 1997), xvi, "played a privileged role within late medieval culture.... the theater was a social site where resistance could be practiced, articulated, enacted, and tried out, protected by the code of theatricality from the full scrutiny of authority even when authority sponsored the performance." The ideological premise of the Corpus Christi plays necessitated this openness to resistance, for the plays would have little persuasive force and spiritual impact if they could not embrace and be embraced by their diverse audiences, sponsors, and performers.

18. With the exception of Rosemary Woolf and Kathleen Ashley, scholars have generally ignored this shift in emphasis. See Rosemary Woolf, *The English Mystery Plays* (Berkeley and Los Angeles: University of California Press, 1972), 227, and Kathleen M. Ashley, "The Resurrection of Lazarus in the Late Medieval English and French Cycle Drama," *Papers on Language and Literature* 22 (1986): 227–44.

19. Christine de Pizan, *The Book of the City of Ladies*, trans. Earl Jeffrey Richards (New York: Persea, 1982), 27.

20. See Sandra McEntire, "The Doctrine of Compunction from Bede to Margery Kempe," in *The Medieval Mystical Tradition in England*, vol. 4, ed. Marion Glasscoe, papers read at Exeter Symposium IV (Cambridge: D. S. Brewer, 1987).

21. See Catherine A. Lutz, "Emotion, Thought, and Estrangement: Western Discourses on Feeling," in *Unnatural Emotions* (Chicago: Chicago University Press, 1988), 53–80.

22. See Alexiou, *Ritual Lament*, esp. 24–35.

23. "Basil of Seleucia's Homily on Lazarus: A New Edition," ed. and trans. Mary B. Cunningham, *Analecta Bollandiana* 104 (1986): 161–84, at 180.

24. *Middle English Sermons*, ed. Woodburn O. Ross, EETS o.s. 209 (London: Oxford University Press, 1940), 272.

25. The most recent scholarship on the cycles indicates that only the York and Chester were conceived as dramatically complete units. The Towneley and the N-Town appear to be composites. Yet it is still possible to identify thematic differences among them, and even a composite grouping of plays can cohere around distinct theological and social ideas.

26. David Mills, "Approaches to Medieval Drama," *Leeds Studies in English*, n.s.,

3 (1969), 60n14, cited in Peter Travis, *Dramatic Design in the Chester Cycle* (Chicago: University of Chicago Press, 1982), 162n25.

27. Lawrence M. Clopper, *Drama, Play, and Game: English Festive Culture in the Medieval and Early Modern Period* (Chicago: University of Chicago Press, 2001), 245.

28. Unfortunately, little is known about the Digby's playwright or audience that might further explain why its heroine's mourning is depicted so differently from the cycle plays. Lawrence Clopper speculates that the "text exhibits some mendicant ideas and is representative of the affective piety promoted by the mendicants, especially among women, and that it would seem to have been written for a community with a significant investment in and devotion to the cult of the Magdalene" (ibid., 247).

29. Alexandra Johnston, "The Christ Figure in the Ministry Plays of the Four English Cycles," Ph.D. diss., University of Toronto, 1964, cited in Travis, *Dramatic Design*, 162n25.

30. See my notes 5 and 6.

31. See my doctoral dissertation, "'Why should calamity be full of words?': The Representation of Women's Laments for the Dead in Medieval English and Shakespearean Drama," Purdue University, 1999.

32. "Lord, if you had been here, my brother would not have died" (John 11:32).

33. "Tunc venient Judei, quorum dicat Primus" (rubric before 426).

34. See Margery Kempe, *The Book of Margery Kempe*, ed. Lynn Staley (Kalamazoo: Medieval Institute Publications, Western Michigan State University, 1996). Every year on Good Friday, for the ten years that her gift of tears consumes her, she weeps and sobs "five er six owyrs togedyr" (57.3320). She weeps an hour "for the sowles in Purgatory; an other owr for hem that weryn in myschefe, in poverte, er in any dises; an other owr for Jewys, Sarasinys, and alle fals heretikys that God for hys gret goodnes schulde puttyn awey her blyndnes that thei myth thorw hys grace be turnyd to the feyth of Holy Chirche and ben children of salvacyon" (57.3326–30). To Margery, weeping and prayer are both "ful swet and acceptabil" to God (78.4417).

35. Allen J. Frantzen, "St. Erkenwald and *The Raising of Lazarus*," *Mediaevalia* 7 (1981): 157–71, at 160.

36. *Oxford English Dictionary*, s. v. "bande," meaning bondage or bond.

37. "Fayntyse" means languor or weakness resulting from melancholy; see *Towneley Plays* Glossarial Index, s. v. "fayntyse."

38. John 11:35 reads simply "Et lacrimatus est Jesus."

39. Seth D. Riemer, "The Dramatic Significance of Christ's Tears in a French and an English Version of the *Lazarus* Play," in *Early Drama to 1600, Acta* (special issue) 13 (1985): 37–47.

40. See Barbara I. Gusick, "Time and Unredemption: Perceptions of Christ's Work in the Towneley Lazarus," *Fifteenth-Century Studies* 22 (1995): 19–41, at 34, and Kathleen M. Ashley, "The Resurrection of Lazarus in the Late Medieval English and French Cycle Drama," *Papers on Language and Literature* 22 (1986): 227–44.

Gusick and Ashley both note that Lazarus's address is in the form of a memento mori sermon.

41. See Laura Severt King, "Sacred Eroticism, Rapturous Anguish: Christianity's Penitent Prostitutes and the Vexation of Allegory, 1370–1608," Ph.D. diss., University of California at Berkeley, 1993, 175–76.

42. Patricia Phillippy identifies this cultural construct of female grief in early modern England. I am grateful to her for sharing with me the unpublished draft of her book *Women, Death, and Literature in Post-Reformation England* (Cambridge: Cambridge University Press, 2002).

5

Constant Sorrow

Emotions and the Women Trouvères

Wendy Pfeffer

Literary texts can be sources of sociocultural information about any time period. From the songs of the women trouvères, we can learn just how women expressed their emotive state within the strict confines of the lyric register. The medieval stereotype of women is that they are, by definition, emotional, in the most negative sense of the term. There are numerous proverbs that express this idea, on the lines of "Femme se plaint, femme se deult, Femme est malade quant el(le) veult,"[1] and the mutability/instability of women is clearly enunciated by the (most likely) male author of the *Contenance des fames*, in his catalogue of women's ills and ill effects, when he states unequivocally,

> Feme a un cuer par heritage
> Qui ne puet estre en un estage.
> Or s'esjouist, or se conforte;
> Or reva, or se desconforte;
> Or semble qu'el soit couroucee;
> Or est pensive, or est lee;
> . . . .
> Or se lie, or se gravie. (lines 27–32, 38)

> [A woman's heart is just not able
> to chart a course that's firm or stable.
> Now she's merry, her spirits soar;
> Now she dreams, she's blue once more;

Now it seems that she is wrathful;
Now she's pensive, now she's cheerful;
. . . .
Now she's gay, then she's no fun.]²

The author continues in this vein for quite a while, to what I believe were hoots of appreciation from his probably predominately male audience. My sense, however, is that women had a very different view of women's emotions, a view expressed in their own terms and in their own writing.

The recent anthology *Songs of the Women Trouvères*³ presents seventy-five songs in the woman's voice. The editors say "woman's voice" because with anonymous songs one cannot be sure that the author was, in fact, a woman. But although it is possible that anonymous male lyricists composed lyrics that sing of women's joys and sorrows, I am convinced it is highly unlikely.⁴ For my purposes, I consider any anonymous Old French song that tells a woman's story using the first person feminine pronoun to be composed by a woman trouvère. Songs included in *Songs of the Women Trouvères* are by named and anonymous authors, in differing genres and registers; only some have extant music. Clearly expressed in these songs is the lyricism of medieval French women of differing social ranks and background, in differing contexts and surroundings. The authors describe a number of emotions, many relating to their status. The singer may be happy because she is in love or unhappy for the same reason; she may be crying because she has an abusive husband or happy because she has successfully cuckolded him; if consigned to a life of religion, she may accept her lot or protest vehemently and emotionally against it. While these songs were not composed as a specific response to the misogynistic portrayal of women's sentiment in other works of Old French, to modern ears the songs do seem to rebut the denigration by male authors and to defend the reputation and emotional balance of the female sex.

Looking carefully at the lyrics in *Songs of the Women Trouvères* and remembering that these songs are but a sampling of medieval women's songs in Old French, several emotions and expressions of emotion stand out. Most clearly evident are expressions of pain, although the precise source of this pain may vary. The way women express this pain in their lyrics will be the primary focus of this essay.

How should a modern reader recognize the pain of the singers of these songs? What comes immediately to mind is vocabulary that evokes this register, words such as *soufrir*, *duel*, and *dolour* with its variants *dolente*, *doloir, dolans*. The authors of these poems can evoke women's pain with metaphors such as *avoir bouche amere*, "to have a bitter taste in the mouth," in song 38, v. 18, an image that still carries punch.[5] These women may be "desesperee," in "tormente," and spend their time crying, for sighs and tears are the primary tool for expressing their emotional pain, and a number of these women do cry. Words for sighs and tears are easily found in our texts. One woman will "plaing et plor et sospir" (song 14, v. 4) [lament and weep and sigh]; another sings, "Plaine d'ire et de desconfort plor" (song 17, vv. 1–2) [Full of anger and despair I weep]; yet another states, "je suix si aloingnie de joie . . . vuel doloir an leu de mener joie" (song 18, vv. 3, 20) [I am so removed from joy . . . I wish to grieve rather than act joyful]. Medieval men and women would both agree that love is painful and potentially even fatal, but the women seem more vociferous in their heartfelt complaints, even as their lyrics conform to the rules of the genre. I would suggest that the women's lyrics are as carefully crafted as those of male trouvères, and that the women are as successful as their male counterparts in letting the listener feel their pain.[6]

Certainly at no point in the lyrics do we find the mutability of emotion evoked by the author of the *Contenance des fames*, although it must be added that the women do not talk explicitly about the constancy of their emotions. The women of the lyrics are disconsolate and generally unconsolable, certainly not inclined to move schizophrenically from one emotion to another.

If we look carefully at one of these songs, more may be gleaned. I propose song 38, actually a *chanson pieuse*, in which the emotions of the female singer are still palpable. The song opens in the same vein as many a courtly song:

Je plains et plors come feme dolente,
Quar j'ay perdu ce que plus m'atalente;
A grant tristour fuïe [est] ma jouvente.
Sans nul confort
Triste sera ma vie jusque a la [mort]. (vv. 1–5)

[I lament and weep like a sorrowful woman,
For I have lost what I care for most;
In great sadness my youth has fled.
Devoid of all comfort
Sad will be my life till the day I die.]

Here we have what would appear to be the stock opening of an unhappy love song—the woman bemoans her fate, for she has lost her youth and, we assume, her lover. It is only in subsequent stanzas that we learn that this is a religious lyric, that the now dead object of affection is Jesus and that the person singing is Mary:

Beau dous cher fis et beau sire et beau pere,
Quant vos de moi feïstes vostre mere,
Por vostre mort doi ge avoir bouche amere.
Sans nul confort
Triste sera ma vie jusque a la [mort]. (vv. 16–20)

[Dear sweet beloved son, dear lord and father,
Because You chose me for your mother,
Your death was bound to leave a bitter taste in my mouth.
Devoid of all comfort
Sad will be my life till the day I die.]

A medieval author has chosen this lyric to express what are imagined as Mary's expressions of grief, using the vocabulary more often associated with characters in courtly romance than with New Testament figures. Mary states, "Por vostre mort bien me doit li cuer fendre" (v. 13) [Your death was bound to break my heart], words not found in any biblical source. I believe that the author of this piece had perhaps suffered some of the woes of Mary, in the loss of a child, and chose to set her own emotional experience in Mary's voice, for a religious lyric would have found a wider medieval audience than the expression of grief of one woman. And the convention of Marian devotion camouflages a display of emotion that might have been criticized in contemporary circles.[7]

In "Par maintes fois avrai esteit requise" (song 18), the Duchesse de Lorraine bemoans the death of her beloved. In this song we learn that her lover is dead and she exclaims:

Par Deu, amins, en grant dolour m'a mise
Mors vilainne, qui tout lou mont gerroie.
Vos m'at tolut, la riens que tant amoie! (vv. 22–24)

[By God, my love, into deep sorrow I have been plunged
By vile death, which wars against everyone.
It has robbed me of you, the one I loved so much!]

This woman wishes her own death, in emulation of Dido (vv. 5–7), because her lover is no more, and even as she tries to reconcile the happy emotions Love should bring her—"ancor me rait Amors joie promise" (v. 19) [Love has again promised me joy]—she prefers despondency: "Si vuel doloir an leu de mener joie: / Poinne et travail, ceu est ma rante assise" (vv. 20–21) [Yet I wish to grieve rather than act joyful: / Pain and torment, such is the penalty imposed on me]. No flighty female emotions here, but heartfelt expressions of grief and sorrow, phrased as artfully and crafted as carefully as any trouvère lament.

Even if the object of female affection lives, the possibilities for unhappiness remain. One female singer laments that she has been conquered by Love and now can only bemoan her fate:

Plaine d'ire et de desconfort
Plor: en chantant m'en rededui.
Sachiez de fi que j'ai grant tort,
Car assez trop hardie fui
Quant mon cuer ne ma boiche mui
A rien qui tenist a deport,
Se por ceu non q'ensi recort
M'ire et mon duel et mon enui. (song 17, vv. 1–8)

[Full of anger and despair
I weep: by singing I recover joy.
You may be sure that I acted very wrongly,
For I was much too bold
When I made moan with heart and mouth
At anything joyful,
Were it not that in this way I express
My anger and my grief and my sorrow.]

Here we do have a woman who can be said to mix laughter and tears, although there is no doubt about her broken heart. Singing gives her comfort, and although the editors translated *rededui* as "recover joy," the Old French verb can also mean the less pleasurable "keep on going" with the sense of "it's singing that keeps me alive." In Middle French, *déduire* comes to mean "développer un discours, un raisonnement, exposer en détail,"[8] and it may be that this woman proposes to do no more in this song than just that—explain to her listeners what has happened to her. She sings to us of her current unhappiness in sufficient detail to provide grist for a psychologist's mill: "Desqu'il ne m'ainme, je me haz" (v. 21) [Since he does not love me, I hate myself], she tells us. And she announces her imminent suicide: "Ensi ma mort quier et porchaz" (v. 24) [So do I seek and pursue my death].

I hasten to add that women were not alone in finding release in music. Male trouvères also considered song a way to deal with strong emotions. Consider the trouvère Blondel de Nesle, who says:

> Se savoient mon tourment
> Et auques de mon afaire
> Cil qui demandent conment
> Je puis tant de chançons faire,
> Il diroient vraiement
> Que nus a chanter n'entent
> Qui mieuz s'en deüst retraire;
> Maiz pour ce chant seulement
> Que je muir pluz doucement.

[If they knew my torment and something of my feelings, those who ask how I can compose so many songs, they would say in truth that no one ought more to be silent. But for only this reason do I sing, that I may die more easily (i.e., to assuage my pain)]. (RS 742, L 104–1, MW 633, lines 1–9)[9]

Song lyrics allowed women to share their grief with us. In this they are no different from male singers. And it is possible that the whole expression of grief is no more than a lyrical feint, just as one must be careful in ascribing to trouvères any sincerity in the emotions expressed in their chansons. But there are other causes of sorrow for medieval women beyond unhappiness in love, notably issues relating to their status. Specifically, women could complain of the status that male society had placed them in. For example, consider women who were forced into religion against their will. Several Old French lyrics record their unhappiness, in words with great resonance today.

> Nonne sui, nonne, laissiés m'aler,
> Je n'i [puis plus arester,
> Ne ja n'i voudrai] vos matines sonner,
> Qui sovent mi font peinne et mal endurer. (motet 67, motetus vv.
> 1–4)

[I am a nun, a nun, let me go,
I can stay here no longer,
Nor do I ever wish to ring your matins,
Which often make me suffer pain and misery.]

While the expression of emotions is not as explicit as in the songs discussed earlier, and the woman is less able to display her sentiments because of the brevity of the eleven-line-long text—though she does say, "De riens ne mi plaist tel vie a demener" (v. 7) [I find nothing pleasing in such a life]—this motet allows us to see another side of medieval life, and the unhappy consequences of decisions made on behalf of unwilling women. A similar tone is found in another motet text where, again, a young woman has been placed in a nunnery against her will:

Mes je sui mise en prison.
De Diu ait maleïçon
Qui m'i mist!
Mal et vilanie et pechié fist
De tel pucelete
Rendre en abïete. (motet 71, motetus vv. 11–16)

[But I have been put in prison.
May God curse
The one who put me here!
An evil, vile, and sinful thing he did
Sending such a young girl
To a nunnery.]

Again a situational complaint and an unhappy woman unable to decide her own fate. I know of no parallel texts wherein male authors complain of their lot in life.

A different status complaint concerns women who are unhappily married, and there are songs that express their emotions as well. One powerful example is motet 73, which begins:

Osteis lou moi
L'anelet dou doi!
Avoir pas vilains ne me doit,
Car, bien sai, cous en seroit
S'avocke moi
Longement estoit. (vv. 1–6)

[*Take it off,*
This ring on my finger!
A boor should not have me,
For I know well he would end up a cuckold
If he were with me
For long.]

While there is no vocabulary in this lyric that can be called "sentimental," nonetheless the feelings of the woman could not be stated more clearly— she wants out, expressed as a threat. Songs voiced by women unhappy in marriage are known generically as *chansons de malmariée*; there are no similar songs for men.

One further point: In medieval French romances, grief is frequently expressed by a rending of garments and a scratching of the face, accompanied by copious tears. Such a scene can be found, for example, in Chrétien de Troyes' *Yvain*, when Laudine sees her husband carried on his bier:

mes de duel feire estoit si fole
qu'a po qu'ele ne s'ocioit;
a la foiee si crioit
si haut com ele pooit plus,
et recheoit pasmee jus.
Et qant ele estoit relevee,
ausi come fame desvee
se comançoit a dessirier
et ses chevols a detranchier;
ses mains detuert et ront ses dras,
si se repasme a chascun pas. (lines 1150–60)

[but she was so crazed with grief
she was on the verge of killing herself;
all at once she cried out
as loudly as she could
and fell down in a faint.
And when she was lifted back to her feet,
like a madwoman
she began clawing at herself
and tearing out her hair;

her hands tore at and ripped her clothing
and she fainted with every step.][10]

Yasmina Foehr-Janssens has observed that anger and grief are paired in medieval French literature: "La colère ne se distingue de la tristesse que dans la mesure où elle pousse à agir celui dont elle s'empare."[11] No lyric composed by a woman comes close to the level of grief or approaches the level of self-violence expressed by Chrétien de Troyes' Laudine. Is this because the lyric used by women composers is more limited in length than romances such as Chrétien's? Such is one plausible explanation.

Or it may be that the very act of composing a lyric provides the vent for expressing emotions like anger or sadness—emotions that the heroine of romance must demonstrate by physical action. That lyrics provide women with an outlet for their emotions has been suggested above. But it is also possible that women composed songs to conceal their feelings, a motive expressed by Christine de Pizan in a virelay that opens quite explicitly with "Je chante par couverture" [I sing to hide my feelings].[12] However, no woman author of the thirteenth or fourteenth century is as candid as the fifteenth-century Christine on this matter.

One further theme found in women's lyrics and not in those of male trouvères is the idea of self-loathing and guilt. The men vent their pain by accusing the lady; in women's lyrics, the lady may turn against herself for not having shown her suitor sufficient attention. This motif is heard very clearly in song 22, where the speaker voices her regrets:

> Lasse, pour quoi refusai
> Celui qui tant m'a amee?
> Lonc tens a a moi musé
> Et n'i a merci trouvee.
> Lasse, si tres dur cuer ai! (vv. 1–5)

> [Alas, why did I refuse
> The one who loved me so?
> He whiled away much time with me
> And found no mercy there.
> Alas, what a cold heart I have!]

This motif becomes the very plot of the fifteenth-century tale *La Belle Dame sans mercy* by Alain Chartier.[13] No medieval male ever accused himself of similar misdeeds. For it is a distinguishing characteristic of women's lyrics that the pain of love can be directed inwards, becoming a self-loathing or guilt not present in male trouvère songs.

By the same token, women in the *jeux-partis* worry not only about making the best choice in men but also about how people around them will view their decision. While male participants in these debates are also concerned about picking the right side of the argument, their concerns are not as socially situated as those of the women. For example, in a *jeu-parti* Lorete uses as an argument "Jai n'an serai blasmee de la gent" (song 2, v. 26) [Never will I be blamed for it]. More strongly, consider the *jeu-parti* between the Dame de Gosnai and Gillebert de Berneville (song 4) where the question raised is, specifically, whom should the lady marry—someone of her own choosing or a husband picked by her friends. The Dame de Gosnai responds:

—Gillebert, c'est grans vieutez
A dame d'user sa vie
Aveuc home qui amez
N'est de lui; mes ne doi mie
Contre tous mes foulz pensez,
S'aim mieux faire pis assez
Par leur los et par leur dis.
A ce me tenrai tout dis
Ne ja ne m'iert reprouvé
Qu'aie conseil refusé. (vv. 11–20)

[—Gillebert, it is great vileness
For a lady to waste her life
With a man who is not loved
By her; but, I must not,
In opposition to everyone else, cling to my foolish thoughts.
Therefore, I would rather act disadvantageously
While heedful of their approbation and opinion.
To this I will always adhere;
Never shall I be reproached
For having refused advice.]

The Dame de Gosnai would rather have the approbation of her friends than marry the man she loves—at least that is the case she argues here.

Medieval women are not always sorrowful; there is some evidence of women's happiness in lyrics too. The words to express happiness are not found as frequently in the women trouvère corpus as is the vocabulary of sadness, for women speak in the happier register less often.[14] However, the Dame de Gosnai assures Gillebert de Berneville that "Amours veult bien et otrie / Que joie et ses biens doublez / Ait dame qui se marie" (vv. 32–34) [Love permits and allows / Twice the joy and pleasure / To a lady who marries]. In this positive register, the Dame de Gosnai is steadfast in her emotion, again contradicting the male perception of flighty female.

In another song, a young lady describes herself:

Car je suis jonette,
Plaisans et doucette,
Rians:
S'amerai tout mon vivant. (song 21, vv. 21–24)

[For I am young,
Charming and sweet,
Full of laughter:
So I will love my whole life long.]

Here the woman promises steadiness in her emotional state. And "S'amerai tout mon vivant" is a positive spin on the sad refrain "Triste sera ma vie jusque a la mort" that we saw in song 38.

Because medieval women lived and composed in a male-dominated society, their display of emotions, as interpreted by men, was always subject to scrutiny and criticism, such as that of the anonymous author of the *Contenance des fames*.[15] Medieval women, simply because they were women, did not have the same liberty as men to express their feelings. The concern of the female debater in a *jeu-parti* about how her arguments would be received reminds us how peculiarly important status and its repercussions were to medieval women.

The question of "status offense" has become a matter for the law in the United States in recent years, and I think the concept of status offense has remarkable applicability to the situation of medieval women. In contemporary American jurisprudence, only a child can be a status offender, for doing something that only a child can do, such as being truant from school.[16] In the Middle Ages, because women's legal status was no higher than children's and perhaps lower, women could also be status offenders, guilty simply because they were women. Medieval women's words were part of the status offense associated with women. Their words were discounted, devalued by men—and the emotions expressed were likewise discounted because expressed by women.

Of the seventy-five songs in *Songs of the Women Trouvères* that mention women's emotions, the vast majority speak of sorrow rather than happiness. I am hesitant to interpret this detail as meaning that women's lives in medieval France were perforce unhappy. I suspect that unhappiness in love makes for a better (and easier-to-sell) song. F. R. P. Akehurst has shown in troubadour lyric that "the matrix sentence to be derived from frequency tables of the usage of the troubadours could be stated as 'Ieu non puesc far amor' [I cannot make love]."[17] In other words, the troubadours' inability to make love is by far the most typical scenario. So too I think that, in Old French lyrics by women, the usual persona presented is not that of a woman who can have what she wants but that of a woman unhappy one way or another with her lot. I suspect, furthermore, that this persona is what the audience expected. As popular audiences in medieval cities expected those who recited *dits* such as the *Contenance des fames* to defame rather than praise, so too did audiences for lyric expect to hear the trials and tribulations of individuals in love, be they male or female.

Although I have not discussed all the songs in Old French that can be attributed to women or that express the woman's voice, it is clear that women did express their emotions in medieval lyric, and that they could use this vehicle to discuss not only the literary conceit of courtly love but also the realities of life, happy or not. These lyrics allow us to hear women complain of parental choices made for them; the songs gave women a place to argue for their wishes and desires; the songs offered women a vent for emotions that would otherwise have been unacceptable to their contemporaries. Their lyrics allowed them to express emotions or, like Christine de Pizan, *chanter par couverture*.

Notes

1. Joseph Morawski, ed., *Proverbes français antérieurs au XVe siècle*, CFMA 47 (Paris: Champion, 1925), 739.
2. Gloria Fiero, Wendy Pfeffer, and Mathé Allain, eds. and trans., *Three Medieval Views of Women* (New Haven: Yale University Press, 1989).
3. Eglal Doss-Quinby, Joan Tasker Grimbert, Wendy Pfeffer, and Elizabeth Aubrey, eds., *Songs of the Women Trouvères* (New Haven: Yale University Press, 2001).

4. For a more detailed discussion of this point, see Wendy Pfeffer, "Complaints of Women, Complaints by Women: Can One Tell Them Apart?" in *The Court Reconvenes: Courtly Literature Across the Disciplines*, ed. Barbara Altmann and Carleton Carroll (Cambridge: Boydell & Brewer, 2003): 125–31.

5. Except as specified, all references to Old French lyrics will be to works in *Songs of the Women Trouvères*. The individual pieces will be identified by their number in that volume.

6. Lisa Perfetti has suggested that medieval women are more conscious of the visible display of their emotions and their effect on others (e-mail correspondence, August 29, 2002). It is hard to identify this attitude in works as short as these lyrics, but there is much truth to her observation.

7. As Perfetti has stated (ibid.), "The religious vocabulary adds legitimacy to a woman's private suffering."

8. Algirdas Julien Greimas and Teresa Mary Keane, eds., *Dictionnaire du moyen français: La Renaissance* (Paris: Larousse, 1992).

9. These abbreviations serve to identify Old French lyric: RS = Hans Spanke, ed., *G. Raynauds Bibliographie des altfranzösischen Liedes* (Rpt. Leiden: Brill, 1980); L = Robert Linker, *A Bibliography of Old French Lyrics* (University, Miss.: Romance Monographs, 1979); MW = Ulrich Mölk and Friedrich Wolfzettel, *Répertoire métrique de la poésie lyrique française des origines à 1350* (Munich: Wilhelm Fink, 1972).

10. Chrétien de Troyes, *The Knight with the Lion or Yvain* (*Le Chevalier au Lion*), ed. and trans. William W. Kibler (New York: Garland, 1985).

11. Yasmina Foehr-Janssens, *La Veuve en majesté: Deuil et savoir féminin dans la littérature médiévale* (Geneva: Librairie Droz, 2000), 58.

12. Christine de Pizan, *Oeuvres Poétiques*, ed. Maurice Roy (Paris: Firmin Didot, 1886–96; repr., New York: Johnson Reprint, 1965).

13. Alain Chartier, *La Belle Dame sans mercy*, ed. Arthur Piaget, 2nd ed. (Geneva: Librairie Droz, 1949).

14. Words for laughter, smiles, pleasure and joy can be found in women's lyrics. However, the multiplicity of meanings behind the Old French *joie*, with English connotations ranging from the cognate "joy" to "sexual pleasure, sexual climax," makes it slightly more difficult to point to uses of this word in these songs as a marker of individual women's happiness. Still, the women use *joie* to refer to a host of pleasures associated with courtship and love.

15. In the lyrics, women present smiles at face value, while male authors are leery of such facial expressions. Men could read smiles as entrapment, if we believe an anonymous male participant in a *jeu-parti*: "Dame, por Deu, or escouteis: / Li jeus et li gais et li ris / Averont maint home mal mis" (song 10, vv. 57–59) [Lady, for God's sake, listen to me: / Play and gaiety and smiles / Have mistreated many a man]. Unfortunately for us, the *jeu-parti* ends with this stanza and so we cannot know the lady's rejoinder.

In a very different context, Robert de Blois counseled women in his *Chastoie-*

ment des dames to say "no" to men politely, gently, and "ne le dites pas en riant" (line 738) [don't say it with a smile/laugh], in part so that no suitor would have difficulty understanding the verbal message. I sense that Robert was almost as distrusting of women as the anonymous author of the *Contenance des fames*. See John Howard Fox, *Robert de Blois, son oeuvre didactique et narrative, étude linguistique et littéraire suivie d'une édition critique de "l'Enseignement des princes" et du "Chastoiement des dames"* (Paris: Nizet, 1985).

16. I offer a Kentucky example; the strict legal definition of status offense is established state by state, but I am confident that a similar legal situation exists throughout North America. According to the Kentucky Juvenile Code (Kentucky Revised Statutes, Title LI 600.020, 58), status offense concerns "any action brought in the interest of a child accused of committing acts, which, if committed by an adult, would not be a crime." I thank Judge Patricia Walker FitzGerald, Jefferson County Family Court, for this reference.

17. F. R. P. Akehurst, "The Auxiliary-Verb-plus-Infinitive Construction in Old Occitan," *Tenso* 2 (1986): 1–20, at 10.

6

A Pugnacious Pagan Princess
Aggressive Female Anger and Violence in *Fierabras*

Kristi Gourlay

Throughout the medieval and early modern periods, gender roles were increasingly prescribed by a body of didactic treatises and fictions that were intended to define etiquette, comportment, moral values, and social roles for aristocratic and bourgeois women. According to these male-authored works, women were to be chaste, modest, pious, and obedient, and strictly to control their anger.[1] They certainly were not encouraged to curse, threaten, defy their parents, or react with murderous rage to adverse situations. Heroines of the Christian literary tradition likewise avoided such aggressive conduct if they wished to live happily ever after with the knight of their dreams. Yet, curiously, all of these dubious behaviors (and the fairy-tale ending) can be attributed to Floripas, the Saracen heroine of the twelfth-century French poem *Fierabras* and its later translations and derivations.[2]

Saracen heroines are sufficiently common in the chanson de geste tradition that scholars have classified them as a literary convention.[3] The setting of their stories is either Spain or the Near East, where the Christians are engaged in conflict with the Muslim "infidel." During this encounter, a conventionally beautiful (in the European Christian sense: blonde, fair, and slender), highly intelligent, and assertive Saracen princess falls in love with a valiant Christian knight who has been captured and imprisoned by her father, a Saracen king or emir. In order to win the knight's love, she promises to convert to Christianity and rescues him, betraying her father, country, and religion in the process. She is usually rewarded for her bold and unorthodox behavior by living happily ever after with her chosen knight. Floripas fits into this convention in every way. She is conventionally beautiful, intelligent, and assertive and helps her chosen knight, Guy of Burgundy, and his companions to escape from her father's prison and capture his castle, holding it until Charlemagne can arrive and vanquish the Saracen foe. A critical difference, however, separates Floripas from other Saracen princesses: she exhibits an explosively volatile temper, a predilection for uttering threats, and a related penchant for deadly violence. Curiously, this unconventional behavior does not hinder her from obtaining her desires: in the final lines of the poem she is baptized (not before urging Charlemagne to hurry up and execute her father) and marries Guy, and the happy couple receives half of her father's former kingdom as a wedding gift. The message of this story seems to be that angry threats and murder will get a girl what she wants: marriage to the man of her dreams and a kingdom to boot—certainly not the message expected from a conventional medieval chanson de geste or romance.

In spite of the unorthodox behavior of its heroine, this story became what has been called "one of the most popular chansons de geste of the later Middle Ages," an assertion that is supported by the large number of copies, adaptations, and translations that were produced in most European languages between the thirteenth and sixteenth centuries.[4] This popularity, and the fact that Floripas' (mis)behavior results in her obtaining exactly what she set out to achieve, would strongly suggest that medieval audiences found Floripas' anger and violence both acceptable and appealing in spite of its transgressive nature. The question is, why does the text not criticize or punish Floripas for her transgressive rage and violence and why does the story become a medieval best-seller in Europe throughout a period when female behavior such as Floripas' was thought to be actively discouraged?

One of the difficulties in assessing Floripas' anger and violence is that little scholarship exists on medieval female anger in either a literary or an historical context.[5] This lacuna is curious, given that angry women are featured in the visual arts, figure in many literary texts, and appear with some frequency in judicial and other archival records, which suggests that female anger was a well-recognized emotion in the premodern period. Unlike male anger, however, female anger was rarely discussed explicitly in medieval texts. To seek an understanding of both Floripas' anger and premodern female anger in general, it is thus necessary to begin with an assessment of what is known about the ways in which medieval society perceived and responded to male anger.

According to the humoral theory proposed by Aristotle, Galen, and others that remained popular in the Middle Ages, "the relationship among four fluids (phlegm, blood, yellow bile [choler], and black bile [melancholy]) was thought to control physical and mental health and to determine a person's basic temperament or 'complexion.'"[6] If these humors got out of balance, the temperament could change: if choler became dominant, the person would have an increased tendency to become angered, hence the term "choleric."[7] The ancient Greeks also distinguished between cold-blooded, calculated anger and hot-blooded anger that was characterized by a "doglike madness symptomatic of rabies."[8] This distinction continued to be accepted by Europeans during the medieval and early modern periods. Accordingly, in fourteenth-century Venice a distinction was drawn between rational, planned, self-interested crimes, which were severely punished, and crimes of passion, which were treated more leniently.[9] Uncontrollable rages were often offered as the explanation for violent crime, as a way of avoiding responsibility for violent action and for justifying murder. Edward Muir cites the sixteenth-century example of Antonio Savorgnan, who evaded responsibility for his violent activity during the carnival of Giovedì Grosso by saying, "I am so angry that I am beside myself and do not know what I am doing."[10] This differentiation between hot- and cold-blooded anger evidently also held true in early modern France where Natalie Davis has demonstrated how acting in *chaude colle*, meaning sudden anger (literally "hot bile"), could excuse a murderer for his deed.[11] Similarly, in medieval England, homicide committed by the temporarily or permanently insane was considered a pardonable offence.[12] Evidently a loss of reason or control was held to be a mitigating factor in any male violence that might result from an angry outburst.

Hot-blooded anger was not the only legitimizing factor in premodern outbursts of violence. Motive also played an important role in determining how society viewed and reacted to anger and resulting violence. Wrath was one of the seven deadly sins, but in the Middle Ages, as Richard Barton observes, theologians "acknowledged that in certain situations it could be legitimate, righteous, and necessary."[13] One such case was anger that arose in defensive response to the grave offenses of defamation of character or verbal affronts to personal honor. In societies in which honor and shame played such a great role, publicly uttered insults could irrevocably sully the name of an individual, calling the honor of his/her family into question.[14] This was especially true in pre-print societies, in which "words constituted action. Neither a substitute nor an alternative for action, they functioned as action. They were thus also actionable."[15] Studies of individual regions and communities support this assertion. Guido Ruggiero found in his study of violence in fourteenth-century Venice that "speech was perceived as a significant form of violent activity."[16] William Ian Miller likewise observes in his study of medieval Icelandic sagas and their historical context that "medieval Icelanders, living in an honor-based culture, perceived little difference in the amount of wrong done by a blow or by a verbal insult. . . . Verbal affronts and physical affronts were collapsed into a single general category of impingements on one's self and one's honor."[17]

While some communities dealt with affronts to honor in peaceable ways, such as taking offenders to court and arranging compensation, the most common response appears to have been angry violence.[18] As Stephen White observes, "to display anger about an action publicly is to construe the action as an injury, as a wrongful act causing harm, damage, or loss, as an offense against a person's honor. So one has a right to get angry and to do what angry people can and should do." He further observes that "those who fail to show anger when they have been shamed are open to criticism and are liable to being shamed by their friends and goaded into anger."[19] Anger was thus the expected response to insult, a response that was often followed by vengeful violence.

The connection between insult-provoked anger and vengeful violence has had a long history. Aristotle wrote: "Anger [is] a longing, accompanied by pain, for a real or apparent revenge for a real or apparent slight. . . . Anger is always accompanied by a certain pleasure, due to the hope of revenge to come."[20] Likewise, in his study of interpersonal violence in Gregory of Tours' sixth-century *Libri Historiarum*, R. F. Newbold found that "indignation and an urge to retaliate against perceived injustices, violation of norms and expectations, or harm to self or others was the main cause of violent action."[21] Scholars conducting regional studies on the later Middle Ages have similarly found this to hold true. In thirteenth-century Provençal village society, for example, Ronald Gosselin observed that the expected response to insults to honor was either compensation or violence.[22] Likewise, A. J. Finch found in his study of the records of the ecclesiastical jurisdiction of Cerisy-la-Forêt in Normandy in the period 1314–1458 that "injurious words" were frequently a provocation for violence.[23] That anger played a motivating role in this violence is unspoken, but clearly evident. Thus, in societies in which personal honor was held to be very important, anger was (and still is) considered a legitimate defensive reaction in response to humiliation, affronts to personal honor, or perceived loss of esteem—a reaction that often resulted in retaliation, either verbal or physical.

Literary representations of male anger support what the historical evidence suggests about medieval views of anger. Such representations were especially common in chivalric literature, in which the defense of honor was critical. Richard W. Kaeuper writes of the "element of rage and sheer battle fury" that is behind the knightly prowess so important to the concept of chivalry, observing that "to read much chivalric literature is to find admired knights regularly feeling rage as they fight; their blood boils; when honour is challenged, they nearly lose their minds."[24] For example, in the influential *Chanson de Roland*, both Christians and Saracens often react to what they perceive to be affronts to their honor with maddened rage. On one occasion Ganelon has a fit of anger when Roland laughs at him, and when the Saracens insult the French, Oliver likewise becomes extremely angry.[25] Similarly, when the Saracen Baligan hears the news of King Marsile's defeat, his anger is so great "he nearly goes mad."[26]

This furious male reaction to insult, and to the dishonor signaled by disappointing news, also holds true for the Saracen and Christian men of the Floripas texts.[27] For example, when Balan hears of Fierabras' defeat by Oliver, he is "doleus et iré" (line 1906) [shamed and enraged]. When insulted by the captured Guy, Balan "à poi n'est forsenés" (4426) [is not a little furious], and orders him to be beaten. Guy in turn "tous est d'ire alumés" (4431) [is all lit up with anger]. Then, when the peers go to rescue Guy and are taunted by Balan's men, Roland "à peu n'est forsené" (3563). Similarly, when Roland is insulted by a Saracen, "le sens cuida derver" (2404) [he nearly loses his mind], and Balan responds in the same way when he witnesses Floripas putting out the fire in the tower and utilizing his precious treasure as a weapon (3786, 3824). Thus both historical and literary evidence suggest that premodern Europeans considered anger, especially hot-blooded anger characterized by a loss of control or temporary madness, to be an acceptable response to affronts to honor.

It is less clear, however, how female anger was perceived and reacted to in the premodern period. Evidence from the visual arts suggests that anger has had a long and enduring association with women: the most common way of representing the vice of anger was in the form of a woman, often a frenzied and violent woman.[28] Art historians maintain that these representations were influenced by the *Psychomachia*, an early fifth-century allegorical epic poem by Prudentius, which tells the story of the war in the soul between the virtues and the vices. True to classical form, Prudentius portrays them as female. In the battle between Patientia and Ira, a frenzied Ira, frustrated by her inability to harm Patientia, goes mad with rage, her mouth foaming and her bloodshot eyes suffused with gall.[29] The battle ends when Ira dramatically commits suicide by impaling herself on her weapon. The *Psychomachia* was soon illustrated, and became one of the most popular didactic works of the medieval period.[30] This personification was adopted by other artists and became a standard way of representing the triumph of virtue over vice in all forms of the visual arts. For example, in a manuscript produced at Moissac at the end of the eleventh century, Ira is portrayed as madly tearing her hair.[31] Likewise, in Giotto's *Last Judgment*, painted on the wall of the Church of Santa Maria dell' Arena in Padua, Ira "has a swollen face, and her head is thrown back. She is tearing her raiment from her breast. Her disordered hair is falling in snake-like coils behind her,"[32] and an early twelfth-century capital in the church of Notre-Dame-du-Port in Clermont-Ferrand depicts the suicide of Ira: a naked woman with flowing hair stabs herself with a short-bladed sword under the inscription "Ira se occidit" [Ira kills herself].[33] Such representations of anger as a maddened woman could only have encouraged the association of women and anger (and loss of control) in the minds of medieval viewers.

The association of women with anger, and the related issue of the reputedly disruptive nature of women, was a subject much discussed in the misogynistic discourse of the Middle Ages.[34] For example, in the early twelfth century Bishop Marbod of Rennes claimed that women are jealous, fickle, greedy, and hot-tempered, and that they instigate quarrels and delight in vengeance, always wanting to get the upper hand.[35] Thought by many to be rebellious, quarrelsome, deceitful, and uncontrollably emotional by nature, women were thus a source of concern for many male clerics and scholars. Yet, surprisingly for such a potentially disruptive emotion, the control of anger is mentioned only in passing in the many behavioral treatises written for women during the Middle Ages and without the detail devoted to other womanly faults like loquacity or ostentation of dress. For example, the late twelfth-century knight and trouvère Garin lo Brun writes only that a lady should not show anger if she is in a bad mood.[36] Likewise, in the late thirteenth century in his *Chastoiement des dames*, Robert of Blois simply advises aristocratic women that they should not show anger or quarrel with others.[37] Similarly, the fourteenth-century Ménagier of Paris specifies to his young wife only that it is inappropriate for a woman to show anger, particularly to her husband.[38] A contemporary, the knight Geoffroy de La Tour-Landry, uses exceptional detail when he tells his three daughters about the danger of anger. He both instructs them that they should not show anger or talk back to their husbands and provides an example of the unhappy fate that comes to a woman who leaves her husband in anger.[39] Female anger thus appears to have been recognized as a possible, and unpleasant, by-product of marriage, one to be discouraged, yet curiously not one that warranted much discussion in manuals of behavior.

This seeming reticence of the behavioral manuals is particularly interesting when compared with evidence from court records and other archival sources. These documents suggest that female anger and resulting violence, at least among the middle and lower ranks of society that they represented, were not uncommon. This anger, like most male anger, appears to have occurred mainly in response to perceived wrongs or insults, particularly insults that called the woman's sexual honor into question. Such insults were especially damaging to women because their honor, and their family's honor, rested almost entirely on their unblemished sexual reputations. Thus the courts seem to have considered any violence that resulted from anger provoked by sexually charged insults to be a forgivable offense. For example, Natalie Davis makes reference to the sixteenth-century case in which Marguerite Panete fought with, and killed, her mother-in-law, who had insulted her by calling her a "villaine putain, paillarde, pourceau" [dirty whore, good-for-nothing, pig]. Marguerite was eventually pardoned for her actions with the provision that she make "satisfaction" to the civil party.[40] In 1536 Mathurine Ginault likewise was pardoned for killing Jeanne Gaultiere, who had called Mathurine "vesse, putain, excommuniée" [fart, whore, excommunicated woman] and said that she slept with priests.[41] What is interesting in these cases is that, unlike men, women who did resort to violence rarely used the *chaude colle* defense alone, but instead were "either silent about their feelings or many-tongued, bringing jealousy, despair, and guilt to the action, along with anger."[42] Davis argues that this is because according to humoral theory, the nature of female anger was different from male anger:

> men were hot and dry, and could be led by fiery yellow bile into both angry killing and the quick passion of angry battle. Women were cold and wet, their anger thickened by phlegm and compromised by melancholy. The "chole" might not be spent in the heat of the moment, but could last like Medea's fury or like the obstinacy of Montaigne's

Gascon women, who "would sooner have bit into hot iron than let go their bite of an opinion they had conceived in anger."[43]

Thus, by its very nature, women's anger was not quick-burning and uncontrolled, and hence justifiable like men's, but smoldering and long-lasting, making it difficult to use *chaude colle* as a convincing defense.

While some women were clearly reacting angrily to insult with physical violence, female anger was expressed more commonly in a verbal form. This is reflected in the historical and judicial records that report angry women responding verbally to insults, threatening neighbors or, most commonly, inciting their men to violence.[44] For example, the twelfth-century historian Orderic Vitalis writes in his *Historia Ecclesiastica* that Helwise, the wife of Count William of Évreux,

> was incensed [irata est] against Isabella of Conches for some slighting remarks and in her anger [per iram] used all her powers to urge count William and his barons to take up arms. So the hearts of brave men were moved to anger [in furore succensa sunt] through the suspicions and quarrels of women [per suspiciones et litigua feminarum], which led to great bloodshed on both sides and the burning of many homes in towns and villages.[45]

Mark Meyerson cites a similar case in fifteenth-century Valencia in which Caterina Gil was reputedly most to blame for the violence that occurred in the feud between her family and the Domingo family. According to the records of the court, she continually nagged at her reluctant husband, even though there was a public truce between the families, telling him repeatedly that he had not done enough to punish the Domingos, and that if he did not do something, then she would.[46] Edward Muir comes to similar conclusions with respect to early modern vendetta ritual in northern Italy, asserting that women "were certainly there in encouraging their men to remember their obligations, in teaching sons to avenge dead fathers, in shaming husbands into countering insults."[47] Women angered by insults to their own or their family's honor thus evidently played a recognized and accepted role in the often violent politics of their communities, but tended to rely more on verbal responses than physical action, which was usually left up to their menfolk.

Female anger is also present in the chansons and romances, but unlike the anger of the women that appears in the records of the court, these outbursts are rarely allowed to go unpunished. Often, literary female anger is expressed by "bad" women in reaction to not getting their way. For example, the thirteenth-century *Roman de Silence*'s wicked Queen Eufeme reacts with uncontrollable rage on several occasions when the hero Silence (who is really a girl raised as a boy to circumvent the laws of her country which prevent female inheritance) refuses to succumb to her amorous advances.[48] The first time this occurs, the lady is consumed with great rage ("plainne de grant rage") and thinks about how to get her revenge (3977). She falsely accuses Silence of forcing himself on her and, when this fails to incite her husband to punish Silence, she is furious and plots to have Silence killed (4248). Later, when Silence rejects her advances again, the lady is again filled with rage and devises a clever plan for revenge (5759–60). On each occasion, her rage appears to be hotly spontaneous and uncontrollable, but this does not preclude her from devising plans for revenge that are deliberate and thought out. Furthermore, her anger is not in response to affronts to her honor, but results from frustration at not getting her way in a matter that would actually compromise her honor if satisfied. Fortunately for Silence, Eufeme's deadly plans do not come to fruition, and Eufeme herself is executed at the end for her misdeeds.[49] Likewise, in the popular Anglo-Norman romance *Bevis of Hampton*, it is anger at the young hero Bevis's passionately outspoken (and true) accusations that cause his evil mother to hit him and then order his death.[50] She is later eliminated from the story by a violent death—a fall from a tower, a fitting punishment for her transgressively violent behavior. Female anger generated by obstacles to selfish goals, particularly when that anger results in violence, is clearly not considered to be acceptable in the literary context of the romances and chansons.

Occasionally "good" literary women do show anger and, like the anger documented in the court records, this anger tends to be in response to threats to their honor or the honor of their families. This literary female anger, however, is rarely constructed as acceptable or justifiable, and generally results in reprimand, if not punishment. For example, in the mid-thirteenth-century French prose version of *Le Roman de Tristan*, Queen Iseut is described as angry and furious when she discovers that Tristan is responsible for the death of one of her kinsmen. She prepares to kill the defenseless Tristan in his bath as an act of vengeance. Before she can do the deed, however, she is stopped by her servant, who voices his disapproval: "Il ne vos apartient pas au moins por ce que vous iestes dame, mes lessiez sor le roi la vengence de ceste chose, car certes il esploitera a vostre honor mieuz que vos ne feriez" [It is not for you, a lady, to avenge this misdeed, but let the king deal with it, and I'm sure he will see that your honor is upheld better than you would].[51] In the second part of *Raoul de Cambrai*, Beatrice almost goes mad with anger when Bernier, disguised as a pilgrim, suggests a remedy for the barrenness of her marriage, which she has successfully avoided consummating in order to remain true to Bernier. Beatrice goes to hit the pilgrim with an applewood staff, but is stopped by her husband, who tells her she is committing a great sin because he is their guest.[52] Finally, in the prologue to Chaucer's *Wife of Bath's Tale*, it is clearly evident that Alisoun is angry when she hits Jankyn and damages his book of "wikked wyves" in order to get back at him for taunting her.[53] Her angry actions, however, result in a beating that leaves her with a contrite husband, but also deaf in one ear.

Thus, the court records suggest that reacting angrily to insult was a socially acceptable response for both men and women in daily life, whereas literary female anger was treated quite differently from literary male anger. Reactions within the text to literary male anger appear to reflect societal norms—namely, that anger was a legitimate, acceptable, and even expected response to an insult to honor. Female literary anger, on the other hand, whatever its cause, generally seems not to have been an acceptable or appropriate response in the courtly cultural context of the chansons and romances. Angry women, both good and bad, are generally punished or reprimanded in some way for their transgression, especially if that anger results in violence.

Floripas' anger, however, is the major exception to this rule. She erupts in violent rage every time someone insults her, gets in the way of her plans, questions her actions, or gives her reason to fear for her life. Yet she does so with complete impunity, even when she kills the offender, and in fact is ultimately rewarded for her behavior. This raises two questions: Is her anger actually legitimate by historical standards? And why is it not treated in the conventional literary way? Initially, her anger appears to be very much in keeping with the socially and legally acceptable conventions of anger established for literary men and the noncourtly men and women of judicial records.[54] In each case, however, the legitimacy of this anger and of the resulting violence is called into question by a closer examination of her motives and by her subsequent actions, which are evidently motivated as much by the desire to eliminate impediments to her plans as by the desire to defend her honor against insult. Her violent reactions are thus very much in the way of "bad" literary women.

Floripas' first angry outburst occurs when the Saracen gaoler Brutamond refuses to let her see the peers because he remembers how a man can see "grant mal par fame alever" (lines 2073–79) [the great evil done by women]. Evidently insulted, Floripas "du sens cuide derver" (2079) [thought she would lose her mind] and threatens him.[55] She then attempts to open the prison herself and, when the gaoler moves to prevent her, she kills him on the spot:

Et Floripas le fiert, bien le sot aviser,
Si que les ex li fist de la teste voler;
Devant lui à ses piés le fist mort c[r]aventer,
Si que onques nel seurent Sarrazin ni Escler.
En la cartre parfonde fist le cors avaler;
Cil fu tost affondrés, car il ne sot noer (2089–94).

[And Floripas the fierce knew to aim well at him, so that she made his eyes fly from his head; he crashed dead before her at her feet, so that no one, neither Saracen nor Slav, could save him. She threw his body down deep into the prison: it quickly sank to the depths because he did not know how to swim.]

She similarly explodes in rage when her father's advisor Sortinbrans dares in her presence to warn Balan of the untrustworthy nature of women. This time, when Floripas hears him, she "le sens cuide derver" [nearly loses her mind] and retorts by insulting him and declaring that she would give him a blow on his nose if women wouldn't reproach her for it (2739–44). In both of these cases, Floripas reacts with anger to slurs on her character and on the character of women in general. However, the legitimacy of her angry, insult-provoked responses is called into question because the perceived affronts to her honor are actually accurate statements that happen to offend her. When the gaoler and Sortinbrans question the trustworthiness of women, in the case of Floripas they are entirely right to do so: on each occasion Floripas is actively in the process of betraying their trust by making possible the release of the peers.

In the remaining two incidents in which Floripas acts with anger and violence, her wrath is sparked by fear that her deception has been discovered and, once again, by the introduction of a potential impediment to her plans. When Floripas takes the rescued peers to her chambers, her governess recognizes them and threatens to turn Floripas and the peers in to her father. Floripas is described in the following way:

> si a le sanc mué:
> Son pere moult redoute et sa grant cruauté.
> A une des fenestres de fin marbre listé,
> Ki fu devers la mer, a la vielle apelé;
> Et ele vint à lui, que ne s'i sot garder,
> Juques vers ses espaules a son cors fors bouté.
> Et Floripas apiele Marmucet de Goré;
> Cil vint courant à lui, ki sot sa volenté.
> Par les jambes le prent, bien i a assené,
> Ens la mer le lancha, ens ou parfont du gué. (2189–98)

[Her blood was stirred up: she feared her father and his great cruelty very much. She called the old woman to one of the windows framed in fine marble which was above the sea. And she came to her [F], because she didn't know to protect herself, and she [F] thrust her body outside as far as her shoulders. Floripas called Marmucet of Goré, who knew her will, and he came running to her. He took her [the governess] by the legs, well instructed there, and threw her into the sea, deep inside the moat.]

Fearing her father's wrath, Floripas is angered and responds within arguably legitimate nonliterary feminine norms for anger and violence in order to eliminate this threat to both her own safety and that of the peers. Like the insults of the gaoler and Sortinbrans, however, her fear is deserved: she is actively disobeying her father and putting his castle into jeopardy. Her subsequent behavior further calls the legitimacy of her actions into question. Rather than expressing appropriate feminine relief at their newfound security, or remorse at the death of her former companion, sentiments that might mitigate her violent actions, Floripas quips rather callously, "Vielle ... or avés deviné; / Par vous n'ierent huimais li François encusé" (2199–2200) [Old woman ... now you've figured it out. The French will never be accused by you]. That this was meant to be humorous is demonstrated by the favorable response of the peers: "Quant nos François l'oïrent, ris en ont et gabé" (2201) [When our French heard this, they laughed and joked].

Floripas' plans are once again jeopardized when her Saracen fiancé, Lucafer of Baudas, becomes suspicious of her lengthy absence and goes in search of her. Upon discovering that her chambers are locked, he rudely and rather dramatically kicks in the door. Floripas' irate reaction to this intrusion and her demand that Roland avenge the deed (2869–71) are arguably justified, as Lucafer's unannounced and forcible entry is not only a further threat to the safety of herself and the peers but an affront to basic good manners and courtly etiquette. Duke Naymes reacts to her request by striking Lucafer so hard that his eyes fly from his head and thrusting his body into the hearth. As with her flippant reaction to the demise of her governess, Floripas once again calls the legitimacy of her actions into question by quipping nastily, "Sire . . . or le laisiés caufer; / Moult aime le foier, il n'a soing de lever" (2941–2) [Sir . . . now let him cook. He really loves the fire, he doesn't care to rise from it]. She is evidently totally unconcerned that her intended spouse was just beaten to death in front of her, but rather is pleased that another threat to her plans has been eliminated. Still the poet makes no comment on her behavior or even implies that she is acting out of the ordinary.

Floripas reacts with wrath on one final occasion. Most surprisingly, her anger is directed at her chosen Christian knight, Guy of Burgundy, who unexpectedly compromises her plans. Guy, the knight for whom she has betrayed her father and religion, is simply not interested in her declaration of love and bluntly rejects her, saying that he can not consider taking a wife without Charlemagne's permission and approval. Floripas is understandably insulted and angered by this rejection and responds dramatically with threats of death: "Quant l'entent Floripas, tout ot le sanc mué, / Et jure Mahomet: 'Se vous ne me prenés, / Je vous ferai tous pendre et au vent encruer!'" (2811–13) [When Florıpas heard this, her blood was all stirred up, and she swore by Mahomet, "If you don't take me, I'll make you all hang and swing in the wind!"]. As in the previous examples, Floripas is reacting to what she perceives as an insult: she has just saved Guy and his companions, at great risk to herself, and the ungrateful knight is totally indifferent to her many charms and publicly shames her by rejecting her marriage proposal in front of the other peers. This time, the legitimacy of her response is outweighed by the fact that Guy is technically in the right in insisting on adherence to the feudal code of behavior that prohibits a vassal from marrying without his lord's permission. Worse, Guy's indifference threatens the whole purpose of her plan, becoming his wife. Evidently sensing that Floripas has little interest in feudal rules and that his life is at stake, Guy sensibly gives in to her demands, to the relief of his companions.

Not only are the motives for Floripas' anger not entirely legitimate, but on two occasions the nature of her anger is also questionable. Floripas' reaction to the words of the gaoler and Sortinbrans are described using terms that are appropriate for acceptable, spontaneous, "hot-blooded" male anger, in ways that indicate a loss of control: "le sens cuide derver" (2079, 2739) [almost lost her mind/senses]. When examined closely, however, these terms prove inaccurate, as her actions clearly show that she is in full control both of her faculties and of the situation and is actively utilizing rational thought. In the case of the gaoler, after her initial threats in response to his justified questioning of her character, the text specifically says that she "coiment" [calmly] called her chamberlain, who "connut son courage et k'el ont en pensé" (2083–84) [knew her intention and what she had in mind] to bring her a weapon. Not only is Floripas calm, but her servants also know her intentions, which suggests those close to her knew her temperament well enough to know what to expect. In other words, Floripas does not simply get angry; anger is an essential part of her disposition. Similarly, her altercation with Sortinbrans indicates that, while angry, she has an acute awareness of her actions and their consequences. She expresses a desire to do him serious harm, but only if she can escape blame by other women (2742). She thus restrains herself *specifically* because she is considering the implication of her actions, a sensible strategy, but one that once again requires a cool head and clear thinking. Furthermore, it seems likely that Sortinbrans escapes without harm because their altercation occurs in a public place where Floripas must be aware that any actual violence on her part could be observed and punished. Clearly Floripas is thinking before she acts, the very process that is *not* supposed to be involved in legitimate, hot-blooded anger and violence.

Thus, Floripas' anger and violence do not adhere to legitimate conventions of anger, male or female, literary or historical. While in each of her angry outbursts Floripas initially appears to be reacting with acceptable anger to insults to her honor, on closer inspection the legitimacy of this anger is called into question. The perceived affronts to her honor are actually accurate factual statements that happen to offend her, and her subsequent violence toward the nonoffenders thus seems extreme, unreasonable, and not entirely justifiable. Furthermore, while her angry reactions are often motivated by fear of repercussions for her deceptive behavior, this fear is well placed, and her actions prove to be primarily in response to not getting her way. As important, despite being described as "almost losing her senses," Floripas is often thinking rationally and in full control of her actions. In spite of the questionable legitimacy of all her angry responses, however, Floripas is not punished or even reprimanded for her behavior; in fact, she is rewarded for it by marriage to Guy. How is it possible to explain the fact that, although she is acting outside both the historical and literary conventions for legitimate anger and violence, this transgression is not only not punished but rewarded?

The most obvious explanation for the acceptance of Floripas' norm-defying anger and her often violent behavior is that she is acting for the "right" side—in this context, Christianity—while contributing directly to the defeat of the "wrong" side, Islam. In the late twelfth century, when the original text was composed, Western Christendom had been engaged in conflict with Islam for centuries. From the time that the Muslims had invaded and conquered the bulk of the Iberian Peninsula in 711, Spanish Christians, aided sporadically by crusaders from the rest of Europe, had been struggling to regain the peninsula from them. Starting with the First Crusade of 1096, the task of returning the Holy Land to Christian hands and keeping it that way became the focus of the energy and resources of most non-Spanish Europeans for the duration of the texts' popularity. In the fourteenth century, the Ottoman Turks and their rapidly expanding empire became the main focus for Christian hostility toward Islam. Christians justified these long, costly, and bloody struggles by their unshakeable belief that, as followers of what they believed to be the one true religion, they were in the right and the Muslims were in the wrong, a belief clearly expressed in the *Chanson de Roland*'s oft-quoted line "Païen unt tort e chrestïens unt dreit" (1015) [The pagans are wrong and the Christians are right]. In the chansons de geste, the Saracens are represented in a way that emphasizes their "otherness" and justifies whatever means necessary to ensure their decisive defeat.[56] In accordance with this ideology, it seems not to matter that Floripas often achieves her goals by methods that do not conform to Christian or chivalrous ideals. Murder, lies, angry outbursts, threats, and treachery, particularly when directed against the enemy, are acceptable as long as the end result is the defeat of the Saracen kingdom for Charlemagne and the Christian Empire.

In addition to supporting the "right" side, Floripas is also, despite her declared intention to convert to Christianity, technically a Saracen throughout the story until her baptism in the final lines of the poem. This status as "other" permits her to act in a manner that defies expectations for European Christian women without posing a threat to those in the audience who might be unsettled by such behavior in a Christian heroine.[57] As the daughter of the sultan of Babylon, a Saracen princess raised in Muslim Spain, Floripas is automatically associated with European conventions of representing Islam. These conventions were created by Western Christian scholars, mainly priests and monks, who studied Islam over the centuries of Muslim-Christian contact for the dual purpose of protecting Christians from the lure of Islam and converting Muslims to Christianity.[58] The resulting didactic literature portrayed Islam and Arabic culture in an imaginatively inaccurate way that was subsequently adopted by poets and used to entertain, but in the process also served to inform. One of the most significant themes associated with this medieval Christian notion of Islam was that of violence.[59] Medieval poets utilized the association of Islam and violence by frequently portraying Muslim characters as being prone to fits of rage when events were not going in their favor. For example, in the *Chanson de Roland*, when King Marsile flees to Saragossa, his wife and people run to their idol of Apollo, curse at it for failing to protect them, and tear away its scepter and crown. They then topple it to the ground and smash it to pieces with sticks (2580–91).

The Floripas texts have a similar example of angry male Saracen behavior. When Balan hears that Charlemagne has crossed the bridge of Mautrible and killed Agolafre, he shouts:

"... Mahomet, com ma lois est fallie!
Mauvais diex recréans, ne valés une alie;
Bien a fait Fierabras, qui ta loi a guerpie:
Mors est et recréans qui mais en vous se fie.
Mes hommes déussiés porter deffenserie;
Par mon cief, mar i as ma honte consentie."
Une machue voit, à .II. mains l'a saisie,
Tous dervés vint courant à la mahommerie,
.III. cos en a donné Mahomet lés l'oïe,
La teste li pechoie et le col li esmie. (5146–55)

["... Mahomet, how my law has failed! Cursed treacherous god, you are not worth a fig. Fierabras, who abandoned your law, did well. Whoever puts his faith in you is dead and treacherous. You should have defended my men. By my head, you have consented to my dishonor." He saw a club, and seized it in his two hands. He ran toward the mosque all enraged, he gave Mahomet three blows to the side of the ear. He smashed the head and he shattered the neck.]

Among Balan's angry outbursts is his attempt to strike his advisor Brullant when Brullant gives him unwelcome advice, and he is prevented from doing so only by Sortinbrans (3726–27). Evidently Balan and the other Saracen men of the chansons have difficulty controlling their anger when confronted with adversity, a characteristic clearly shared by Floripas.

This representational convention of the "hot-tempered" nature of Saracens may be partially drawn from ancient and contemporary medical theories of *complexio*, or the balance of the qualities of hot, cold, wet, and dry that resulted from the mixture of elements in the human body. According to Galen and his later medieval followers, *complexio* varied among peoples from different geographical areas: those who lived in cool climates were supposed to be colder and moister in complexion, and those who lived in hot climates were more likely to have hot and dry complexions.[60] While in the earlier Middle Ages scholars like Isidore of Seville associated sub-Saharan Africa with a hot climate, Suzanne Conklin Akbari observes that by the fourteenth century it was the East, or the Asian continent, that had come "to be known as a place of overwhelming heat, understood in both a literal and a moral sense."[61] So it is not surprising that Muslims, associated with hot locations such as the Near East, North Africa, and Spain, would have been expected to have hot complexions along with the heated emotions that could arise from such a complexion. Muslim women, while female and therefore colder and moister than men in complexion, would still have been considered hotter than their northern Christian counterparts. Thus, according to both representational conventions and contemporary medical theory, anger and violence are natural to Floripas as a Saracen woman. This Saracen behavior is permitted because her rage and violence ultimately benefit the Christians and contribute to the Saracen defeat.

Quite apart from her adhering to behavioral expectations for Saracens and acting on behalf of the "right" side, I would argue that "belle" Floripas' anger and her tendency to kill or threaten anyone who gets in her way are examples of the many parodic inversions that characterize the Floripas texts.[62] Immediately prior to Floripas' first act of violence, her murder of the gaoler Brutamond, the poet introduces Floripas as "La plus gentil puciele dont onques fu parlé" (2005) [the most noble girl of whom was ever told] and provides a detailed catalogue of her physical attributes, which are identical to those used to describe most Christian heroines. She is slender, with long golden hair, shining eyes, and skin as white as summer flowers (2004–42).[63] This conventional description sets up the audience's expectations for appropriate courtly feminine behavior, expectations that are completely overturned as soon as "Floripas la fiert" (2089) (Floripas the fierce) beats the gaoler to death.[64] The presence of a conventionally beautiful, "cortoise" (courteous, refined) heroine who erupts in rage, threatens, and kills like the worst of villains would have been a novelty to audiences used to more decorous heroines who rarely displayed any kind of emotion, particularly anger. Such a novelty must have entertained and amused audiences and may help account for the long-lasting and international appeal of the story.[65] That Floripas' unconventionally violent behavior was intended to amuse is supported by the fact that each of the murders committed by her, or at her instigation, is either preceded or followed by dryly witty comments, comments that are received with laughter by the peers. As Norman Daniel comments in reference to the chansons de geste, "In these poems, violence is fun."[66]

The ability of female anger and violence to entertain is one that I would argue is present in other genres of medieval literature. In the *Roman de Silence*, for example, Queen Eufeme reacts in a rather extreme manner to Silence's rejection of her sexual advances. In order to make it look as though Silence has raped her, Eufeme tears her own hair, punches herself in the nose, and tramps upon her wimple, all the while holding on to Silence and uttering insults such as "crazy bastard" and "dirty scum!" (lines 4076–94). The idea of the queen beating herself in the face with one hand while hanging on to the cause of her rage with the other, continually berating him for an imaginary crime, must have amused audiences. The fabliaux are similarly filled with women who violently abuse their husbands to comic effect, and depictions of husband beaters likewise found great popularity in the visual arts.[67] As Natalie Davis observes, "the point of such portraits is that they are funny and amoral: the women are full of life and energy, and they win much of the time."[68]

Even the vita of the virgin martyr Saint Juliana contains elements of physical humor. Like many virgin martyrs, Juliana is tortured and then put to death because she refuses to marry her pagan betrothed unless he converts to Christianity. But unlike other virgin martyrs who are the victims of male violence, Juliana is also a perpetrator of violent deeds. After the usual beatings and torture by father and suitor, Juliana is thrown in prison, where she engages in an extended physical altercation with a demon who makes the mistake of trying to corrupt her faith. On the advice of God, she first beats the demon with the chains that bind her until he pleads for mercy, then, totally on her own initiative, she drags him behind her when she is taken to be executed, and finally throws him into a latrine. While

Juliana's treatment of the demon is at least initially in response to divine instruction, I would argue that the ongoing violent confrontations between her and the ridiculous, rather pathetic demon must have been intended to amuse. The two characters invert the usual convention of pagans tormenting saints, and their altercations contribute little to the spiritual meaning of the text. The fact that the demon himself specifically acknowledges that she is making a fool of him ("me ridiculum facere"), combined with the fact that she ultimately throws him in a latrine, a place traditionally associated with scatological humor, suggests that the author of the vita knew that Juliana's treatment of the demon would evoke a laugh from the audience and most likely cause them to remember her story.[69] It thus seems very possible that literary physical and verbal altercations initiated by women with men of authority were intended to entertain and amuse medieval audiences.

In addition to being amusing, the inversion of audience expectations serves to contest conventional gender boundaries, while at the same time ultimately upholding them. Humor and related role inversion are well recognized as providing a safe means of critical expression,[70] and Roberta Krueger has noted that problematic female characters are often the "catalyst for a resistant, critical interpretation of courtly ideology."[71] As demonstrated, Floripas exhibits characteristics usually associated with legitimate male patterns of anger, violence, and aggression, yet she does so in a clearly female body, as the heroine of the story. This behavior, while in direct opposition to conventional literary norms for appropriate feminine behavior, does recall the evidence of judicial records for similar behavior conducted by noncourtly women. By allowing Floripas to react with anger to situations that would anger men or women of lower social status in the same circumstances, the Floripas texts present anger as a behavioral option for women of higher social status. Thus, while inverting a convention with humorous results, the texts also acknowledge that noble women are able to, and probably do, get angry at insults to their honor, recognizing that female anger is a legitimate, or at least understandable, response to certain situations for women of all classes. As Natalie Davis has suggested with respect to early modern representations of sexual inversion, such images of "disorderly women" may be functioning "not ... to keep women in their place ... [but] to widen behavioral options for women within and even outside marriage."[72] As we have seen, however, Floripas acts in this way as a non-Christian, and her anger, being in response to comments that while insulting are actually factually accurate, is not really legitimate according to medieval standards for acceptable anger. These facts may serve to undercut any acknowledgement of female anger so that Floripas' behavior might be more acceptable to more conservative audience members, contesting conventional female roles while at the same time upholding them.[73]

In addition to finding the parodic nature of her behavior amusing, some men may also have found her aggression and volatility titillating. It is clear that audiences were captivated by depictions of female warriors who abandon feminine gender roles to fight according to male roles, a conclusion that is supported by the ongoing popularity of the Amazons and other literary women warriors throughout the medieval and early modern periods.[74] While it is not known for certain why the idea of warrior women attained such popularity with audiences, one possibility is that for male audience members the combination of women, anger, and violence may have held erotic appeal. Certainly aggression and violence toward women has held an unfortunately enduring and widespread erotic appeal,[75] and evidence suggests that violent women too may have held a similarly erotic appeal. Such an argument is supported by the evolution of the warrior maiden Camilla's character from Virgil's original portrayal of her in the *Aeneid* to her portrayal in the twelfth-century poem *Eneas*. Camilla, introduced as a warrior girl in book 7 of the *Aeneid*, is described in fifteen lines that focus on her skill as a fighter, making no direct reference to her beauty (803–17). Likewise, when she reenters the story in book 11, Virgil does not dwell on her appearance but presents her as a fellow warrior (498–521). By the twelfth century, however, the audience of *Eneas* is treated to more than one hundred lines that make continued reference to Camilla's incredible (conventional) beauty, paired with her strength as a warrior. This connection is made explicit in the scene preceding her death, where a Trojan tauntingly says:

> en belle chambre soz cortine
> fait bon combatre o tel mescine.
> Venistes ça por vous moustrer?
> Je ne vous veul mie acheter.
> Pour quant blanche vous voi et bloie:
> .IIII. deniers ai ci de Troie,
> qui sont moult bon, de fin or tuit;
> ceuz vous donra por mon deduit
> une piece mener o vous;
> je n'en seray point trop jalous,
> bailleray vous aus escuiers.

Bien vous veul vendre mes deniers:
se tant y perch, point ne m'en plaing,
vous en avrez double gaaing:
l'un ert que de mon or avrez,
l'autre que vostre bon ferez;
mais ne vous souffiroit naient,
je cuit, se il estoitent cent;
vous en porriez estre lassee,
mais ne seriez mie saoulee. (7153–72)

[It is good to do battle with such a maiden in a beautiful chamber under a bed-curtain. Have you come here to show yourself off? I do not wish to buy you, although I see that you are fair and blond. I have here four Trojan deniers, which are very good, of fine gold. I will give these to you to have a moment of pleasure with you. I will not be too jealous of it, but will share you with my squires. I wish to make you earn well my deniers: if I lose, I won't complain, you will have double profit: one part in having my gold, the other in taking your pleasure, but that won't suffice for you, I think, even if there were one hundred of us; you may become tired, but you won't be satisfied.][76]

The most unsettling thing about this passage, especially given the focus of the poet on Camilla's appearance, is the way in which the Trojan reduces her status from a valiant warrior maiden, who has just performed admirably on the battlefield, to a sexual playmate whose favors he wants to buy, like those of a prostitute. In *Eneas* the clear connection drawn between Camilla's warrior status and her sexuality thus provides an especially revealing example of the increasing literary pairing of beauty and female violence.

Like Camilla, Floripas is clearly presented as being physically desirable while at the same time displaying a remarkable capacity for anger and violence, a combination of traits that likewise may have been found erotic by some members of the audience. The appeal may have been that, in spite of the fact that the Church was instructing European men to seek out docile, obedient, even-tempered women for spouses, some men may have entertained "safe" fantasies about women who were more independent, passionate, and expressive. Other men may have been attracted by the fantasy of a challenging chase. In a culture in which the hunt and conquest of various sorts was such a dominant part of courtly ideology, the sexual victory over an angry and aggressive woman, especially a high-status woman of the enemy, would have been that much more difficult and challenging and therefore more sweet.

Floripas' anger and aggressively violent streak likely appealed to different audience members for different reasons. Her beauty and passionate nature, violence, and "otherness" may have held exotic or erotic appeal for some men who fantasized about more spirited wives, and appealed to the sense of humor of others through its unconventional pairing of a beautiful princess and a volatile temper tending toward brutal violence. Some medieval audience members may have cheered her on because her actions ultimately serve to benefit the Christians and eliminate problematic Saracens. More important, her anger and violent reaction to insults directed toward both her honor and women in general may have been intended and/or interpreted as a negative commentary on misogynist views similar to that later expressed by Chaucer's Wife of Bath.[77] Likewise, her anger and the aggressively violent manifestations of that anger seem to have provided another safe space in which to explore alternative models of female behavior, one that recognized that noble women did get angry and in some situations were justified in doing so. Her conversion to Christianity and safe initiation into the feminine domestic sphere of marriage at the end of the story likewise ensure that all of her transgressions can be considered a part of her non-Christian, unmarried past by those audience members uncomfortable with seeing them as an innate part of her character and, by extension, of all women's. In Floripas, European Christians are offered the chance to safely contemplate female anger and violence in a way that need not necessarily be associated with their own women but could still resonate with women who might identify with Floripas in spite of her Saracen origins. The fact that the story lends itself so well to such a multiplicity of interpretations goes a long way toward explaining its enduring appeal to European audiences throughout the medieval and early modern periods.

Notes

This essay is an abbreviated version of the final chapter of my Ph.D. thesis, "'Faire Maide' or 'Venomous Serpente': The Cultural Significance of the Saracen Princess Floripas in France, England and Spain, 1200–1500," Centre for Medieval Studies, University of Toronto, September 2002.

1. See Diane Bornstein, *The Lady in the Tower: Medieval Courtesy Literature for Women* (Hamden, Conn.: Archon, 1983).

2. There is no known copy of the original poem extant, but it is generally accepted that it was composed in France by an unknown poet during the late twelfth century.

See Marianne J. Ailes, "A Comparative Study of the Medieval French and Middle English Verse Texts of the *Fierabras* Legend" (Ph.D. diss., University of Reading, 1989), 61–93, and Joseph Bédier, "La Composition de la *Chanson de Fierabras*," *Romania* 17 (1888): 22–51. I have based my analysis of *Fierabras* on the nineteenth-century A. Kroeber and G. Servois edition of BN f.fr. 12603, in vol. 4 of *Les Anciens Poètes de la France*, ed. F. Guessard (Paris: F. Vieweg, 1860), because it is the only modern edition of this early fourteenth-century verse version, one that appears to have significantly influenced the majority of later versions. There are, however, some questions about the reliability of the Kroeber and Servois edition. See André de Mandach, "The Evolution of the Matter of Fierabras" in *Romance Epic: Essays on a Medieval Literary Genre*, ed. Hans-Erich Keller (Kalamazoo, Mich: Medieval Institute Publications, 1987), 130–31, and Marc le Peron, "Liste des vers sautés, ajoutés ou déformés dans l'édition du ms. 'A' par A. Kroeber et G. Servois du 'Fierabras' (Paris, 1860)," in *Au carrefour des routes d'Europe: La Chanson de geste*, Xe Congrès International de la Société Rencesvals pour l'Étude des Épopées Romanes, Strasbourg 1985 (Aix-en-Provence: Université de Provence, 1987), 2:1216–28.

3. While not all Saracen princesses are the same, scholars have identified twenty-eight texts that include various forms of the convention. See Micheline de Combarieu, "Un personnage épique: La Jeune Musulmane," *Mélanges de langue et littérature françaises du moyen âge offerts à Pierre Jonin* (Aix-en-Provence: CUERMA, 1979), 183–96; F. M. Warren, "The Enamoured Moslem Princess in Orderic Vital and the French Epic," *PMLA* 29 (1914): 341–58; and Charles A. Knudson, "Le Thème de la princesse Sarrasine dans la Prise d'Orange," *Romance Philology* 22(1969): 449–62. Jacqueline de Weever, *Sheba's Daughters: Whitening and Demonizing the Saracen Woman in Medieval French Epic* (New York: Garland, 1998), is another interesting study of the Saracen princess but is based on a limited understanding of the texts and their historical context.

4. André de Mandach has made a detailed study of the Floripas/Fierabras texts and has documented at least forty manuscripts dating between the thirteenth and fifteenth centuries: fifteen written in French, one each in Occitan, Provençal, and Latin, four in Anglo-Norman, three in Middle English, eight in Irish, and seven in Italian. In addition, a French prose version by Jehan Bagnyon was printed in Geneva in the late fifteenth century and went through at least twenty-six reprintings throughout Europe in the following centuries, especially in France and Switzerland. It was also translated into English, German, and Spanish, and the story was transported at some time during the sixteenth century to the Americas, where it still exists in various forms. See *La Geste de "Fierabras,"* Naissance et développement de la chanson de geste en Europe 5 (Geneva: Librairie Droz, 1987), 165–86.

5. In *Anger's Past: The Social Uses of an Emotion in the Middle Ages*, ed. Barbara H. Rosenwein (Ithaca: Cornell University Press, 1998), there is only one essay that deals with women, and it is in a highly specialized context that makes reference to only one seventh-century text. Jennifer Willging's article "The Power of Feminine Anger in Marie de France's 'Yonec' and 'Guigemar,'" *Florilegium* 14 (1995–96): 123–

35, is more about feminine responses to loveless marriages than about anger. William V. Harris includes a short chapter on female anger in *Restraining Rage: The Ideology of Anger Control in Classical Antiquity* (Cambridge, Mass.: Harvard University Press, 2001), but the social and religious context of classical antiquity was considerably different. Scholarship on the early modern period is richer in its offerings. Natalie Zemon Davis initiated work on women's anger in the context of letters of pardon in *Fiction in the Archives: Pardon Tales and Their Tellers in Sixteenth-Century France* (Stanford: Stanford University Press, 1987), and Gwynne Kennedy has recently published *Just Anger: Representing Women's Anger in Early Modern England* (Carbondale: Southern Illinois University Press, 2000).

6. Kennedy, *Just Anger*, 7.

7. Nancy G. Siraisi, *Medieval and Early Renaissance Medicine: An Introduction to Knowledge and Practice* (Chicago: University of Chicago Press, 1990), 105–6.

8. Edward Muir, *Mad Blood Stirring: Vendetta in Renaissance Italy*, reader's ed. (Baltimore: Johns Hopkins University Press, 1998), 143–44.

9. Guido Ruggiero, *Violence in Early Renaissance Venice* (New Brunswick, N.J.: Rutgers University Press, 1980), 175.

10. Muir, *Mad Blood Stirring*, 120–21. See also 145.

11. Davis, *Fiction in the Archives*, 36–76. Davis describes examples of remission tales that involve acts of violence committed in fits of anger that are pardoned by the king.

12. Thomas Andrew Green, *Verdict According to Conscience: Perspectives on the English Criminal Trial Jury, 1200–1800* (Chicago: University of Chicago Press, 1985), 30, and Naomi D. Hurnard, *The King's Pardon for Homicide before A.D. 1307* (Oxford: Clarendon Press, 1969), 159–70.

13. Richard E. Barton, "'Zealous Anger' and Aristocratic Relationships," in Rosenwein, *Anger's Past*, 155.

14. Most scholarship on honor cultures in both the modern and premodern periods has focused on the Mediterranean. See, for example, Julian Pitt-Rivers, *The Fate of Shechem; or, the Politics of Sex: Essays in the Anthropology of the Mediterranean* (Cambridge: Cambridge University Press, 1977); David D. Gilmore, ed. *Honor and Shame and the Unity of the Mediterranean* (Washington, D.C.: American Anthropological Association, 1987); and J. G. Péristiany, ed., *Honour and Shame: The Values of Mediterranean Society* (Chicago: University of Chicago Press, 1966). While no full-fledged study has yet been undertaken for western Europe, ethnohistorians like Mark Meyerson are now attempting to draw parallels between the medieval and early modern cultures of northern and southern Europeans who, while living in very different cultural milieus, seemed to have been influenced by similar concepts of honor and shame.

15. Helen Solterer, *The Master and Minerva: Disputing Women in French Medieval Culture* (Berkeley and Los Angeles: University of California Press, 1995), 11–12.

16. Ruggiero, *Violence*, 125.

17. William Ian Miller, *Humiliation: And Other Essays on Honor, Social Discomfort, and Violence* (Ithaca: Cornell University Press, 1993), 83.

18. For peaceful means of dispute resolution, see Daniel R. Lesnick, "Insults and Threats in Medieval Todi," *Journal of Medieval History* 17 (1991): 71–83, esp. 71, and J. A. Sharpe, *Defamation and Sexual Slander in Early Modern England: The Church Courts at York*, Borthwick Papers 59 (York, Eng.: Borthwick Institute, 1980).

19. Stephen D. White, "The Politics of Anger," in Rosenwein, *Anger's Past*, 140, 144.

20. *Rhetoric* 2.2.1, quoted in Miller, *Humiliation*, 226n23.

21. R. F. Newbold, "Interpersonal Violence in Gregory of Tours' *Libri Historiarum*," *Nottingham Medieval Studies* 38 (1994): 3–17, at 9.

22. Ronald Gosselin, "Honneur et Violence à Manosque (1240–60)," in *Vie privée et ordre public à la fin du Moyen-Âge: Études sur Manosque, la Provence et le Piémont (1250–1450)*, ed. Michel Hébert (Aix-en-Provence: Université de Provence, 1987), 45–63.

23. A. J. Finch, "The Nature of Violence in the Middle Ages: An Alternative Perspective," *Historical Research* 70 (1997): 249–68, at 263. Of course, most of these studies are based on an analysis of court records and thus are a reflection of the attitudes of only that sector of the population that was making use of the court system. Those of higher social status do not tend to appear with much frequency in these records, yet this does not mean that they were not using violent means to settle disputes over honor. See also Elizabeth S. Cohen, "Honor and Gender in the Streets of Early Modern Rome," *Journal of Interdisciplinary History* 22 (1992): 597–625, and Mark D. Meyerson, "'Assaulting the House': Interpreting Christian, Muslim, and Jewish Violence in Late Medieval Valencia," in *Children of Abraham: Jews, Christians, and Muslims in the Middle Ages*, ed. A. Dykman and M. Taccioni (State College: Pennsylvania State University Press, forthcoming).

24. Richard W. Kaeuper, *Chivalry and Violence in Medieval Europe* (Oxford. Oxford University Press, 1999), 144.

25. All quotations are from Gerald J. Brault, ed. and trans., *The Song of Roland: An Analytical Edition*, vol. 2 (University Park: Pennsylvania State University Press, 1978). See also the *Lais* of Marie de France ("Lanval," lines 325, 363–66) and Chaucer's *Canterbury Tales* (Summoner's and Friar's) for other examples of male anger in response to insult.

26. The word used in the text is not *ire* but *doel* (line 2789), but George Fenwick Jones argues convincingly in *The Ethos of the Song of Roland* (Baltimore: Johns Hopkins Press, 1963), 84, that "although *doel* is sometimes consociated with pity or affection, it is more often associated with anger and shame; and therefore the deeper meaning of the word must be shame, humiliation, or indignation more often than sorrow, as most translators have believed."

27. The examples that follow are only a few of the many in the text. It should be noted that these terms are identical or very similar to those used to describe Floripas' anger, a fact that will be discussed later.

28. Joanne S. Norman, *Metamorphoses of an Allegory: The Iconography of the Psychomachia in Medieval Art* (New York: Peter Lang, 1988), 8. Most of the representations of the virtues and vices that Norman goes on to describe are of women. See also Adolf Katzenellenbogen, *Allegories of the Virtues and Vices in Medieval Art: From Early Christian Times to the Thirteenth Century* (London: Warburg Institute, 1939; reprint Toronto: University of Toronto Press, 1989), 19–20. Pages cited are from the 1989 edition.

29. Prudentius Clemens Aurelius, *Prudentius*, ed. and trans. H. J. Thomson (Cambridge, Mass.: Harvard University Press, 1949), 1:286.

30. Katzenellenbogen, *Allegories*, 1–3. There are sixteen illustrated manuscripts extant dating from the ninth to the late thirteenth century. Jennifer O'Reilly indicates that parts of this work are preserved in more than three hundred medieval manuscripts and exerted influence on other writers; see *Studies in the Iconography of the Virtues and Vices in the Middle Ages* (New York: Garland, 1988), 4, 13. See also Emile Mâle, *The Gothic Image: Religious Art in France of the Thirteenth Century*, trans. Dora Nussey (New York: Harper, 1958), 98–130; and Lester K. Little, "Anger and Monastic Curses," in Rosenwein, *Anger's Past*, 9–35.

31. Katzenellenbogen, *Allegories*, 11–12, with reference to Paris, BN MS. Lat. 2077.

32. Morton W. Bloomfield, *The Seven Deadly Sins* (East Lansing: Michigan State College Press, 1952; reprint Michigan State University Press, 1967), 103. Citations are from the 1967 edition.

33. Norman, *Metamorphoses of an Allegory*, 30.

34. Studies on medieval misogyny include R. Howard Bloch, *Medieval Misogyny and the Invention of Western Romantic Love* (Chicago: University of Chicago Press, 1991); Francis Lee Utley, *The Crooked Rib: An Analytical Index to the Argument about Women in English and Scots Literature to the End of the Year 1568* (Columbus: Ohio State University, 1944); Susan L. Smith, *The Power of Women: A Topos in Medieval Art and Literature* (Philadelphia: University of Pennsylvania Press, 1995).

35. Marbod of Rennes, "De meretrice," in *Liber decem capitulorum*, Migne *PL* 171, col. 1698. See Alcuin Blamires, ed., *Woman Defamed and Woman Defended: An Anthology of Medieval Texts* (Oxford: Clarendon Press, 1992), 100–103, for an English translation of the whole chapter.

36. Bornstein, *Lady in the Tower*, 34, with reference to Garin lo Brun, "L'Enseignement de Garin lo Brun," ed. Carl Appel, *Revue des Langues Romanes* 33 (1889): 409–29.

37. Bornstein, *Lady in the Tower*, 59, with reference to Robert of Blois, *Robert von Blois: Sämtliche Werke*, ed. Jakob Ulrich, 3 vols. (Berlin: Mayer und Müller, 1889).

38. *Le Ménagier de Paris*, ed. Georgine E. Brereton and Janet M. Ferrier (Oxford: Clarendon Press, 1981), bk. 1, sec. 6.

39. *The Book of the Knight of the Tower*, trans. William Caxton, ed. M. Y. Offord, EETS s.s. 2 (London: Oxford University Press, 1971), 101–2.

40. Davis, *Fiction in the Archives*, 103, with reference to AN, JJ237, 1r, letter of remission dated June 1524 for Marguerite Panete, wife of Mathieu de La Faye of a village in the Bourbonnais.

41. Davis, *Fiction in the Archives*, 201n60, with reference to AN, JJ249B, 118r-v. Davis notes many other similar cases, 98–103.

42. Ibid., 103–4. See also 82–83.

43. Ibid., 81, with reference to Montaigne's "Défense de Sénèque et de Plutarque," *Essays*, 2.32.548.

44. This latter response to anger was particularly noticeable in the medieval Icelandic sagas where, as William Ian Miller notes, "women are expected to goad their men-folk to vengeful action" (*Humiliation*, 104). In her study of heroic women in the Icelandic sagas, Jenny Jochens makes reference to Rolf Heller's work, which identified fifty-one cases of women who goad and nag their husbands into deeds of crime and revenge in the forty extant sagas and short stories; see "The Medieval Icelandic Heroine: Fact or Fiction?" in *Sagas of the Icelanders: A Book of Essays*, ed. John Tucker (New York: Garland, 1989), 106–7.

45. *The Ecclesiastical History of Orderic Vitalis*, ed. and trans. Marjorie Chibnall (Oxford: Clarendon Press, 1969–80), vol. 6, bk. 8, 14–15.

46. He finally gave in to her demands. Mark D. Meyerson, "Violence Against Women and the Power of Women in Late Medieval Valencia," unpublished paper, 10–11.

47. Muir, *Mad Blood Stirring*, 191.

48. *Silence: A Thirteenth-Century French Romance*, ed. and trans. Sarah Roche-Mahdi (East Lansing, Mich.: Colleagues Press, 1992). All references are to this edition.

49. The hero Lanval likewise rejects the queen's advances in Marie de France's lay "Lanval" with very similar results (lines 305–10).

50. See "Bevis of Hampton," in *Four Romances of England*, ed. Ronald B. Herzman, Graham Drake, and Eve Salisbury (Kalamazoo: Medieval Institute Publications, Western Michigan University, 1999), lines 302–42, where Bevis rightly accuses his mother of arranging the death of his father, an aging knight, so that she might marry her lover. The Middle English version (ca. 1324) is descended from the earlier Anglo-Norman *Boeuve de Haumton*.

51. Old French in *Le Roman de Tristan*, ed. Renée L. Curtis (Munich: Max Hueber, 1963), 1:175, lines 9–13. English translation in *The Romance of Tristan*, trans. Renee Curtis (New York and Oxford: Oxford University Press, 1994), 350. In Gottfried von Strassburg's early thirteenth-century German version of the poem, it is the young Isolt who attempts to avenge her uncle's death before being stopped by her mother.

52. *Raoul de Cambrai*, ed. and trans. Sarah Kay (Oxford: Clarendon Press, 1992), line 7113.

53. Geoffrey Chaucer, *The Riverside Chaucer*, ed. Larry D. Benson, 3rd ed. (Boston: Houghton Mifflin, 1987), lines 790–93.

54. This similarity is supported by the fact that her anger is usually described in the identical terms used to describe male responses in the text to similar situations in which male honor is insulted in some way. The terms used to describe Floripas' anger are "sens cuide derver" (2079, 2739), "coureça" (5280), and "le sanc mué" (2181, 2189, 2869). For the same terms applied to male characters, see lines 1077, 2404, 2701, 3786, and 3824.

55. The fact that she is insulted by this comment is highlighted in the fifteenth-century prose version of *Fierabras*, where Floripas "fut bien marrye de ceu qu'il l'avoit ainxi davant tous ses gens escondite rudement et commancza a rougir et a penser qu'elle feroit" (726–28) [was very furious at this, that he had thus spoken rudely before all her people, and began to redden and think that she would strike (him)]. She evidently continues to dwell on the insult, because she calls her seneschal and asks him to beat the gaoler so as to set an example to others. See *Fierabras: Roman en prose de la fin du XIVe siècle*, ed. Jean Miquet (Ottawa: Éditions de l'Université d'Ottawa, 1983), an edition based on BN f.fr. 4969 (ca. 1410) and BN f.fr. 2172 (ca. 1460).

56. Dorothee Metlitzki, *The Matter of Araby in Medieval England* (New Haven: Yale University Press, 1977), 160.

57. The fairies and women from the otherworld who are commonly found in romances are an additional type of "other" who are likewise permitted to act in more aggressive ways than Christian heroines. See "The Wooing Woman in Anglo-Norman Romance," *Romance in Medieval England*, ed. Maldwyn Mills, Jennifer Fellows, and Carol M. Meale (Cambridge and Rochester, N.Y.: D. S. Brewer, 1991), 149. See also Anna Hubertine Reuters, "The Forward Heroine–Fairy Mistress," in *Friendship and Love in the Middle English Metrical Romances* (New York: Peter Lang, 1990), 91–108.

58. Peter the Venerable, abbot of Cluny, was one such scholar and is credited with initiating the study of Islam in Europe. See James Kritzeck, *Peter the Venerable and Islam* (Princeton: Princeton University Press, 1964), 14, 15, 24, 51–69. Peter and other Christians like Alexander du Pont in his *Roman de Mahomet*, Guibert of Nogent, Gerald of Wales, and Alan of Lille helped create and perpetuate a popular and long lasting imaginary vision of Islam and the Arab world. See Marie-Thérèse d'Alverny, *La connaissance de l'Islam dans l'Occident médiéval*, ed. Charles Burnett (Aldershot: Variorum, 1994); Thomas E. Burman, *Religious Polemic and the Intellectual History of the Mozarabs, c. 1050–1200* (New York: E. J. Brill, 1994); María Rosa Menocal, *The Arabic Role in Medieval Literary History: A Forgotten Heritage* (Philadelphia: University of Pennsylvania Press, 1987), 38–42; Norman Daniel, *The Arabs and Medieval Europe*, 2nd ed. (New York: Longman, 1975), 263–98.

59. Norman Daniel cites the example of the thirteenth-century Dominican William of Tripoli, who wrote that "one article of belief of theirs runs like this: 'the faith of the Saracens arose by the sword of Muhammad, and will perish by the sword

which will be God's.'" His contemporary Ricoldo da Monte Croce likewise maintained that "the religion of the Saracens is violent and was brought in by violence, and so among them it is held to be quite certain that it will last only as long as the victory of the sword will remain with them." See *Heroes and Saracens: An Interpretation of the Chansons de Geste* (Edinburgh: Edinburgh University Press, 1984), 95. See also Rana Kabbani, *Europe's Myths of Orient: Devise and Rule* (London: Macmillan, 1986), 5, 16; Menocal, *Arabic Role*, 39–45. This association was only strengthened after the fall of Constantinople to the Ottoman Turks in 1453, when contemporary writers emphasized reports of the excessive cruelty and inhumanity of the Turks. See Robert Schwoebel, *The Shadow of the Crescent: The Renaissance Image of the Turk, 1453–1517* (New York: St. Martin's Press, 1967).

60. Siraisi, *Medieval and Early Renaissance Medicine*, 101–4. See also Richard J. Durling, ed., *Burgundio of Pisa's Translation of Galen's Peri Kraseon "De complexionibus"* (New York: Walter de Gruyter, 1976) and Ian Maclean, *The Renaissance Notion of Woman: A Study in the Fortunes of Scholasticism and Medical Science in European Intellectual Life* (Cambridge: Cambridge University Press, 1980). The thirteenth-century encyclopedist Bartholomaeus Anglicus, following his seventh-century predecessor Isidore of Seville, also differentiated between the natures of northern and southern (and Eastern) men based on their respective climates. See Suzanne Conklin Akbari, "From Due East to True North: Orientalism and Orientation," in *The Postcolonial Middle Ages*, ed. Jeffrey Jerome Cohen (New York: St. Martin's Press, 2000), 19–34.

61. Akbari, "From Due East," 29–30.

62. I am relying on Martha Bayless's definition of parody, in *Parody in the Middle Ages: The Latin Tradition* (Ann Arbor: University of Michigan Press, 1996), 3, as "an intentionally humorous literary (written) text that achieves its effect by (1) imitating and distorting the distinguishing characteristics of literary genres, styles, authors, or specific texts (*textual parody*); or (2) imitating, with or without distortion, literary genres, styles, authors, or texts while in addition satirizing or focusing on nonliterary customs, events, or persons (*social parody*)." She continues that "in the later medieval period . . . social parody was by far the more popular category of the genre and served as the vehicle for a significant proportion of medieval satire. . . . Rather than being restricted to a form of intertextual commentary, parody was pressed to the service of larger social issues" (5). See my Ph.D. thesis for a full discussion of parodic inversion in the Fierabras/Floripas texts and its significance.

63. She is described similarly once again at the end of the story when she undresses for baptism. See D. S. Brewer, "The Ideal of Feminine Beauty in Medieval Literature, Especially 'Harley Lyrics,' Chaucer, and Some Elizabethans," *Modern Language Review* 50 (1955): 257–69; Alice M. Colby, *The Portrait in Twelfth-Century French Literature* (Geneva: Librairie Droz, 1965).

64. *Fiers* is a word used to describe heroic warriors, male or female. See George Jones, *The Ethos of the Song of Roland* (Baltimore: John Hopkins University Press, 1963), 66.

65. Gerald Herman, "Unconventional Arms as a Comic Device in Some Chansons de Geste," *Modern Language Quarterly* 30 (1969): 326–27, has also argued that there is an element of humor in the "violent damsels" of the chansons. The three examples he cites, however, are of women who are forced to use violence to fend off a suitor or abductor. In contrast, Floripas' violence is in response to what she has perceived as an insult to her honor. Norman Susskind argues that other things that medieval Europeans found amusing were "démesure" or outrageous behavior, foreigners (Lombards, Jews, pagan gods), or women if they performed "unwomanly" deeds; see "Humor in the *Chansons de Geste*," *Symposium* 15 (1961): 186, 189, 190.

66. Daniel, *Heroes and Saracens*, 118.

67. See Smith, *Power of Women*, for many artistic and literary examples of women who get the upper hand in marriage.

68. Natalie Zemon Davis, "Women on Top," in *Society and Culture in Early Modern France*, ed. Natalie Zemon Davis (Stanford: Stanford University Press, 1975), 124–151, at 134–35.

69. This humor is not as incongruous as it might seem in such a sacred context. As V. A. Kolve has observed about humor in the religious context, "such laughter could be put to good use: it could make doctrine memorable"; see *The Play Called Corpus Christi* (Stanford: Stanford University Press, 1966), 130. For the vita of St. Juliana in modern English, see Jacobus de Voragine, *The Golden Legend: Readings on the Saints*, trans. William Granger Ryan (Princeton: Princeton University Press, 1993), 1:160–61. On religious humor, see also Bayless, *Parody in the Middle Ages*, 177–212.

70. See Davis, "Women on Top," for inversional behavior as either supporting or overturning the status quo. As Kathryn Gravdal notes, in such parodic treatments "poets and audiences seek one form of resolution, albeit artistic, to the social conflicts and anxieties of their historical world"; see *Vilain and Courtois: Transgressive Parody in French Literature of the Twelfth and Thirteenth Centuries* (Lincoln: University of Nebraska Press, 1989), 19.

71. Roberta L. Krueger, *Women Readers and the Ideology of Gender in Old French Verse Romance* (Cambridge: Cambridge University Press, 1993), xiv.

72. Davis, "Women on Top," 131.

73. Ann McMillan finds similar interpretive ambiguities in Eustache Deschamps' representation of the Neuf Preuses; see "Men's Weapons, Women's War: The Nine Female Worthies, 1400–1640," *Mediaevalia* 5 (1979): 113–39, at 128.

74. See Deborah Fraioli, "Why Joan of Arc Never Became an Amazon," in *Fresh Verdicts on Joan of Arc*, ed. Bonnie Wheeler and Charles T. Wood (New York: Garland, 1996), 189; Abby Wettan Kleinbaum, *The War Against the Amazons* (New York: New Press, 1983); Simon Shepherd, *Amazons and Warrior Women: Varieties of Feminism in Seventeenth-Century Drama* (Brighton: Harvester Press, 1981); Wm. Blake Tyrell, *Amazons: A Study in Athenian Mythmaking* (Baltimore: Johns Hopkins University Press, 1984); McMillan, "Men's Weapons, Women's War." Women warriors seem to have held particular appeal in early medieval times in

northern Europe. See Carol J. Clover, "Maiden Warriors and Other Sons," *Journal of English and Germanic Philology* 85 (1986): 35–49; Clover, "Regardless of Sex: Men, Women, and Power in Early Modern Europe," *Speculum* 68 (1993), 363–87; Jenny Jochens, *Old Norse Images of Women* (Philadelphia: University of Pennsylvania Press, 1996), 87–112.

75. On the connection between violence and sexuality in classical and medieval texts, see Amy Richlin, "Reading Ovid's Rapes," in *Pornography and Representation in Greece and Rome*, ed. Amy Richlin (Oxford: Oxford University Press, 1992); Kathryn Gravdal, "Chrétien de Troyes, Gratian, and the Medieval Romance of Sexual Violence," *Signs* 17 (1992): 558–85; and Gravdal, *Ravishing Maidens: Writing Rape in Medieval French Literature and Law* (Philadelphia: University of Pennsylvania Press, 1991). For discussion of the popular virgin martyr vitae that often focus on the torture of the beautiful and naked virgin in a manner that could be construed as erotic, see Jocelyn Wogan-Browne, "Saints' Lives and the Female Reader," *Forum for Modern Language Studies* 27 (1991): 314–32, and "The Virgin's Tale," in *Feminist Readings in Middle English Literature: The Wife of Bath and All Her Sect*, ed. Ruth Evans and Lesley Johnson (New York: Routledge, 1994), 165–94.

76. *Eneas: A Twelfth-Century French Romance*, trans. John A. Yunck (New York and London: Columbia University Press, 1974).

77. Thanks to Lisa Perfetti for kindly bringing this to my attention.

7

Calefurnia's Rage
Emotions and Gender in Late Medieval Law and Literature

Sarah Westphal

Legal practitioners and theorists have long recognized a conflict between emotion and reason in legal decision making. This conflict is especially strong in the courtroom, where judges and juries alike are expected to keep their feelings in check when deliberating the outcome of a trial in order to preserve objectivity in the cause of justice. For example, instructions issued to a jury by the State of California in the penalty phase of a trial required that jurors "not be swayed by mere sentiment, conjecture, sympathy, passion, prejudice, public opinion, or public feeling." Their weighing of aggravating or mitigating factors were not to be "guided by emotions, sympathy, pity, anger, hate, or anything like that because it is not rational if you make a decision on that kind of basis."[1] The constitutionality of these instructions to erase one's feelings was challenged in the lower courts but ultimately upheld by the United States Supreme Court, which confirmed the central idea that emotions can be harmful. But not all emotions. On one hand the justices recognized the value and legitimacy of some kinds of feeling in legal decision making, but on the other hand they agreed that untethered and inappropriate emotions undermine rationality and fair judging. This distinction, they reasoned, is spontaneously known to jurors, who can be counted on to discern the difference between constructive and destructive emotions and to accept such instructions as ruling out only the negative or untethered forms of feeling.

Since ancient times, philosophers and rhetoricians have warned about the negative impact of undisciplined emotions on rational thinking.[2] In this paper I will examine the conflict between reason and emotions as it was framed in the later Middle Ages in literary and legal sources from central Europe. Medieval legal theorists and medieval authors of fiction who were aware of the law also addressed the role of emotions in the courtroom. Like their modern and ancient counterparts, they had a divided view of emotions. They reasoned that some kinds of emotion—or, better, some forms of emotional expression—are appropriate in forensic debate but that others must be excluded in order to protect the law's integrity and to serve the goals of justice.[3] In the sources that I am about to examine, additional lines of reasoning pertaining to gender and to race clarify and reinforce the distinction between appropriate and inappropriate emotions. I will show that "bad" emotions, regarded in legal theory as essentially feminine, were held at bay in the courtroom by denying women direct access to the institutions and processes of law. Because women were thought to be unable to control their emotions, they were not given the same judicial capacity—dynamically defined as the ability to act—as men.[4] The terms of exclusion were not rigid, however, as I will show with reference to a fictional medieval trial in which both race and gender operate to determine who could and who could not have full legal powers.

I have adapted the concept of legal theory from Merry Wiesner Hanks's discussion of the legal status of women in law codes, in learned debate, and in German society in the *sixteenth* century. Although my texts were composed from the thirteenth through the fifteenth century, long before the academic debates on female nature that Wiesner Hanks cites, they achieved similar rhetorical goals—namely, to justify the exclusion of women from a variety of legal functions. And, like later texts, medieval sources also performed the theoretical task of translating abstract notions of gender into rules and norms regarding marriage, control of property, criminal punishments, and guardianship or power over oneself or one's children.[5] The contents of medieval as well as early modern law codes are further theoretical in that they do not necessarily reflect real social arrangements or lived historical experience. This disjunction between what written collections of legal norms and customs depict as happening and what actually may have happened in medieval community cannot be too strongly emphasized. Nor do medieval law codes necessarily harmonize with the evidence of other kinds of primary legal source material such as wills, contracts, or trial transcripts which become available at the latter end of the period under consideration. These give a more varied and more complex picture of women's agency in the law. For the thirteenth century, though, virtually the only legal sources available are theoretical. And finally, though their norms and practices may or may not have been observed, for many the customary laws reflected an ideal human community. Their codification of a social ideal is still another way in which they constitute theory.[6]

My focus will be the earliest custumal, or collection of legal norms and customs, written in the German language. Known as the *Sachsenspiegel*, it was composed about 1235 by a man named Eike von Repgow, who was well educated though probably not academically trained. The *Sachsenspiegel* is the single most important law text from the German territories that covered large portions of central Europe. It has been valued in traditional scholarship as a witness to private (customary) and feudal law in Germany during the centuries after Charlemagne, a period for which direct written evidence of the law is extremely scarce.[7] The *Sachsenspiegel* was not law in the most official sense of the word—it was not an edict issued by a ruler, nor did it contain statutes issued by a city council—although it increasingly became associated with the notion of imperial authority.[8] It was a written fixation or adaptation of legal knowledge and practices that had long existed orally. The importance of the *Sachsenspiegel* lay not only in what it preserved from earlier times but also in the impact it had on subsequent legal thinking. It was massively influential. It exists today in some 450 manuscripts produced from the thirteenth through the fifteenth century as well as in printed sixteenth-century editions. It has been said that there is no such thing as "the *Sachsenspiegel*" but only a multitude of *Sachsenspiegeln*. The title refers not to a single text but to "the entire species of law book realized in all its adaptive diversity."[9] Its authority was recognized in Prussia as late as 1794.[10] Both urban and territorial codes were based on a *Sachsenspiegel*. One important and early reworking of the *Sachsenspiegel*, the High German *Schwabenspiegel*, has special importance for this paper, as will be explained below. The *Schwabenspiegel* was produced in Augsburg at the end of the thirteenth century under Franciscan influence. It, too, still exists in hundreds of manuscripts.

One additional aspect of the *Sachsenspiegel* tradition is important for understanding the gendering of emotion in legal theory. Four manuscripts have magnificent illustrations of most of the legal acts or transactions described in the *Sachsenspiegel* text. These four are referred to by the name of the city in which they are preserved today as the Wolfenbüttel, Heidelberg, Oldenberg, and Dresden manuscripts.[11] The illustrations are placed in (usually) five horizontal bands or registers to the left of the text. The purpose of the illustrations was primarily mnemonic. Persons charged with practicing the law could remember it better with the aid of pictures. But these illustrations also have a life of their own. Not only do they reflect the text, they also interpret it or add new information. Occasionally they seem to comment on each other up and down the registers on a single folio just as juxtaposed passages of text reinforce each other by analogy.

Eike's original *Sachsenspiegel* from 1235 no longer exists but one thing is nearly certain. It or its earliest adaptations contained the pithy anecdote about a woman named Calefurnia and how her untethered rage disrupted a court of law. Calefurnia is a fiction, but her story made its way through much of the *Sachsen-* and *Schwabenspiegel* tradition. The sheer number of manuscripts and the bewildering complexity of their relationships do not permit a clear overview of exactly how far her story traveled or exactly how it was retold as the customs were reworked and renewed in different settings and subjected to different local influences. It is safe to say that some knowledge of Calefurnia was held through numerous generations of people who came into contact with the written, vernacular law in the forms produced by the *Spiegel* tradition.

I quote from Maria Dobozy's English translation of the illustrated Wolfenbüttel manuscript produced around 1300.[12] Calefurnia is pictured in both word and image arguing a case before the emperor in the highest court in the land. Presumably she is arguing on her own behalf in a personal matter and not as a pleader or advocate on behalf of another person, since there is not a second figure in the image. The substance of her case is never revealed. The text anecdote of Calefurnia begins with the general principle of law that arises from her actions: "No woman may be pleader, nor may she bring a suit without a guardian. Calefurnia forfeited this [right] for all [women] when she misbehaved before the emperor in a fit of rage [MLG *torn*, MHG *zorn*] because her demands could not proceed without a spokesman.[13] Of course, any man may be a pleader and a witness, and bring suit and defend himself except in the district in which he is outlawed or if he is in royal outlawry. But he may not do so in a religious court if he is outlawed by royal authority."[14]

This passage presents Calefurnia as the Eve of legal theory on gender, a negative exemplary figure whose shortcomings, including rage, lack of self-control, misbehavior, and lack of respect for the emperor, are generalized to all womankind. The *Sachsenspiegel* is generally reticent on the topic of emotions, despite its interest in regulating human interactions that are naturally fraught with feeling, such as conflict among heirs over the inheritance of property. Its most important view on emotions beyond the Calefurnia passage is in the prologue that states that "no one [charged with the act of judging] should let himself be diverted from the law, not for love or jealousy, wrath or gain." Wrath in matters of judgment, the prologue continues, is reserved to God alone.[15] But in the Calefurnia passage, untethered emotions that threaten the integrity of the law and usurp the divine prerogative of wrath are the center of interest. The author embodies them as female and places them under the authority of a male guardian. Calefurnia's setback grounds the expulsion of all women as active agents in legal process and does the ideological work of keeping undisciplined emotions, the kind that judges and practitioners are expected to avoid, at safe distance. The emperor embodies judgment without anger. In the same flow of logic, the passage guarantees the rights of all men to direct participation in court unless they have been individually outlawed.[16]

The text of the Wolfenbüttel *Sachsenspiegel* says nothing specific about Calefurnia's misbehavior toward the emperor. The illustration that accompanies the text in all four manuscripts, however, gives a visual clue about what she did in her wrath that had such final consequences for all womankind. The picture in the Wolfenbüttel manuscript shows Calefurnia with the refined facial attributes of a wellborn woman, not the coarser features of a peasant. Her left hand gestures toward the emperor in the *Klagegebärde*, or plaintiff's gesture, echoed in numerous illustrations in the *Sachsenspiegel*, and her right arm and hand are lowered in the typical corresponding position. So far her image is completely standard for someone bringing a suit. The Dresden and Heidelberg manuscripts seem to capture her aggression in an overt leaning posture, a kind of in-your-face orientation toward the enthroned emperor, but in Wolfenbüttel and Oldenberg she has a more upright posture suggesting a somewhat more dignified attitude.[17]

But dignity and correctness are only half the picture. Calefurnia's similarity to images of numerous other pleaders in the *Sachsenspiegel* is coupled with shocking difference. All four manuscripts also depict what has been described, because of its hairiness, as a "brushlike object" next to Calefurnia's rear end.[18] Heidelberg shows the "brush" with a "handle," actually a line or pen stroke indicating that the "brush" is to be associated mentally and spatially with Calefurnia's derriere. This object has no explanation in the texts of the illustrated *Sachsenspiegel* manuscripts. The silence of the text would nearly seem to prompt a user of the manuscript, perhaps a young man faced with learning the law in order to fill his heredi-

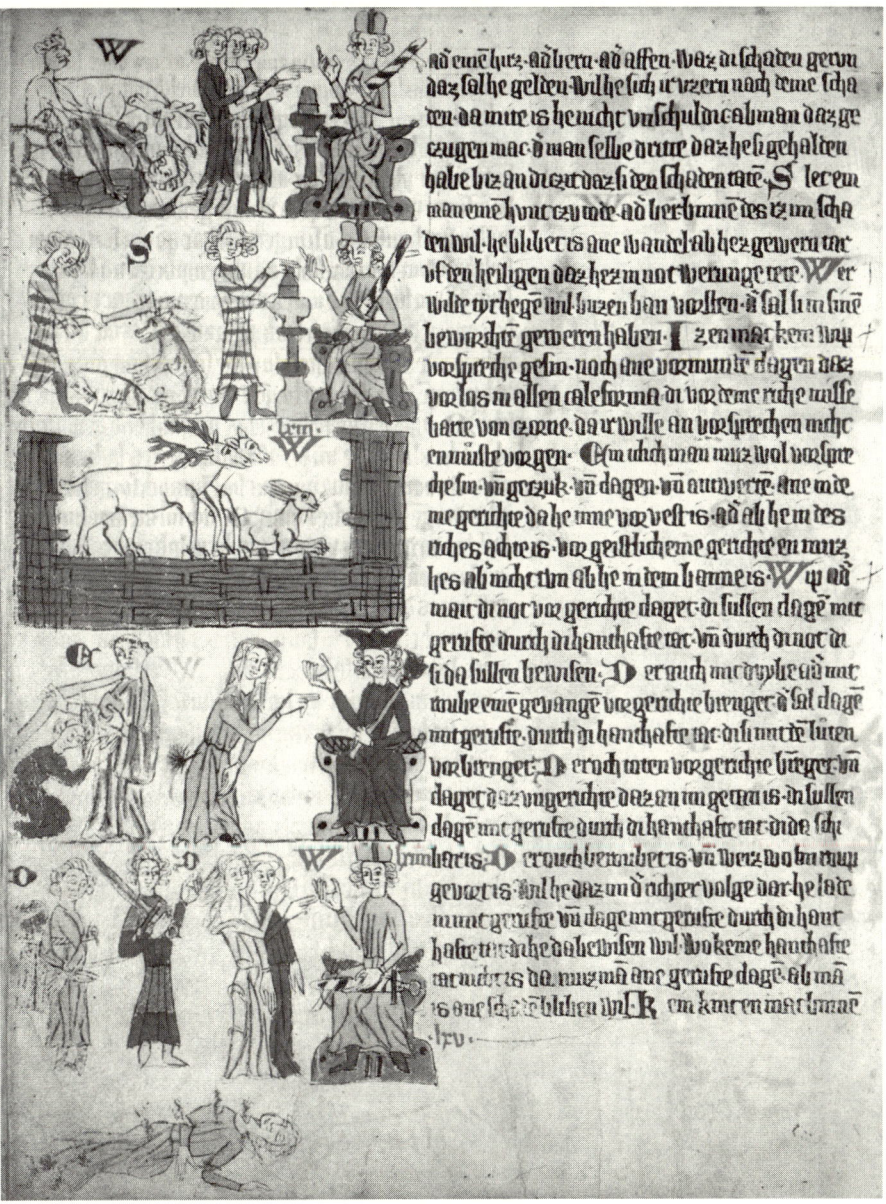

Illustrated *Sachsenspiegel,* Cpg 164, fol. 10v. The image of Calefurnia is in the fourth row from the top. By permission of the University Library, Heidelberg.

tary role as a judge, to question the object's identity. A possible solution, however, is offered in one version of the *Schwabenspiegel* where it is reported that Calefurnia's rage, her attack on the emperor, lay in letting him see her private parts from the rear—or her rear-end private parts ("hindere scham" [rear pudenda]).[19] In simple words, she mooned him, exposing her behind along with some, or all, or perhaps none, of her genitalia. The confusion of female *con* and *cul*, which may be visible in this image, is standard fare in the fabliaux, according to E. Jane Burns.[20] The illustrators of all four manuscripts, working in a single iconographic tradition, show Calefurnia facing the emperor, making her case with the plaintiff's gesture while symbolizing her misbehavior with a round, bristly mass suggesting something shameful and normally unseen. Caviness and Nelson comment, "the illustrator has done his best to represent this event with decorum."[21]

Conceptually, rage is doing heavy gender work in the *Sachsenspiegel*, setting up a dividing line between those who have full legal capacity (most adult men) and those who can approach the law only through the mediation of a man. Rage is a key concept in the *Sachsenspiegel*'s construction of gender as hierarchical difference along the boundary of sex. It is a term of representation that simultaneously creates relations of identity among women as a group (since all women are banned through Calefurnia) and relations of difference between groups of women and men.[22] Gender belonging is ultimately anatomical and its repercussions are metonymical: Calefurnia's exposed nether parts are substituted for her speaking head in a seemingly perfect instance of the decapitation of the always already castrated woman as theorized by Cixous in her essay "Castration or Decapitation?"[23] Calefurnia is silenced, so she "speaks" for womankind with other orifices. The gender work performed in the *Sachsenspiegel* by the story of Calefurnia's anger reproduces the masterly gesture, on the level of theoretical discourse in the law, of knowing women in order to dominate them.[24] The theoretical hierarchy of male over female, or of reason over emotion, or of appropriate emotions over inappropriate ones, maps onto this construction of sexual difference.

In the representation of Calefurnia, legal theory is gender theory. A principle in the law is justified by attributing a negative characteristic, anger, to an entire group. Her rage, however, cannot be fully interpreted without the historical depth and the historical estrangement attained through philological, textual, and cultural analysis. The word for "rage" that appears in the Low German of the *Sachsenspiegel* is *torn*, and in the

High German of the *Schwabenspiegel* it is *zorn*.[25] The brothers Grimm's dictionary offers several pages of discussion of this word, but one definition, in fact one of the oldest, is particularly salient. "We should probably not regard the movement of emotion as the original meaning, but rather 'battle, fighting with actions and words.'"[26] Moreover, this meaning is "still richly attested" [noch reichlich belegt] in Middle High German in sentences such as "here was battle without enmity" [hie was zorn ane haz], referring to combat between brothers of the Round Table, Iwein and Gawein. *Zorn* refers not (only) to an internal state, a psychology or frame of mind, but also to actions observable on the outside, the wild use of weapons in combat, or a hostile exchange of words. In his study of the *Nibelungenlied*, Jan-Dirk Müller explains *zorn* as the habitus of the hero, his normal mode of being which accommodates immense capability in battle.[27] Exceptional women also can have heroic anger. Müller cites one passage from the *Nibelungenlied* in which *zorn*, as "the expression of immense physical exertion in battle," is attributed to a woman.[28] Prünhilt, the "Amazon" princess from Iceland, has decreed that she will marry only the man who can defeat her in three tests of physical strength. When she competes with a suitor in a game that involves throwing boulders, she is described as *zornec* and the reader or listener is intended to see her awesome physical effort. But when she is defeated at her own game and destined to marry the victor, she becomes red with rage ("in zorne rôt"), which Müller interprets in the more modern and (to us) more familiar sense as a spontaneous welling up of angry feelings from inside, a reaction to honor lost, a boiling of the blood.[29]

Heroic anger, of course, is positively valued in secular medieval culture and mainly reserved for men. Prünhilt's case shows that exceptional women were represented as participating in men's *zorn*, though with limited success or compromised results and as an overt challenge to the real hero, Siegfried. Her strength in battle is a foil for the brilliance of Siegfried. Calefurnia's rage, a representation from a similar cultural location, both does and does not share in these definitions. It does in the fundamental sense that her rage implies little or no psychology. Calefurnia has no story and therefore no imputed inner life. She does not redden as does the defeated Prünhilt. *Zorn* resides only in her outward action. Her mooning the emperor *is* her rage, and her wrath is literal in her act. Yet it differs in that mooning is merely the formal equivalent of heroic strength, wild use of arms in battle, or awesome physical exertion in a warlike game. Although it shares the sense of enormity or even notoriety, it has none of the positive overtones that characterize the *zorn* ascribed to male heroic or chivalric actors. It is funny or shocking, not inspiring. Calefurnia's weapon is her bottom. She assaults with the view of her baseness and her sexual difference. She is seen to condemn herself. Her quarrel produces not fame but infamy, and it taints every woman now and forever through the universalizing power of theory.

The brothers Grimm's meaning of *zorn* as a battle of words is resonant in the legal context of the *Sachsenspiegel*, since law was regarded positively as a verbal battle that was analogous to physical combat.[30] Battle with words was precisely what forensic oratory was held to be. Moreover, *zorn* in legal contexts, as Jan-Dirk Müller has pointed out, referred to what we would now call a legal standpoint or position. For example, it designated a disturbed relationship between a lord and a vassal signified by actions amounting to physical distancing that had genuine legal implications.[31] A vassal who refuses to come to the lord's court when summoned or who departs without taking proper leave is staging *zorn* with little or no reference to his feelings on the inside. In the legal fiction I will discuss below, the *zorn* of Queen Venus toward an alleged oath breaker, which she enacts with expressions and gestures, signifies a legal standpoint. In the Middle High German romance of *Iwein* (Yvain), Laudine gives up her *zorn* toward Iwein when she becomes persuaded, through Lunete's forensic rhetoric, to marry him for reasons of state. When she says, "by God I will relinquish my anger" [weizgot ich lâze mînen zorn] toward the man who has murdered her husband, she is not talking about her feelings but about her willingness to be reconciled with him as a political expediency.[32] Similarly, a party to a legal suit who refuses reconciliation, one of the major goals of medieval justice, is holding a formal position of *zorn*.

The juridical meanings of *zorn* have a partial overlap as well. One might view Calefurnia's *zorn* as a legal position of refusal of the emperor's requirement that she have a guardian. Such a position would have been absurd, though, since the emperor was himself the agent of divine justice on earth.[33] This belief is especially strong in the *Sachsenspiegeln*. The *Sachsenspiegel* tradition, though rooted in community life, was identified with the authority of the emperor from the earliest times, and this identification strengthened as the tradition grew. The *Sachsenspiegel* explicitly presents itself as *Kaiserrecht* or imperial law, given to the Saxons by Charlemagne.[34] In some manuscripts this notion is reinforced in that the *Sachsenspiegel* is copied with the *Buch der Könige*, a text that traces biblical history from Abraham forward.[35] The emperor is justice, divine in origin and expressed in the customs. Paradoxically and predictably, Calefurnia's pursuit of justice turns out to be a defiance of justice (misbehavior before the emperor) making her *zorn* the quintessential irrational action/emotion that medieval legal thinkers sought to banish from the practice of law—though perhaps with limited success, as Enders has demonstrated with numerous arguments tracing the origins of medieval drama in medieval courtroom practice. But in the minds of those who perpetuated the *Sachsenspiegel* tradition, it was what resulted when women became enmeshed in the affairs of men, in battle or in the courts.

The story of Calefurnia was not invented by Eike von Repgow, nor did it arise unmediated from the community experience reflected in the Saxon customs. It was inherited by medieval legal theory from Roman law. The most important Roman source for Calefurnia's bad behavior is the *Corpus juris civilis*, commonly called the Code of Justinian, compiled between 530 and 533 C.E. by scholars and legal experts at the command of the Byzantine emperor Justinian himself. Its reinvention for the medieval West began in Italy (Bologna) in the last decades of the eleventh century, and by the twelfth century manuscripts were circulating in central and northern Italy, though "perhaps not yet in Provence or north of the Alps in general, where an interest in Roman law was nonetheless fairly strong."[36] Burchard of Biberach (d. after 1231), provost of Ursberg from 1215 to 1226, made a note in his chronicle that seems to mark the beginning of interest in what had come to be known simply as the law books: "Up to now they [libri legales] had been neglected and no one had studied them"—but now they are studied, he implies.[37] Thus the first phase of interest, that of the glossators, was just under way when the *Sachsenspiegel* was composed in the 1230s. It is not known where Eike himself or his earliest copyists picked up the story of Calefurnia, or how much he knew of its source, or even to what extent Roman law impacted the earliest decades of the *Sachsenspiegel* tradition. What can be asserted is that he recycled a "foreign" chunk of Roman law as if it were homegrown in Saxony, thereby naturalizing the story of Calefurnia and reinforcing its gender theory as custom.

Calefurnia's Roman model, a woman named Carfania, is found in the large segment of the *Corpus juris civilis* that is known as either the Digests or the Pandects (these are alternate names referring to the same volumes of the *Corpus*). Her story is near the beginning of book 3, title 1 of the Digests, which had become one of the standard school texts at the end of the twelfth century.[38] The rubric for title 1, "Concerning the Right of Application to the Court," discloses the topic of the text as who may and who may not appear before the emperor in a matter of law, either on his or her own behalf or as an advocate for another person. It determines who is an actor in a law court and who is a spectator; who speaks, and who is spoken for. What is at stake in title 1 is the dignity of the judge (the law itself), the orderliness of the courtroom, and the avoidance of frivolous applications. Logically, these concerns are interrelated.[39]

In both the *Sachsenspiegel* and the Digests of Justinian the law that protects the Law, so to speak, is the law of gender. Roman law, however, is more comprehensive and more systematic than Saxon law rooted in Germanic community practices. In the *Digests* there are three classes of people with differing rights of application to the court: those with full capacity (adult men), those who are excluded entirely (minors and deaf people),[40] and those who have partial rights. Having partial rights meant you could bring suit or mount a defense on your own behalf but not on behalf of another person. You could not represent another. Adult women are consigned to the intermediate position, the group of people who have partial legal capacity. Others with only partial or "self-rights" include blind men, because "they cannot see and respect the insignia of the magistracy and pay them proper respect," and men who are infamous because they "suffer their body to be used like that of a woman" or who are false accusers or who hire themselves out to fight wild beasts. Like women, they can be plaintiffs or defendants but not lawyers. They have no role as an official in the courtroom, nor can they represent the law itself in the role of advocate.[41] In short, they are incapable of respect (blind men) or of representation (women, false accusers, those who fight beasts, sodomites) because they do not reproduce the normative, adult male legal subject. Deep taboos concerning the body, sexual contact, and animal contact seem to underlie this concept of who can speak for another in a legal capacity.

Justinian's scholars explain the assignment of women to the group with partial capacity: "The origin of this restriction was derived from the case of a certain Carfania, an extremely shameless woman, whose effrontery and annoyance of the magistrate gave rise to this Edict."[42] The Latin word here translated as "extremely shameless" is *improbissima*, whose implication—simultaneously "substandard" and "over the top"—captures the oxymoron of Carfania's effrontery.[43]

Roman law has been described as "a mine of precious materials that [medieval] jurists, as specialists arrogating to themselves a monopoly on the theorization of social relations, could recuperate and reutilize."[44] The invention of Calefurnia's *zorn* in the Saxon law is the most striking aspect of her recuperation to the cultural situation of Middle Europe in the thirteenth century. Gone is the Roman idea that certain groups of people including women are incapable of representation because of social stigma or taboos concerning the body and sexuality. The problem as seen in the Saxon law resides mainly with women (and certain outlaws in some manuscripts) and involves control. Calefurnia cannot discipline herself, so she requires control in the form of a guardian to preserve the dignity of the court. For whatever reason, anger had become the key legal idea, and its theorization was gendered. The evolution of the name from Roman Carfania to Saxon Calefurnia points to her new, medieval essence of anger in syllables suggesting Latin *calere* (to grow warm, to glow) and *furnus* (oven). It is almost as if the notion of annoyance, attributed to the magistrate in the Roman source, is transferred to Calefurnia and magnified as *zorn*. *Zorn* is distanced from its positive, masculine heroic and legal or political applications and reinterpreted or engendered comically as mooning the emperor. Formally viewed, the *Sachsenspiegel* maximizes Justinian's restriction on women's legal capacity by moving them into the category of minors, or those who cannot represent even themselves. In a sense, woman's position in Roman law is better, and the lack of agreement between Roman and Saxon law may have had some advantages for historical women in their dealings with the courts in settings where both traditions were valued. Yet the concept of gender guardianship for women as being the equivalent of minors remained intact through the German Middle Ages and the early modern period when new justifications such as the assumed mental weakness of women were introduced.

There is another stream of thought, arising in both Christian and popular culture, that flows into the concept of Calefurnia's *zorn* in the *Sachsenspiegel*. It helps explain why her *zorn* was perceived so negatively. It can be immediately apprehended in sayings that illustrate woman's anger as particularly virulent, for example Hans Sachs's "There is no anger worse than a woman's anger" [kein zorn ist über frawen zorn].[45] Warnings about the anger of woman are also found in the Bible and the Apocrypha. Probably the most important biblical source on female rage is the book of Ecclesiasticus, or Sirach. Because it appears in neither the Jewish nor the Protestant canon, Ecclesiasticus is not as well known today as in the medieval past. But in the Middle Ages this quite long book was routinely quoted. In the Douai-Reims translation of the Latin Vulgate Bible the key text on woman's anger reads: "There is no head worse than the head of a serpent: / And there is no anger above the anger of a woman. It will be more agreeable to abide with a lion and a dragon, than to dwell with a wicked woman. / The wickedness of a woman changeth her face: and she darkeneth her countenance as a bear: and showeth it like sack-cloth" (Eccles. 25:22–24).

This concept of emotion differs from the heroic or forensic ones discussed above. It is more a blind, driving force. Its roots are in antiquity or the ancient Near East and it is intrinsically linked to womanhood, already setting up the lines of gender difference adapted by the Middle Ages' more gestural concepts of anger. Martha Nussbaum memorably describes this brand of emotion—which can include love, grief, and so on, as well as wrath—as follows:

> Like gusts of wind or the swelling currents of the sea, [emotions so conceived] push the agent around, surd unthinking energies. They do not themselves embody reflection or judgment, and they are not very responsive to the judgments of reason. (This picture of emotion is sometimes expressed by describing emotions as "animal," as elements of a not fully human nature in us. It has also been linked with the idea that emotions are somehow "female" and reason "male"— presumably because the female is taken to be closer to the animal and instinctual, more immersed in the body.)[46]

Nussbaum passes over this theory of emotion as "hardly worth spending time on" since it was "never strongly supported by major philosophers," some of whom "dislike the emotions intensely."[47] Yet it appears to be very close to the theory of anger as female and perilous—more dangerous than the blind aggression of lions and dragons—found in the above verses from Ecclesiasticus.

The Bible was the most sacred law text of the Middle Ages. The Bible, the *Corpus juris civilis*, and the collections of canon law together comprised the overarching and universal realm of ideal law from which, or within which, the territorial codes such as the *Sachsenspiegel* exerted their authority. The *Sachsenspiegel* has extensive direct as well as indirect or conceptual links to the Bible. Guido Kisch has published an important work pointing out places in the *Sachsenspiegel* text where there are quotes, allusions, or even rough vernacular translations of Bible passages.[48] Eike's awareness of the Bible was extensive, and the *Sachsenspiegel* is interwoven with biblical truths.

Contextual evidence from the *Sachsenspiegel* links Calefurnia to the angry woman of the Bible through the imagery of animals. Ecclesiasticus 25:24 is terrifying in the way it morphs the angry face of the wicked woman into a black, hairy bear. The story of Calefurnia, told to justify the imposition of a guardian on any woman who comes before the law, is the culmination of a series of provisions on kept creatures, literally the custodianship of animals. The section in the Wolfenbüttel manuscript translated by Dobozy starts after a thematic break in the text with mention of how God gave man dominion over the beasts. There follows a discussion of the protection of animals in game preserves, then a statement of the responsibility of a person who "keeps a mean dog, or a tame wolf, or a deer, or a bear, or a monkey" if such an animal should cause harm, then the provision that a man who kills a mean dog in self-defense shall not pay a penalty to the dog's owner, then the obligation to enclose wild animals that are kept outside of a preserve—and then, in the same flow of logic, the assertion that women shall have guardians in the law, followed by Calefurnia's fit of rage to explain why.[49] The parataxis points up the analogy that is being constructed: control of animals is parallel to control of women like Calefurnia. Her fit of rage amplifies the image of mean dogs, tame wolves, and domesticated bears, perilous domestic partners indeed. Considering her antics in the presence of the emperor recorded by the *Schwabenspiegel* and pictured without comment in the illustrated *Sachsenspiegel* manuscripts, she is also somewhat like a tame monkey. These associations linking women's nature to animal nature also can be found in the biblical source text on female rage; thus the *Sachsenspiegel*'s contextual argument that animals need responsible management and women need guardians.

Reasoning from contextual juxtaposition is characteristic of the fine structure of the *Sachsenspiegel* text. Eike tends "to give a reason for decisively important provisions [in the law] and, by drawing on parallels—even when the parallels are not directly related to the matter at hand—to make visible the principles that are fundamental to the richness of Saxon legal life."[50] Such a use of parallels, or argument by analogy, justifies the important provision on gender guardianship. It is evocative of proverbial discourse. Moreover, in the Wolfenbüttel as in the other illustrated manuscripts, the register with the image of Calefurnia and her unmentionable "brush" is on the same folio with the images of domesticated beasts and game preserves. The "brush," which is not mentioned in the text of the *Sachsenspiegel*, may perhaps resemble an animal's tail in this visual setting. The layout of the images gives visual reinforcement to the analogies that emerge from the written context. There is codicological evidence to support the claim that these parallels were intentional or at least understood to be meaningful by subsequent users of the *Sachsenspiegel*. The context linking the control of domesticated beasts with gender guardianship is unchanged in at least a portion of the later manuscript transmission. That is, over time there is alteration in the topics of the provisions following the Calefurnia story but, in the editions I have been able to consult, there is little change other than amplification in the provisions on the control of animals leading up to it. This context is also intact in the otherwise very unstable *Schwabenspiegel* tradition, at least as it is reflected in published editions.[51]

The discussion of Calefurnia that I have presented so far concerns what might be called elements of closure. Anger, as a multidimensional and historical notion, is what justifies the exclusion of women from the law as primary actors or fully capable subjects. Yet the story does not end there. Precisely the narrative element of Calefurnia, the colorful character of the woman plaintiff who dares to show the emperor her backside, opens a space of imagination that is not contained by legal theoretical discourse but finds its way into literature. By the same token, the appeals of fictional characters like the evil wife give Calefurnia her endurance as a theoretical construct.

I want to show the productivity of the idea of Calefurnia in a literary text composed in 1453 by Hermann von Sachsenheim, a man who received legal training and is known to have had a long relationship of service to the rulers of Württemberg. His text,[52] called *Die Mörin* or *The Moorish Woman* after one of its main characters, has been described by the legal scholar Hans Fehr as "the most comprehensive trial poem of the [German] Middle Ages" [das eingehendeste prozessuale Dichtwerk des Mittelalters] and as a gift to legal historians.[53] And in fact two German scholars of legal history, Friedrich Wilhelm Strothmann and Hugo Loersch, publishing in 1930 and in 1871 respectively, deciphered the intricacies of trial process, argumentation, and the points of formal law that one encounters in *Die Mörin*. Yet they paid scant attention to what, in this connection, are the most striking elements of the story: the complainant and her advocate are both women, one of them is black-skinned, and the issue of their anger looms large throughout the text.[54]

Hermann von Sachsenheim knew some version of the *Sachsenspiegel*, as one might expect of a man of his learning and position. There are references to it in the text. Yet despite his meticulous attention to legal realism, surely based on his experiences as well as his learning, he ignored gender guardianship as a formal requirement. *The Moorish Woman* thus pushes the boundaries of legal theory and has the character of a controlled experiment in fiction.[55] What would happen if one put women back into the courtroom as litigants and advocates? How and why would their anger express itself in action? Hermann provides hilarious answers to these hypotheticals, entertaining and unsettling the reader and testing the boundaries of gender made flexible by literary fiction before reinforcing the closure that the Calefurnia of the *Sachsenspiegel* is intended to justify: because of their wrath, better to keep women at arm's length after all.

Die Mörin is not a well-known text, so a cursory explanation of its plot will introduce my observations. The trial is set in the island country of Queen Venus-Minn, a land of many religions and ethnicities located in the vaguely imagined East. The complainant is the queen herself. She is aided in her suit by three women, all queens in their own right, who give her advice during the frequent recesses. The prosecutor is the very dark skinned Moorish woman named, interestingly enough, Brunhilt after the boulder-tossing Germanic heroine. They function in the courtroom as if gender guardianship never existed. The defendant, a knight of Swabia named Hermann, is also the first-person narrator of the text. His advocate is another European knight, the elderly Eckhart, who embodies the chivalric ideals of a better time now past. Like the queen, Hermann is advised by three supporters, all men, who are also court officials: a notary, a bailiff, and a marshal. In this contest of the queens versus the bureaucrats, the judge is King Danhuser (Tannhäuser), the husband of Queen Venus and thus entangled in a hopeless conflict of interest. Humor arises in the striving of the bureaucrats to persuade King Danhuser to perform his husbandly duties and take control of his rampaging, angry queen.

The trial addresses an issue that late medieval culture took seriously despite the comedy that arises in Hermann's literary courtroom. That issue is the seduction, deception, and abuse of women. The defendant is being tried for his unethical actions in matters of sex, actions the prosecution characterizes as the equivalent of murder. The defense team's strategy is to redefine the narrator's alleged transgressions not as crimes but as normal masculine heterosexual behavior. They manage to reduce the charge from something resembling murder to mere boasting about his conquests, a charge the narrator flatly denies. Hermann is also charged with breaking an oath of allegiance to the queen. For her part, the queen is unable to prove the charge of oath breaking since she cannot produce witnesses. Suspense arises when the jury, composed of twelve peers of the realm, declares itself divided, six in favor of the plaintiff and six in favor of the defendant. King Danhuser must cast the deciding vote, and he finds in favor of the queen, condemning the defendant to the gallows. The sentence, though, is never carried out. The trial ends in a wonderful compromise in which everybody except the prosecutor Brunhilt carries off a piece of victory. The defense uses the newfangled device of appeal to a higher court. Venus is allowed to choose the location of the new trial, and she settles on Strasbourg, a city known to favor her customs and rule. The king deems the appeal too expensive and too dangerous to carry out: How can he afford to transport his entire court overseas? What if there are storms at sea? Thus the defendant is able to return home safe and secure that the matter has permanently rested.

Brunhilt and Queen Venus are consistently and continuously described in *Die Mörin* as angry, and the reader—along with the men on the defense team—must read or decipher their *zorn* as a legal standpoint, or as irrational emotion, or as some highly combustible mixture of all the possible meanings of the word. The life of the defendant depends on getting the meanings of women's anger right and finding effective methods to cope with it. Eventually the women are outmaneuvered by procedural intricacies. Their anger is made to seem risible by their comparative lack of legal skill. The men, by intentional contrast, are never described as angry in the forensic realm of *Die Mörin* even though they are involved in a trial that rides roughshod over justice at the direction of wrathful women.

The women's *zorn* against the men is played out across the semantic fields I have been reconstructing in my discussion of the Calefurnia anecdote. I will focus my remarks on the Moorish woman, since in her character the issue of anger is reinvented as an issue of race. There are passages in which Brunhilt is angry in the technical, legal way of holding to a standpoint or position in a forensic battle. For example, she arrives at the trial to begin her prosecution "in grim anger," which is the objective state her public persona established with gesture or expression, proper to her adversarial role in a case involving the death penalty (line 706). Elsewhere her anger, like Calefurnia's, is an outward reaction to silence imposed upon her as a woman and a lady. This is seen when Brunhilt confronts the narrator for the first time and summons him to court. He has just been magically captured and flown in a trunk from Europe to the island of Queen Venus. There follows a hearty exchange of insults between the two, stopped only when an anonymous knight steps in to scold Brunhilt: "it is not fitting for pure ladies to permit prisoners to converse [with them]." Brunhilt reacts: "in anger she bit her lip / so that blood ran down her front" [Von zorn sie in ain lefczen baiß / das ir das bluot hernacher ran] (418–19). The knight's invocation of constraints of class and gender compel Brunhilt to hold her tongue, but her undisciplined emotion of anger expresses itself in violent lip biting. Heroic *zorn* is also ascribed to the Moorish woman through her heroic namesake Prünhilt of the *Nibelungenlied* tradition. The point of similarity between the two, however, is not physical strength but a perceived ability to inspire fear in men. One critic has described the Moorish Brunhilt as "the rabid, mannish woman who teaches fear to the (chauvinist) world of men" [das rabiante Mannweib . . . die eine (chauvinistische) Männerwelt das Fürchten lehrt].[56] Although this characterization is more Wagnerian or Freudian than medieval, the *Nibelungenlied* does supply the raw materials for the virago in the powerful "Amazon" bride Prünhilt who hangs King Gunther from a nail in the wall on their wedding night to preserve her virginity and her strength. In fact, the modeling of the Moorish woman on the heroic Prünhilt is an early instance of the reception of this traditional heroine as a virago or a frightening woman who is known less for her deeds than by the paralyzing effect she has on males.

Something new, the significance of race, is added to the mix in the depiction of Brunhilt as black. Hermann creates, in narrative form, a theoretical argument that divides reason from emotion not simply in terms of gender but complicated by the category of race. In brief: The light-skinned Venus is capable of reconciliation—of cooling her anger—at least to the extent that the defendant is released with his life after promising to appear in court in Strasbourg. The title character of *Die Mörin*, the very dark-skinned woman who serves as the prosecutor on behalf of the complainant Queen Venus-Minn, does not join the reconciliation but rather stands alone at the end in her pursuit of vengeance through legal means, however corrupted or inept, against the narrator-defendant. Thus in the dominant value system of the text, her anger is truly a surd force that cannot respond to judgments of reason, nor to the lofty goal of medieval justice that lay in reconciliation.

At the end of the *Die Mörin* Brunhilt stands alone and unsupported in her *zorn*, her continued opposition to the narrator. Blackness, never a neutral descriptor, takes on a negative ethical meaning as the refusal to be reconciled to what has emerged as the common good. Significantly, once the king hands down the death sentence (which is never carried out), the other characters start referring to her as "black Brunhilt" [Brunhilt swarcz] which brings out the ethical negativity now ascribed to her appearance (3750, 3755). She is a Calefurnia with a cause, the prosecutorial spirit that refuses to compromise, and so is better outmaneuvered in trial practice, isolated at court, or placed under a guardian's control. When she arrives too late to stop the compromise that will set the narrator free, she is described with resonant metaphors as an unbaptized animal, the maw of Satan, growling like a bear. The story harshly condemns Brunhilt's *zorn* in this final image in which she is seen to have the bearlike, blackened face of the angry, wicked woman of Ecclesiasticus as a racialized attribute.

Alexandra Sterling-Hellenbrand has argued that medieval German Arthurian romances create spaces (literally: topographical places) of experimentation for the construction of gender and race in the process of narration before imposing closure in the form of dominant cultural values.[57] Similarly, the condemnation of Brunhilt at the end of *Die Mörin* is the final assessment of her, but not the only way offered by the text to judge her character and her anger. A more sympathetic angle of vision is derived from the literary tradition established by the most popular medieval German romance, Wolfram's *Parzival*, another text known to Hermann von Sachsenheim and often recalled by him in *Die Mörin*. Brunhilt's anger in this transformation is not merely irrational resistance to the lofty goals of justice; it is possibly justifiable when contextualized by the cause of the trial itself, the unethical treatment of women by men. This narrative double image of the Moorish woman is created through Hermann's powers of irony, his ability to say one thing and mean another, and the productivity of the Calefurnia concept.

The black Brunhilt is related to the black Queen Belakane created by Wolfram in book 1 of *Parzival*, one of the classic texts of the German High Middle Ages and well known by Hermann von Sachsenheim.[58] I use "related" in a general sense, as an antecedent who, like the Queen of Sheba, creates space for the representation of black womanhood. But I use it in a specific sense as well. Queen Belakane, like Dido, is an abandoned woman in Wolfram's *Parzival*, deserted with child by Gahmuret, the knight who shortly afterwards becomes the father of the hero Parzival by a white woman. As Alfred Ebenbauer puts it, "Belakane dies, like Dido, the tragic death of the abandoned woman; and this death is no chivalric adventure and no courtly gallantry. Wolfram knows that."[59] Belakane's son Feirefiz reappears in the romance several thousand lines later seeking revenge against his father for the abandonment of his mother. Ebenbauer shrewdly observes that Feirefiz, though "angry" with his father, cannot escape the benefits of his father's splendid legacy of fame. The theme of Gahmuret's guilt vanishes in *Parzival*, trivialized—Ebenbauer claims—by racialized attitudes held by Wolfram's audiences and coded in his text that would more readily accept the abandonment of a black woman, even a queen, than a white woman.[60] Writers who followed Wolfram and worked in his tradition, however, dwelt on the plight of the abandoned Belakane, not (only) on the splendor of Gahmuret. These authors include Ulrich von Etzenbach, the author of *Reinfrid von Braunschweig*, and Albrecht von Scharfenberg, author of *Der jüngere Titurel*. In the latter, for example, the black inhabitants of Zazamanc, Belakane's country, want to kill the shipwrecked hero when they see his white skin and Gahmuret's coat of arms. They desire revenge for their queen who was deserted like a concubine and driven to an untimely death.[61]

The purpose of the trial in *Die Mörin*, from the women's standpoint, is to bring the narrator to justice for the seduction and abandonment of other women who cannot speak for themselves. The narrator is accused of performing on a quotidian basis the kind of cruelty toward women that Gahmuret had performed on a world-historical stage in fiction. Brunhilt is not an abandoned woman, but in her blackness and her virago chastity she is the perfect embodiment of *zorn* as the prosecutorial spirit, nurtured by literary tradition, that takes to task men, and particularly the elite white men who would have formed a large part of the audience in a court such as Mechthild's. She is a figure of vengeance in the unspoken name of Belakane, far more determined than Feirefiz to get her restitution—and a scourge for the shame-ridden conscience of the male subject as constructed by the literary tradition and perhaps by the social norms of the era as well. Ebenbauer counts the black Brunhilt among the literary descendants of Queen Belakane, but his brief discussion of her role consists mainly of references to Welz on the topic of the virago.[62] He does not develop the implications of his insight because he does not see the issue of seduction and desertion that the prosecution in *Die Mörin* sets out to address. The title Hermann von Sachsenheim gave to the text, *Die Mörin*, places the abandoned woman victim (Belakane) and the frightful *zorn* of the prosecution (black Brunhilt) in an important and visible place. Printed editions state on the title page that the text is a warning to men who would practice chivalry. The nature of the warning is obviously embodied by black Brunhilt, the Calefurnia with a case, whose anger may fall on those who behave unethically like Gahmuret, or his shadow the narrator, in their treatment of women.

In conclusion, this essay has shown that legal thinkers who created and perpetrated the influential *Sachsenspiegel* tradition in central Europe addressed a problem that was known in antiquity and, as the Supreme Court decision cited at the outset of my argument demonstrates, continues to be important today. The problem is the conflict between reason and emotions or the proper role of emotions in legal decision making. I have argued that medieval legal theorists in the *Sachsenspiegel* tradition tried to keep destructive or irrational emotions at a safe distance in the courtroom by diminishing the legal capacity of women. Gender guardianship is the remedy offered for this reduction of legal power caused, in the view of the *Sachsenspiegel*, by women's undisciplined anger.

The anecdote of Calefurnia is a founding myth inherited from Roman law but naturalized as Saxon custom by numerous *Sachsenspiegel* manuscripts that circulated in central Europe throughout the later Middle Ages. The Roman concern with issues of representation that affect not only women but also certain men—those who are "used" as women, those who earn a living fighting wild animals, et cetera—was diminished in the twelfth century by Eike von Repgow or his immediate successors in the *Sachsenspiegel* tradition. They had an overriding concern with gender and anger, or with the gender of anger, in legal fora. Calefurnia's act of mooning the emperor pictured in the four illustrated *Sachsenspiegel* manuscripts adds elements of shock and comedy to the concept of woman's *zorn* found in the text. I have linked Calefurnia's insult and the resulting silencing of women to the feminist critique of patriarchy through the work of Cixous, Burns, and Solterer. I have drawn on semantic and cultural studies to show that woman's wrath, like heroic anger, was expressed with external gestures but lacked the positive, inspiring aspects attributed by medieval secular culture to male heroic or chivalric deeds. Understood as a legal standpoint, Calefurnia's wrath is simply irrational, since it is directed at justice itself, embodied by the emperor. Her insult to the dignity of the law suggests the comedy of fabliau-like stories, a genre that was growing in popularity in Germany in the later thirteenth century. In fact, this is one instance where literary stereotypes seem to drive or support the reasoning of legal theory. Notions of the danger of women's wrath were also fostered by Christian and popular culture through often quoted Bible passages, above all the lines from Ecclesiasticus describing the frightful image of the blackened face of the angry woman. From this standpoint gender guardianship is analogous to the control of wild beasts, an argument actually made through the juxtaposition of passages and images on these topics in some *Sachsenspiegel* manuscripts.

The finding that Calefurnia is nourished by literary culture, both heroic and chivalric, leads to a concluding discussion of one of the most important German legal fictions from the later Middle Ages. Hermann von Sachsenheim's *Die Mörin* is a highly realistic trial depiction. Two women, one white and one black, act together as complainant and prosecutor in a court of law. But although Hermann seems to push the limits of legal theory by creating a world in which gender guardianship does not exist, his emphasis on the women's wrath and their corrupt use of the legal system offers tacit support for the requirement of gender guardianship. Race, however, is a complicating factor. The wrath of the black woman has some positive elements, since it reacts to a problem that late medieval culture took seriously and often explored in literature: the abuse of women through seduction and abandonment. Some German authors who preceded Hermann used dark-skinned characters in their stories of abandonment. In this tradition, blackness represents the plight of the victim and the guilt of the perpetrator. This positive meaning of blackness is changed, however, as *Die Mörin* reaches its conclusion. The white woman is able to give up her anger and join a compromise with the dominant interests of the king and his courtiers. The black woman by contrast is incapable of such distance, and her blackness is reduced to her singular, unrelenting rage.

Notes

1. California v. Brown, 479 U.S. (1986), 538 ff. Cited by Martha C. Nussbaum, *Poetic Justice: The Literary Imagination and Public Life* (Boston: Beacon Press, 1995), 55, 132n3.

2. On ancient views see Nussbaum's "Rational Emotions," chapter 3 of *Poetic Justice*.

3. For example, the acceptable practice of lawyers feigning the emotions of their clients as part of making their case is discussed by Jody Enders, *Rhetoric and the Origins of Medieval Drama* (Ithaca: Cornell University Press, 1992), who writes: "Already enjoined in handbooks to imitate actors, classical and medieval orators took that analogy to fascinating dramatic extremes" (56).

4. Manlio Bellomo, *The Common Legal Past of Europe, 1000–1800*, trans. Lydia G. Cochrane (Washington, D.C.: Catholic University of America Press, 1995), 8.

5. Merry Wiesner Hanks, "Frail, Weak, and Helpless: Women's Legal Position in Theory and Reality," in *Regnum, Religio et Ratio: Essays Presented to Robert M. Kingdon*, ed. Jerome Friedman (Kirksville, Mo.: Sixteenth Century Journal Publishers, 1987), 161–69, at 162–63.

6. On the mirror symbolism in the title *Sachsenspiegel* (*Saxon Mirror*), see Maria Dobozy, trans. and intro., *The Saxon Mirror: A Sachsenspiegel of the Fourteenth Century* (Philadelphia: University of Pennsylvania Press, 1999), 7–9.

7. Peter Johanek, "Rechtsschriftum," in *Die Deutsche Leteratur im Späten Mittelalter 1250–1370: Reimpaargedichte, Drama, Prosa*, ed. Ingeborg Glier, vol. 3,

part 2 of *Geschichte der deutschen Literatur von den Anfängen bis zur Gegenwart* (Munich: C. H. Beck, 1987), 396–431, at 397.

8. Johanek, "Rechtsschriftum," 415–16; Dobozy, *The Saxon Mirror*, 17.

9. Dobozy, *The Saxon Mirror*, 34.

10. Ibid., 1.

11. The illustrations from all four illustrated manuscripts that pertain to women's legal status can be viewed at the website created by Madeline Caviness and Charles Nelson, "Women's Bodies, Women's Property: Limited Ownership Under the Law; German Customary Law Books Illustrated in the Fourteenth Century," hosted by Tufts University Archives and Special Collections (accessed November 2004), http://dca.tufts.edu/features/law/. In addition, images can be viewed in the facsimile and CD-ROM editions of the manuscripts as well as online, as indicated below:

Dresden manuscript signature: Dresden State and University Library M 32 (Calefurnia image, fol. 34v); facsimile: *Die Dresdener Bilderhandschrift des Sachsenspiegels*, ed. Karl von Amira, 2 vols. (Leipzig: Hiersemann, 1902–26); *Der Dresdner Sachsenspiegel*, ed. Heiner Lück (Graz: Akademische Druck- und Verlagsanstalt, 2002); website: "Die Dresdner Bilderhandschrift des Sachsenspiegels," Sächsische Landesbibliothek—Staats- und Universitätsbibliothek Dresden, http://www.tu-dresden.de/slub/proj/sachsenspiegel/sachs.html (excellent background information and some images but not fol. 34v).

Heidelberg manuscript signature: Heidelberg University Library, Cpg 164 (Calefurnia image, fol. 10v); facsimile: *Die Heidelberger Bilderhandschrift des Sachsenspiegels: Kommentar und Anmerkungen*, ed. Walter Koschorreck, 2 vols. (Frankfurt am Main: Insel, 1970); CD-ROM: *Die Heidelberger Bilderhandschrift des Sachsenspiegels*, ISBN 3–8253–0848–0 (Heidelberg: C. Winter Universitätsverlag, 1999); website: "Manuscripta mediaevalia—Digitalisierte Handschriften," http://www.manuscripta-mediaevalia.de/hs/hs-online.htm (the image of Calefurnia can be accessed by clicking on the icon for Cpg 164 on the homepage; once the manuscript is accessed, simply flip through the folios, numbered very lightly in pencil on each upper right recto, to 10v).

Wolfenbüttel manuscript signature: Herzog August Library, Cod. Guelf 3.1 Aug. 2o (Calefurnia image, fol. 40v); facsimile: Eike von Repgow, *Sachsenspiegel: Die Wolfenbüttler Bilderhandschrift Cod. Guelf. 3.1 Aug. 2o*, ed. and trans. Ruth Schmidt-Wiegand, 3 vols. (Berlin: Akademie, 1993); website: "Sachsenspiegel-online," Herzog August Bibliothek and Fachhochschule Braunschweig/Wolfenbüttel, http://www.sachsenspiegel-online.de/cms/ (project to digitalize entire manuscript not yet complete; some images excluding fol. 40v with Calefurnia).

Oldenberg manuscript signature: Landesbibliothek Oldenberg, Cim I 410 (Calefurnia image, fol. 60v); facsimile: *Der Oldenberger Sachsenspiegel: Codex Picturatus Oldenburgensis CIM I 410 der Landesbibliothek Oldenberg*, ed. Ruth Schmidt-Wiegand, 2 vols. (Graz: Akademische Druck- und Verlagsanstalt, 1995).

12. Wolfenbüttel, Cod. Guelf. 3.1 Aug. 2o.

13. There is a confusion of cause and effect in the original German language (quoted in note 14) that is accurately carried over into the English translation. Calefurnia's actions are said to be the origin and cause of gender guardianship and yet her anger also appears to be a reaction to it—that is, gender guardianship is already in place. One explanation might be Eike's awareness that gender guardianship already existed in Roman law. As Lisa Perfetti has suggested, "The Sachsenspiegel assumes women's anger at their exclusion [in Roman law] and then, nonsensically, makes this anger the cause rather than the effect of their exclusion" (e-mail correspondence, June 20, 2002).

14. Dobozy, *The Saxon Mirror*, 112. The Middle Low German text from the critical edition by Eckhardt reads: "it ne mach nen wif vorspreke sin noch ane vormunde klagen; dat verlos en allen Calefurnia, de vor deme rike missebarde vor torne, do er wille ane vorsprekene nicht ne muste vordgan. Iewelk man mut wol vorspreke sin [unde tugen unde klagen unde antwarden], ane binnen deme gerichte, dar he inne vervestet is, oder of he in des rikes achte <gedan> is; [vor geistlekeme gerichte ne mut he is aver nicht dun, of he to banne is]." *Sachsenspiegel: Landrecht,* ed. Karl August Eckhardt, 3rd ed., Monumenta germaniae historica: Fontes iuris germanici antiqui, n.s., 1.1 (Göttingen: Muster-Schmidt, 1973), 181–82.

15. Dobozy, *The Saxon Mirror*, 67.

16. It is important to note that outlaws in the *Sachsenspiegel* fall into several classes, some of whom could appear before the law with the help of a guardian. Like women, outlaws with access to representation are set back from the law but remain sui juris, or possessing rights of their own. This similarity between women and some outlaws would seem to explain the association of ideas in this passage. Caviness and Nelson comment that the illustrations show a cleric agreeing to advocate for a male outlaw, thus presenting a solution to his problem, but for women they show only the source of the problem in Calefurnia (http://dca.tufts.edu/features/law, accessed November 2004).

17. Caviness and Nelson, http://dca.tufts.edu/features/law.

18. Walter Koschorreck, *Der Sachsenspiegel in Bildern: Aus der Heidelberger Bilderschrift ausgewählt und erläutert von Walter Koschorreck* (Frankfurt am Main: Insel, 1976), 80. The image of Calefurnia from the Heidelberg manuscript can be viewed online, in facsimile, and on CD-ROM, all as listed in note 11.

19. Caviness and Nelson, http://dca.tufts.edu/features/law.

20. E. Jane Burns, *Bodytalk: When Women Speak in Old French Literature* (Philadelphia: University of Pennsylvania Press, 1993), 34.

21. Caviness and Nelson, http://dca.tufts.edu/features/law. With her fair face and foul back side, Calefurnia is reminiscent of the allegorical figure of Lady World that is found in contemporary literature and sculpture (Freiburger Münster) in which a beautiful, queenly woman has horrid, decaying flesh full of toads and worms on her back side.

22. Teresa de Lauretis, *Technologies of Gender: Essays on Theory, Film, and Fiction* (Bloomington: Indiana University Press, 1987), 4–5.

23. Hélène Cixous, "Castration or Decapitation?" trans. Annette Kuhn, *Signs* 7.1 (1981): 41–55.

24. Helen Solterer, *The Master and Minerva: Disputing Women in French Medieval Culture* (Berkeley and Los Angeles: University of California Press, 1995), 58. See also Mariella Rummel, *Die rechtliche Stellung der Frau im Sachsenspiegel-Landrecht* (Frankfurt am Main: Peter Lang, 1987), 110–14. Rummel does not see the requirement of guardianship as arising from theories of woman's nature but rather from the archaic character of legal and trial process, especially the need to bear arms. She comments on the story of Calefurnia as the justification for a custom that was no longer really defensible.

25. I use "anger," "wrath," and "rage" as interchangeable English translations for *torn/zorn*. Although the wrath of God is a theological concept, it is not relevant to my claims about Calefurnia.

26. "Als ursprüngliche bedeutung dürfte aber nicht die gemüthsbewegung als solche anzusehen sein, sondern 'kampf, streit mit thaten und worten.'" Jacob Grimm and Wilhelm Grimm, *Deutsches Wörterbuch*, ed. Gustav Rosenhagen, 16 vols. (Leipzig: S. Hirzel, 1954), 16:90.

27. Jan-Dirk Müller, *Spielregeln für den Untergang: Die Welt des Nibelungenliedes* (Tübingen: Max Niemeyer, 1998), 206. On the highly conventional, public, visible expressions of anger by lordly men in political narratives from the Middle Ages, see also Stephen D. White, "The Politics of Anger," in *Anger's Past: The Social Uses of an Emotion in the Middle Ages*, ed. Barbara Rosenwein (Ithaca: Cornell University Press, 1998), 127–52.

28. Müller, *Spielregeln*, 206: "[der] Ausdruck des gewaltsamen körperlichen Einsatzes beim Wetkampf."

29. Müller, *Spielregeln*, 206.

30. Enders, *Rhetoric*, 141–48.

31. Müller, *Spielregeln*, 207.

32. Hartmann von Aue, *Iwein*, ed. G. F. Benecke and K. Lachmann, rev. Ludwig Wolff, 7th ed. (Berlin: Walter De Gruyter, 1968), vol. 1, line 2062.

33. Dobozy, *The Saxon Mirror*, 17.

34. Ibid.

35. Johanek, "Rechtsschriftum," 415.

36. Bellomo, *Common Legal Past*, 60.

37. Ibid.

38. Ibid., 63, 128.

39. S. P. Scott, ed. and trans., *The Civil Law* ... (trans. of *Corpus juris civilis*), 17 vols. in 7 (1932; repr., New York: AMS Press, 1973), 3:3.

40. Deaf people are excluded since they cannot hear the decrees of the judge and could thus be found contumacious by mistake.

41. Title 1 places detailed qualifications on the groups of men in the intermediate classification that work to the advantage of some. For example, an exception to the provision against sodomites admits those who have been forcibly "violated by rob-

bers or enemies" (Scott, *The Civil Law*, 4). A blind man with the rank of senator may be a judge. There is no such amelioration for women. Caviness and Nelson observe several instances in which the *Sachsenspiegel*, too, gives a benefit of the doubt to men but assumes the worst of women.

42. Scott, *The Civil Law*, 4.

43. The Latin passage is: "origo vero introducta est a Carfania improbissima femina, quae inverecunde postulans et magistratum inquietans causam dedit edicto." *Corpus iuris civilis: Text und Übersetzung auf der Grundlage der von Theodor Mommsen und Paul Krüger besorgten Textausgaben*, vol. 2, *Digesten 1–10*, trans. and ed. Okko Behrends et al. (Heidelberg: C. F. Müller Juristischer Verlag, 1990), 266.

44. Bellomo, *Common Legal Past*, 58.

45. Grimm and Grimm, *Deutsches Wörterbuch*, 105.

46. Nussbaum, *Poetic Justice*, 56.

47. Ibid., 60.

48. Guido Kisch, *Sachsenspiegel and Bible* (Notre Dame, Ind.: University of Notre Dame, 1941).

49. Dobozy, *The Saxon Mirror*, 111–12.

50. Johanek, "Rechtsschriftum," 407. In German: "entscheidend wichtigen Sätze eine Begründung mitzugeben und durch heranziehung von Parallelen—auch wenn sie nicht unmittelbar mit der gerade behandelten Materie zu tun haben—die Prinzipien sichtbar zu machen, die der Fülle des sächsichen Rechtslebens zugrundelegen."

51. Eckhardt, *Sachsenspiegel: Landrecht*, 181–82; *Der Schwabenspiegel in der Ältesten Gestalt: Landrecht Hrsg. von Wilhelm Wackernagel (1840); Lehnrecht Hrsg. von Heinrich Christian von Senckenberg (1766)*, ed. Karl August Eckhardt, Bibliotheca rerum historicarum Neudrucke 3 (Aalen: Scientia, 1972), 193; *Schwabenspiegel Langform Z*, ed. Karl August Eckhardt, Bibliotheca rerum historicarum Land- und Lehnrechtsbücher 8 (Aalen: Scientia, 1974), 141; *Schwabenspiegel Kurzform: I. Landrecht, II. Lehnrecht*, ed. Karl August Eckhardt, 2nd ed., Monumenta germaniae historica: Fontes iuris germanici antiqui, n.s., 4.1–2 (Hannover: Hahn, 1974), 331. Each of these editions has a scholarly apparatus with information about the sequence of paragraphs in the manuscript sources.

52. Hermann von Sachsenheim, *Die Mörin: Nach der Wiener Handschrift ÖNB 2946*, ed. Horst Dieter Schlosser (Wiesbaden: F. A. Brockhaus, 1974).

53. Hans Fehr, *Das Recht in der Dichtung* (Bern: A. Francke, 1931), 285.

54. More recent scholarship has been attentive to the literary dimensions of the text, including its unmitigated irony, its wit, its genre, the subjectivity of its first-person narrator, the historical context of its production, and the coded historical references in the text itself. The most significant critical work is Peter Strohschneider, *Ritterromantische Versepik im ausgehenden Mittelalter* (Frankfurt am Main: Peter Lang, 1986), with a good discussion of the historical context of the court of Hermann's patroness Mechthild von der Pfalz. Strohschneider particularly em-

phasizes the communicative strategies of the text as it was received in a closed, courtly setting.

55. It is significant that Hermann dedicated his text to a powerful woman, Mechthild von der Pfalz. Her brother is also named in the dedication. Hermann's relationship to Mechthild was the enabling context in which he carried out his experiment with gender theory. Yet there are no grounds to assume that Mechthild herself is reflected in any of the characters, as Alfred Karnein has shown in "Mechthild von der Pfalz as Patroness: Aspects of Female Patronage in the Early Renaissance," *Medievalia et Humanistica: Studies in Medieval and Renaissance Culture*, n.s., 22 (1995): 141–70.

56. Dieter Welz, "Witz, Komic und Humor in der 'Mörin' des Hermann von Sachsenheim," *ZfdA* 109 (1980): 337–61, at 347.

57. Alexandra Sterling-Hellenbrand, *Topographies of Gender in Middle High German Arthurian Romance* (New York and London: Garland, 2001).

58. Wolfram von Eschenbach, *Parzival*, trans. A. T. Hatto (Harmondsworth: Penguin Books, 1980), 39–40.

59. "Belakane stirbt (wie Dido) den tragischen Tod der verlassenen Frau; und dieser Tod ist kein ritterliches Abenteuer und keine höfische Galanterie. Wolfram weiss das." Alfred Ebenbauer, "'Es gibt ain Mörynne vil dick susse Mynne': Belakanes Landsleute in der deutschen Literatur des Mittelalters," *ZfdA* 113 (1984): 16–42, at 24.

60. Ibid., 24–25.

61. Ibid., 30–31.

62. Ibid., 39.

8

Waxing Red

Shame and the Body, Shame and the Soul

Valerie Allen

It seems ludicrous to refer to our genitals as our "shamefuls," yet in medieval England they thought nothing of it: Chaucer's Parson excoriates men who wear garments that "thurgh hire shortnesse ne couere nat the shameful members of man."[1] Clothing conceals what should not be shown: "God haþ ȝyuen cloþing to man . . . his schameful lymes to hil [protect] & to hide."[2] The association between the genitals and shame is ancient. "Pudenda," Latin for "genitals" and also an English word, derives from *pudor* (shame). Greek employs the same association—*aidōs* (shame), *aidoia* (genitals)—and its pre-Attic occurrences indicate initial independence from the Judeo-Christian story of Eden.[3] Eden nonetheless remains our point of departure. Before sinning, "Either forsothe was naked, Adam, that is, and his wijf," but "thei shameden noȝt," translating the Vulgate's *non erubescebant*.[4] The metonymic relation between cause and effect—between shame and the blush—tacitly lies within *erubescere* (to redden out). After Eden, the naked body is a blushing body.

During the Middle Ages there does not seem to be that feminization of "pudenda" that emerges explicitly in the early modern period. John of Trevisa, for example, uses "genitals" and *pudenda* interchangeably.[5] Instances in the *Oxford English Dictionary* of exclusively feminine "pudenda" date from the seventeenth century, while "genitals" generally refer to the male sex organs; German *die Scham*, rare today but common enough in the nineteenth century, refers specifically to female sex organs. The gendering of the shamefuls was never absolute in English but also never entirely absent. Nowadays "genitals" refers indiscriminately to either sex, while "pudenda" is fast becoming obsolete. Medieval terminology, less sexually fixed than the early modern period's, yet demonstrates in other ways how the shame that arises from bodily exposure is feminized. Shame's causes are many in the Middle Ages; we might even call shame the primal medieval emotion, so ubiquitous and various are its applications. But we should not lose from view its central nexus with nudity—with female nudity, as we shall see—and that the blush, shame's sign, befits a woman more than a man.

It is true, mind you, that medieval romance heroes blush furiously and often. When the Green Knight derides Arthur's court, it grieves the "lord," and "þe blod schot for scham into his schyre face / and lere. / He wex as wroth as wynde."[6] Shame also floods Gawain when, recounting his adventures to the court, "þe blod in his face con melle / When he hit schulde schewe, for schame."[7] Shame arises here from the slight to chivalric rather than sexual honor, and let's not ignore how it results in physical action. Instead of cringing as a woman (or coward) might, Arthur strides purposefully toward the Green Knight, at least until Gawain takes over the offensive.

In contrast, feminine blushes tend to converge on moments of sexual impropriety or of fear of it, and the behavioral effect is usually silence and shrinking. Shamefacedness makes Criseyde, when visiting the temple, stand "in litel brede."[8] Lucrece, on the point of rape, is speechless and unable to look up: "A word, for shame, forth ne myght she brynge, / Ne upon hem she durste nat beholde."[9] When the formel eagle blushes with *shame* at the royal tercel's declaration of love, "She neyther answered wel, ne seyde amys, / So sore abasht was she."[10] Men also blush from sexual modesty, but even then the shame can assume the form of violence: when propositioned by Queen Morgan that he "do hir pleasure," Sir Alexander replies, "A, Jesu defende me. . . . For I had levir kut away my hangers than I wolde do her ony suche pleasure!"[11] Geoffrey of Vinsauf, discussing metonymy, denotes the blush as the sign of anger: "What does fear produce? Pallor. What does anger cause? A flush. . . . We refashion the statement thus: fear grows pale, anger flushes."[12] Arguably, it is oftentimes hard to tell shame from anger in a man.

A male's blushes express a wider, less specific range of cultural experience. Dishonor has as much if not more to do with his social degree as it does with endangered chastity. It is the professional fraudulence of his former boss that makes the Canon's Yeoman blush: "Evere whan that I speke of his falshede, / For shame of hym my chekes waxen rede."[13] When Walter first announces to her father his marital intentions toward

Griselde, the impoverished man's reaction is like that of a young maiden: "This man astonyed so / That reed he wax; abayst and al quakynge / He stood; unnethes seyde he wordes mo."[14] On hearing the news, Griselde has her own fit of maidenly quaking, but the nesting of her shame within her father's is arresting. The daughter's bashfulness comes from being courted, the father's from Walter's breach of estate by soliciting one so far beneath his social rank.

There are certainly occasions when the woman's shame is strictly social, as in the story of Avice, a free female rear-vassal who married William of Boucres, another free rear-vassal. Lambert of Ardres, writing in the thirteenth century, recounts how "she had scarcely lain down on the boards of her marriage bed at Boucres, when men came from the lord of Hames and demanded the club-cherl tax from her. But she blushed for a little while, coloring out of shame and fear, and protested that she was completely ignorant of what the club-cherl tax was, that she was entirely free, and that she came from a free family."[15] The description is couched in strikingly interior terms. While the image of Avice on her marriage bed is clearly a figure of speech—no one actually burst into her chamber on her wedding night—the phrasing conjures up exactly such a vision, implying an association between the insult of imputed servility and the violation of her very womanhood.

It is not that women are inattentive to the calibrations of social degree, but rank itself is mediated through sexual identity. In the thirteenth-century *Ancrene Wisse*, the priest counsels the female penitent to put a name in her confession on those circumstances and details that identify her sin for what it is. Those circumstances reveal how her sin takes its name according to her estate, which itself is measured in terms of her sex:

> Ich am an ancre. A nunne. A wif iweddet. a meiden. a wummon þ me lefde se wel. a wummon þe habbe ear ibeon ibearnd wið swuche þing. & ahte þe be tere forte beon iwarnet. Sire hit wes wið swuch mon. & nempni þenne. munek. Preost. oðer clearc. & of þ ordre. a weddet mon. a ladles þing. a wummon as ich am.[16]

> ["I am an anchoress," or "a nun," or "a married woman," or "a maiden," or "a well trusted woman," or "a woman who has been burnt by such things before and ought to have been more wary." "Sir, it was with such and such a kind of man," and then identify him—"a monk," "a priest," or "a cleric, and of what order," "a married man," "an innocent creature," "a woman just like myself."]

As the legacy of Eden, shame in theory pertains without gender or rank; but once the sin is given its individuating circumstance, it assumes a sexed body and an estate. Again the *Ancrene Wisse* shows its sensitivity to womanhood as an ordained estate, to the collapse of all predicables into that of femininity alone:

> Sire ich am a wummon & schulde bi rihte beo mare scheome ful to habben ispeken as ich spec. oðer idon. as ich dude. for þi mi sunne is mare þen of a wepmon. for hit bi com me wurse.[17]

[Sir I am a woman, and should be the more ashamed to have spoken as I spoke, or to have done what I did. Therefore my sin is greater than if a man had committed it, for it became me worse.]

The confessor anatomizes the sin in exquisite detail, as scrupulously as if conducting a scholastic *disputatio* about *esse*. Indeed, the circumstances of sin—its *quis, quid, ubi, per quos, quociens, quomodo,* and *quando*[18]— sound remarkably like Aristotle's categories so dear to medieval ontology. According to the sex of the penitent, sin and shame assume a different being, for "what," asks Augustine, "more closely concerns a body than its sex?"[19] If shame is a more widely diffused emotion in medieval male experience, in woman it signifies more purely, retaining its essential mark of sexual lack and exposure.

Aristotle sheds light on the emotion when he observes that shame is appropriate, even praiseworthy, only in the weaker or lower orders of being.[20] The young are particularly well adapted to shame (*aidōs*), because, driven by passion rather than reason, they often err; shame, which is a species of the emotion of fear—namely, fear of disgrace[21]—aids them in holding other passions in check. Thus, if the fear of disgrace is stronger than the fear of death in battle, then shame, though not a virtue in itself, has occasioned the virtue of courage. Shame keeps vigil over the waywardness of weak vessels; its motion is self-defensive rather than externally repressive. Following the cue of Aristotle, Aquinas classifies it as one of the parts of the virtue of temperance;[22] significantly, he calls shame *verecundia*, which carries the force of "modesty," rather than *pudor*.[23] *Verecundia* in this heightened sense of modesty protects, not constrains. By virtue of its doctrine of original sin, Christian morality valorizes shame, which for Aristotle is a mark of privation and weakness, because it seeks to compensate for and protect against the spiritual frailty that is our universal condition. Doubly frail because she is weaker in reason and body than is a man, woman needs shame to cover and support her.

Augustine also puts a theological spin on shame by finding willful insubordination at its core. For him, dissociation between rational and sensory desire characterizes original sin. Before the Fall, all muscular movement occurred at the behest of the will, and harmony reigned between sensory and rational desire; in the postlapsarian dispensation, sensory desire gains its own motion, thereby overturning the preeminence of reason. Sensory appetite becomes autonomous. As soon as Adam and Eve sinned, Augustine maintains, they recognized their nakedness, and their sexual members operated without the sanction of reasoned intention:

> It is reasonable then that we should feel very much ashamed [*pudere*] of such lust, and reasonable too that those members which it moves or does not move by its own right, so to speak, and not in full subjection to our will [*arbitrium nostrum*], should be called "shameful parts" [*pudenda*], as they were not before man sinned.... [It] is not that they were unaware of their nakedness, but that their nakedness was not yet base [*turpis*] because lust did not yet arouse those members apart from their will.[24]

What is at issue is the assumption of autonomy by that which should remain subservient. Woman's need for mastery and her identification with the body are memorably depicted in Paolo Veronese's allegory of "La Virtù, che frena il Vizio": Virtue, represented by a man, looking heavenward, holds a bridle with the bit inserted into the mouth of Vice, represented by a woman who stares at the ground with the angriest eyes. In his other hand, he carries a rod. In the Fall, sense appetite breaks free of the authority of rational appetite and, in doing so, both feminizes the sensory and sensualizes the feminine; woman, subject to man, shames herself in doing her own thing.

In shame lies death. Augustine's definition of death—that "by which soul and body are sundered" [*qua separantur anima et corpus*][25]—places mortality at the moment when the body-soul union is lost. The primal fragmentation of self-identity, this "separation" of rational from sensory desire in the Fall anticipates the final separation of body from soul and soul from God. Such wrong autonomy brings shame and death in its wake.

What emerges from Augustine's analysis is that shame—along with the sin that occasions it—is all about blood and muscles, involuntary dilations and contractions, and the imperviousness of the flesh to the will and words. The loins, says Plato,[26] are situated farthest from the brain, too far from the head to hear the voice of reason. So when they act unilaterally, shame shrivels up those contumaciously distended members like snails recoiling into their protective carapace. Conversely, when loss of honor is imminent, the blush restores the loss by sending blood back to members that cannot swell and be strong.

Commenting on book 4 of the *Ethics* of Aristotle, Aquinas explains the movements of shame, which is a species of fear, upon the body:

> All the passions are accompanied by some corporeal change. Shame [*verecundia*] and fear [*timor*]—which is concerned with the danger of death—have a general resemblance in that each passion is judged by a change in the color of the body.
>
> But they have particular differences, since people who are ashamed blush [*rubescere*], while those who fear death turn pale. The reason for this difference is that the spirit and the humors naturally rush to the place feeling the need. Now, the seat of life is the heart, and so when danger of death is feared, the spirit and the humors speed to the heart. Consequently, the surface of the body being as it were deserted, grows pale. On the other hand, honor [*honor*] and confusion [*confusio*] are numbered among external things. Therefore, since a man fears the loss of honor by shame [*verecundia*], he blushes as the humors and spirits stream back to the surface.[27]

The blush defensively returns blood to the pale cheeks, so that "face" will not be lost, for loss of honor is registered in the outer limbs and most of all in the face, the seat of knowledge. True to the homeostatic principles of ancient medicine, excess (of blood) counteracts the defect (of honor) to sustain the creature in virtuous equilibrium. When shame "flees" from "wantonness" (*proterviam fugitans*),[28] the motion is a literal shrinking of limbs; eyes are averted, bodies curl up, tongues are tied. Criseyde, in the temple, "stood ful low . . . ay under shame's drede."[29] The blush acts as antidote to the gesture of recoiling, and restores the flow of vital spirits: when Gawain is confronted by Bertilak about his keeping of the girdle, "alle þe blode of his brest blende in his face / þat al he schrank for schome."[30] The blush puts back together a body shamed by having lost its honorable integrity.

Christianity makes shame central to subjective experience in a way that Greek antiquity does not. Where in Greek ethics shame is decorous only in the weak, in a confessional context everyone—knight or villein, adult or youth, man or woman—is shamefully weak before God, and the blush is the recognition of the fact. Reliance upon spontaneous blushing informs the mood of the confessional and its ideology of affect. The importance of *Ancrene Wisse* in the fashioning of affective subjectivity, and of devotional female selfhood in particular, has been well established.[31] From its directions for confession emerges a cultivation of blushes and tears as active participants in the work of redemption. When the poor widow cleans her house, she damps the fine dust the better to expel it; so also should tears douse the powder of small sins.[32] Just as the Red Sea had to be crossed in order for the Israelites to proceed to the salvation of the Promised Land, so the redness of shame must be endured to attain absolution and redemption.[33] No shiny gemstone could please God better than a red face in confession.[34] Shame's blazon balances, as in a ledger, the penitent woman's shamelessness in committing the sin, and acts out on the body the inner sacramental work of grace: "þe cwike rude of þe neb. deð to understonden þ te sawle þe wes bla. & nefde bute dead heow. haueð icaht cwic heow & is irudet feire"[35] [The lively redness of the face gives us to understand that the soul, which was pale, and had only the hue of death, has assumed the hue of life and has reddened beautifully]. Woman, moister of complexion than is a man, is naturally built for such emotional expression. Tears and the rush of blood in a blush furnish her with a vocabulary of piety better than do any words.[36]

The supposition at work in such devotional writing is that the blush follows *pudor* as one heartbeat follows another. It is what Augustine calls a natural sign (*signum naturale*), a term he uses in *De Doctrina Christiana* in distinction to designated or conventional signs (*signa designata*).[37] The former are effects that follow necessarily from their cause; the latter signals sent with the express intention of signifying. Put differently, with *signa designata* the relation between signifier and signified (or cause and effect) is capable of being otherwise. *Signa naturalia*, on the other hand, are a sure thing, signifying their cause as certainly as smoke betokens a fire and feet leave tracks. There is no choice about *signa naturalia*, and if a blush is a natural sign of shame, then it can no more be suppressed than it can be forced; it has no intentionality as such.

Yet the blush is not entirely unequivocal; nor is shame. Dante describes himself as "alquanto del color consperso che fa l'uom di perdon talvolta degno" [suffused somewhat by the color that sometimes makes a man worthy of pardon].[38] "Sometimes"? Augustine sidles away from specifics, announcing that the question of whether a man's cry of pain is involuntary or intended is not pertinent to his discussion.[39] Aquinas also shows some double-mindedness when attempting to categorize shame: is it a passion or a virtue?[40] If a passion, then it is an involuntary response to certain stimuli (or, in Augustine's terms, *signum naturale*); if a virtue, then the effect of rationally motivated choice (*signum designatum*). His answer is that shame shares in both; essentially a passion, it nonetheless possesses aspects of virtue and can therefore be called a praiseworthy passion. Shame happens somewhere between reason and passion, mind and body, choice and necessity. It tracks the existential line between flesh and the soul; it straddles, it *is* the boundary between choice and those disobedient, bothersome members. Both conjoining them and wedging them forever apart, shame belongs to a discourse of the in-between.

Shame happens between people. It circulates, like the rush of blood that it is; so do gazes. Each blush in *Sir Gawain and the Green Knight*—King Arthur's before the Green Knight, Gawain's before Sir Bertilak, Gawain's before the court at Camelot—occurs before the gaze of another. Shame requires an audience, occurring only once one *sees* that one is being looked at. It forms a crucial stage in the construction of self-awareness, an abysmal moment in which one sees oneself being seen being seen; reflections are reflected in the reflections of eyes. Shame constructs subjective identity not as autonomous entity but as being-in-relation. It implies that the shamed subject's sense of self is to a high degree externally regulated by the one before whom shame is felt, and to that extent it differs philosophically from guilt, which internalizes that principle of censure within the (guilt-ridden) subject.[41] Woman, who has no name until given one by father or husband, embodies being-in-relation more fundamentally than the male.

Primarily identified as *passio* or suffering, the "passion" of shame nevertheless also partakes of virtue and hence of action; one performs shame. This active sense problematizes the traditional depiction of woman as the passive, shamed object of the male gaze, of which Virginia being "eye-fucked"[42] by the rapacious Apius is a paradigmatic example.[43] Middle English *blishen*[44] means to "shine brightly," to "blush red," and to "gaze upon," suggesting strongly that blushing comes less from being looked at than from looking, that Adam's and Eve's shame came from seeing the other's nakedness rather than from exposure of self; hence, that to blush means to know, to see.

Knowing and seeing, an ancient identification, mark loss of purity as much as they mark understanding. By implication, "blindness" suggests freedom from shame. Augustine is quick to point out the error in thinking that Adam and Eve were literally blind before sinning—a misunderstanding arising from a wrong reading of the phrase that, after sinning, "the eiȝen of both ben openyd."[45] But innocence does require a certain blinkering of the eyes—a figurative blindness—as the *Fasciculus Morum* points out when expounding the vice of lechery.[46]

Occurring at the interstice between mind and body, viewer and viewed, shame inevitably touches male confessor as well as female penitent. His attempt to achieve that figurative blindness—looking at her but with pure thoughts—doesn't seem to work. Wycliffe remarks on how, in facing each other during confession, shriver and female penitent often come unstuck: "Prestis & wymmen shulde turne her faces to-gider, & speke of lustful þoutes & dedis, which myȝt do harme to hem boþe, but þis lawe ȝyueþ occasioun to do synne as it falliþ oft."[47]

Spiritual "blindness" must be sought by some other means. Myrc instructs that, when hearing confession, the priest himself must cowl his face and listen to the confession with a mild demeanor. By lowering his head, the confessor tries to assume the condition of prelapsarian Adam, where his eyes "are not opened," where he may not be violated by the object of his gaze. The recommendation to look away applies to all, but when the penitent is a woman, the instructions acquire an anxious precision:

> But when a wommon cometh to þe,
> Loke hyre face þat þou ne se,
> But teche hyre to knele downe þe by,
> And sum-what þy face from hyre þou wry,
> Stylle as ston þer þow sytte,
> And kepe þe welle þat þou ne spytte.
> Koghe þou not þenne, þy þonkes,
> Ny wrynge þou not with þy schonkes,
> Lest heo suppose þow make þat fare,
> For wlatynge þat þou herest þare,
> But syt þou style as any mayde
> Tyl þat heo haue alle I-sayde.[48]

No peeping at her, turn away your face, no spitting, no coughing, don't fidget, sit tight or else she'll think you're wincing at the awful things she's coming out with. A woman is telling her sordid secrets to a priest, a man. She sees that she is being "watched" (that is, listened to) by a priest, a man;

each twitch or shuffle feels like a gaze that is both disgusted and aroused. The confessing "I" "eyes" herself with male eyes that mirror her shame and, in mirroring it, double it. The rupture that opens up here within the woman between the "I" who sinned and the "I" who now regards herself self-consciously gapes as wide as the gender gap itself.

The plethora of prescription registers the impossibility of expunging sexual awareness entirely from the exchange between priest and female penitent. In a situation already fraught with mutual difficulties of knowing where to look or how to hold one's body, the female penitent must find a way to put her lechery into words that reveal the sin without exposing too much:

To euch preost mei ancre schriuen hire of swucche utterliche sunnen þe to alle bifalleð. Ah ful trusti ha schal beon o þe preostes godlec. þ ha allunge schaweð to. hu hire stonde abute flesches temptatiuns. ȝef ha is swa ifondet. bute ideaðes dute. þus þah me þuncheð þ ha mei seggen. Sire flesches fondunge þ ich habbe oðer habbe ihaued geað to uorð up o me þurh mi þeafunge. . . . Ne dear ich þ ha deopluker ne witerluker schriue hire to ȝung preost her abuten. Ant ȝet of þis inohreaðe him walde þunche wunder.[49]

[An anchoress may confess herself to any priest about outer sins that happen to us all, but she must be very trusting of the priest's goodness to whom she completely reveals how she stands in relation to temptations of the flesh, if she be so tempted. But it seems to me she could say something like this: "Sir, a fleshly temptation that I have or have had comes upon me very strongly through my consent. . . ." I dare not suggest that she confess herself more deeply or more clearly about these things to a young priest; and yet even this would already seem to him vile.]

The need for exposure and the danger of too much exposure continue an Edenic discourse of nudity that runs through the penitentials as pronounced metaphor for spiritual innocence. The record of confession must be "nakyd . . . & noȝt coloured in therk & fayre woordys."[50] Julian of Norwich says, "The holy gost ledyth hym to confession, wylfully to shew hys synnes nakydly and truly with grett sorrow and with grett shame."[51] "Naked" is originally the past participle of the active Middle English verb *naken*, meaning to "strip" or "bare oneself." The singleness of the modern form fixes nudity grammatically as a passive state, while the Middle English verb retains an activity now lost. So used we are to thinking of a (spiritually) naked woman as vulnerable object, patient of the searching questions put to her by the physician of her soul, that we forget the simple truth that even the most unskilled of ecdysiasts knows—this is *her* act.

In the gendered scene of the confessional where female penitent is shrived by the male confessor, her "nudity" is particularly at issue. Her speech must be a "naked text"—no euphemisms, no frills. The priest, writing the *Ancrene Wisse* for his "dear sisters," exhorts spiritual nudity as raucously as a wolf whistle:

> Schrift schal beo naket. þ is naketliche imaket. . . . Sire ha seið þe wummon. ich habbe iheued leof mon. oðer ich habbe ibeon ha seið fol of me seoluen. þis nis nawt naket schrift. biclute þu hit nawt. do awei þe totagges. Vnwrih þe. & sei. Sire godes are ich am a ful stod meare. a stinckinde hore. . . . Make hit i schrift steort naket.[52]

> [Confession must be naked, that is, plainly made. . . . "Sir," a woman says, "I have had a lover." Or "I have been careless about myself." This is not a naked confession. Don't wrap it up at all. Do away with the trimmings. Reveal yourself and say, "Sir, God's mercy, I am a foul stud mare, a stinking whore. . . . make your sin stark naked."]

But there can be too much nudity, or the wrong sort. In putting a name on the ugly sin, she can go too far:

> ʒcf þi fa a ful nome & cleope þi sunne fule. Make hit i schrift steort naket. þ is. ne hel þu nawiht of al þ lið þer abuten. þah to fule me mei seggen. Me ne þearf nawt nempnin þ fule dede bi his ahne fule nome. ne þe schendfule limes bi hare ahne nome. inoh is to seggen swa. þ te hali schrift feder witerliche understonde hweat tu wulle meanen.[53]

> [Give your foe a foul name, and call your sin foul; make it stark naked in confession, that is, do not hide anything connected with it. However, one can speak too foully. It is not necessary to name the foul act by its own foul name, nor the shameful members by their own names. It is enough to speak so that the holy father confessor clearly understands what you mean.]

Framed even as it is in the rhetoric of contrition, her confession of lust makes present the past insubordinacy of her members. Naming her shamefuls gives them self-motion, and breaks up the ideal organization of her body; that which should be covered, silent, and restrained thrusts into the foreground in unsightly fashion. Body parts operate on their own, without reference to the whole. The classic *descriptio* of the romance heroine with its decorous omission of inappropriate detail—witness Blanche's portrait where "her lymmes" are on view only "in so fer as I had knowynge"[54]—patterns the separate members, uniting parts into the whole without which, in Aristotelian terms, a work cannot be beautiful (*kalos*).[55] To take an image from Chaucer's *Miller's Tale*, imagine a female bottom stuck out the window: the part becomes the whole, in both senses of the homophone; it should be offstage; it's obscene (*ob scaena*)—"quodcumque ostendis mihi sic, incredulus odi"[56] [in disgust and disbelief am I confronted with whatever such you show me]. When women's shameful members are on display, then hermeneutics as well as Alison's ass go out the window. Absolom mistakes her butt for her head; the peasant of Gautier Le Leu's *De deus Vilains* thinks that his hostess's bare bottom sticking out from under the coverlet is the head of his sick companion;[57] the cowardly knight of *Berangier au lonc cul*, challenged by his wife disguised as a knight either to fight or to kiss her ass, chooses the latter and is stunned by the length of the crack;[58] even the devil, as Rabelais recounts, can't recognize a woman's "comment a nom" [what's-its-name] for what it is,[59] mistaking it for a horrible wound. The nearest Rabelais can get to naming the spectacle is a pun. Having prophesied about Panurge's proposed marriage, the sibyl then turns and moons him ("leurs monstroit son cul"), at which he says, "Voy là le trou de la Sibylle" [Look, there's the sibyl's cavern].[60] Ignominy literally means loss of name, loss of the *nomen*. *Ars grammatica* falters in front of a woman's what's-its-name. While "pudenda" may be the agreed signifier for you-know-what, the word can only wave in the general direction of you-know-what, for the very denomination is a refusal to put a name on it. Like sodomy, pudenda may just as well be called "those things that cannot be named."[61] The name of a thing denotes that thing in its entirety; if a part assumes the status of a whole, language no longer signifies properly or literally but figuratively, and the natural union between *res* and *verbum* turns into the knowing liaisons of rhetorical device. The confessional may seem far removed from the fabliau, but the problem of putting a name on her shamefuls is common to both.

A woman who forces a man to *blish* at and "know" her pudenda, either literally or figuratively by means of a confession that names her members too exactly, gets her own back for the Edenic edict that made them shameful in the first place. Her "naking" is a passively aggressive act, for she makes herself the object of the shamed gaze; she shames by means of her shamefuls. Where a man—Arthur, Gawain, Sir Alexander—acts directly on his shame, woman acts by indirection; her body talk is crooked.

In contrast to spiritual nakedness stands *colour*, which both is the morally neutral rhetorical term for adornment of language and carries a more insidious sense of counterfeiting. As a rhetorical term, "color" usually denotes an "easy ornament," *ornatus facilis*, which implies a cosmetic rearrangement of sounds in contrast to a difficult ornament, which involves a real change of meaning in words. Easy and difficult ornaments are themselves then categorized as figures of speech, in contradistinction to figures of thought, the most sustained and difficult of verbal mutations. "Color" can be used more generally to denote any kind of rhetorical figure; it's this kind of color of which Chaucer's Franklin denies knowledge.[62] But strictly speaking, it denotes linguistic adornment of the most superficial kind; it bears the sense of a covering garment, since the Latin noun *ornatus* means "attire" or "equipment." In exegetical terms, *colour* corresponds to the letter of the law as opposed to its spirit, and aligns itself with the carnal, with woman.

For Lollardism *colour* occurs frequently in the vocabulary of disparagement of false, dissembling language.[63] In the confessional, no "colour of sin"[64]—no fudging—should remain in one's statement. Self-accusation must be direct, "noȝt excusyng þi-self in colouris."[65] By a metonymic shift, color, meaning dye, comes also to refer to the cloth it colors, and thus returns us to the sense of the blush as a garment or covering.[66] Colors block out the pudenda of sin in the same way false shame estops the words of confession. The standard poses and liturgical formulae that constitute the sacramental event of confession run the inherent danger of insincerity. Aware of the possibility, the writers of the penitentials seek anxiously to make each confession as good as the first time, demanding a perpetual sacrifice of tears and blushes as surety for an unknowably bottomless sorrow of heart.

When Augustine speaks of how there was no need for our first parents to blush before they sinned, he refers not simply to their lack of discomfort with their nudity but more profoundly to the sense in which they perceived it. With no clothes as an option, nudity must mean something different. Nudity there needed no self-reference, and hence no name. To name a thing implies the ability to name its opposite, and with no clothing for contrast, one could not "nake," one could not be stripped in any privative or transgressive sense. Prelapsarian nudity denotes an ontological wholeness without need of supplement of clothes or ornament. It is, as it were, already clothed and all kitted out—an indissoluble unity, with no possibility of the undoing that stripping entails, or the fragmentation of the body brought about by mooning or flashing; a self-presentation that has no secondary or hidden meaning and no ambiguity; an utterance totally univocal. Pure nudity is as impossible as Kant's *Ding an sich*,[67] as unspeakable as a woman's what's-its-name, as unknowable as a true confession whispered from the heart.

Freud once wrote an essay on the antithetical meanings of words, in which he demonstrates a significant number of words that can also mean their opposite; the more ancient the concept, the greater its ability to contain contradiction. Both language and the unconscious reveal a preference "for combining contraries into a unity or for representing them as one and the same thing."[68] The underlying logic is that we only formally name and conceptualize a thing once we can identify its opposite, hence that identity is relational rather than intrinsic, and the apparent semantic independence of concepts represses an implied contrary meaning. Understood theologically, words after the Fall lost their ability to signify univocally, and every act of naming at some level named its contrary. Consider then that the Middle English word *schameless* possesses a contradictory meaning no longer present today. Alongside the retained sense of being impudent, Middle English *schameless* means "free of shame": "the trouthe is schameles ate ende, / Bot what thing that is troutheles, / It mai noght wel be schameles."[69] *Schameless* can mean either "guilty" or "innocent." In order to blush, one has to "know" the concealment of a garment in order to know that one is without it; it is at once protective veil and coy ornament, a "color" from the most innocent to the most insidious of senses. In postlapsarian times it is impossible to be naked without shame, just as it is impossible to speak without ornament and possible counterfeit. The only properly naked utterance is silence. The only decorous way to be naked is to be invisible. By the same self-canceling logic, the only good virgin is a dead virgin.[70] Paradoxically, the garment of the blush is the sign by which one can be seen to be spiritually naked, just as for Tertullian the veil is the sign of the virgin underneath it.[71] This is as provoking as the problem of whether the light's really off when the fridge door is shut. Nakedness can be known only by a garment. Shame is fatally double and indirect, and woman its true bearer.

In the epistemological uncertainty of the confessional, one can never be sure that shame is not false. The manuals counsel that one go to confession often, just in case the last confession wasn't performed entirely in the nude, as it were, and in the right kind of nudity at that: *nuditas virtualis* rather than *nuditas criminalis*. Go frequently,

> uor þet me not yef heþ wel yby yssriue / oþer uorþenchinde. zuo me ssel ofte winne ayen / þet me heþ lesse ynoȝ y-do.[72]

[lest I have not been well shrived or fully repentant. Thus shall I repeat often what has not been done sufficiently.]

> Confiteor. hali weater. Beoden. hali þohtes. Blesceunges. Cneolunges. Euch god word. euch god werc. wessched smeale sunnen þe me ne mei alle seggen.... Schrift schal beo dredful. þ tu segge wið Ierome. Quoci ens confessus sum. uideor michi non esse confessus. As ofte as ich am ischriuen. eauer me þunched me unschriuen. for eauer is sum forȝeten of þe totagges.[73]

[The confiteor, holy water, prayers, holy thoughts, blessings, genuflections, every good word and every good deed, wash the small sins that one cannot fully declare.... Confession must be fearful, so that you say with Jerome, "Quociens confessus sum, videor michi [mihi] non esse confessus": As often as I confess, I always think myself unconfessed. For some of the details are always forgotten.]

The nakedness required by confession is the innocent nakedness of prelapsarian Eden; anything else is mooning or stripteasing. Since an innocent confession is a contradiction in terms, we are left with the disturbing possibility that every woman's blushing confession of lust is at some level a shameless flaunting, that woman can never properly confess lust, and thus never be truly cleansed of it.

When a woman casts off her smock, she "cast hir shame away,"[74] so how can her shame be sincere when she's naked? The only sincere blush is invisible. The only good virgin is a dead virgin. Back to the *Ding an sich*. Leave it to Rabelais:

> But this morning I came across a fine fellow carrying two little girls, two or three years old at most, in a saddlebag just like Aesop's, one in front and one behind.... Then I asked him: "My good man, are those

two young girls virgins [*pucelles*]?" "Brother," he answered, "for two years I've been carrying them like this. I watch the one in front continually, and in my opinion she is a virgin—although, that said, I wouldn't put my finger in the fire for it. As for the one I carry around behind me, I really haven't a clue."[75]

Notes

1. Geoffrey Chaucer, *Canterbury Tales*, X.422. All references to Chaucer are taken from *The Riverside Chaucer*, ed. Larry D. Benson, 3rd ed. (Boston: Houghton Mifflin, 1987).

2. *Þe Pater Noster of Richard Ermyte: A Late Middle English Exposition of the Lord's Prayer*, ed. Florent Gérard Antoine Marie Aarts (The Hague: Martinus Nijhoff, 1967), 19, line 26.

3. See entries in Henry George Liddell and Robert Scott, eds., *Greek-English Lexicon*, rev. ed. (Oxford: Clarendon, 1996), for Hesiod and Heraclitus as sources for *ta aidoia* meaning "shameful members."

4. Middle English taken from John Wycliffe's *The Holy Bible, Containing the Old and New Testaments* . . ., ed. Josiah Forshall and Frederic Madden (Oxford: Oxford University Press, 1850), Gen. 2:25.

5. *On the Properties of Things: John Trevisa's Translation of Bartholomaeus Anglicus' "De Re Proprietatibus,"* ed. M. C. Seymour et al., 3 vols. (Oxford: Clarendon, 1975), iv.48.

6. *Sir Gawain and the Green Knight*, ed. J. R. R. Tolkien and E. V. Gordon, 2nd ed. (Oxford: Clarendon, 1967), lines 317–19.

7. Ibid., lines 2503–4.

8. Chaucer, *Troilus and Criseyde*, I.179.

9. Chaucer, *Legend of Good Women*, lines 1835–36.

10. Chaucer, *Parliament of Fowls*, lines 446–47.

11. *Works of Sir Thomas Malory*, ed. Eugène Vinaver, 2nd ed. (Oxford: Clarendon, 1967), 2:643.

12. Geoffrey of Vinsauf, *Poetria Nova*, trans. Margaret F. Nims (Toronto: Pontifical Institute of Mediaeval Studies, 1967), 51.

13. Chaucer, *Canterbury Tales*, VIII.1094–95.

14. Chaucer, *Canterbury Tales*, IV.316–18.

15. Lambert of Ardres, *The History of the Counts of Guines and Lords of Ardres*, trans. Leah Shopkow (Philadelphia: University of Pennsylvania Press, 2000), 81.

16. *Ancrene Wisse: The English Text of the Ancrene Riwle; Edited from MS. Corpus Christi College Cambridge 402*, ed. J. R. R. Tolkien, EETS o.s. 249 (London: Oxford University Press, 1962), 163 (fol. 86b, lines 12–17).

17. *Ancrene Wisse*, 163 (fol. 86b, lines 8–12).

18. John Myrc, *Instructions for Parish Priests*, ed. Edward Peacock, EETS o.s. 31, reprint (New York: Greenwood, 1969). See Latin rubrics, p. 44.

19. Augustine of Hippo, *City of God against the Pagans*, vol. 2, ed. and trans. William M. Green (Cambridge, Mass.: Harvard University Press, 1963), V.6.

20. Aristotle, *The Nicomachean Ethics*, ed. and trans. H. Rackham, rev. ed. (Cambridge, Mass.: Harvard University Press, 1934), IV.9.

21. Aristotle's identification of shame as fear forms the standard definition for scholasticism and is a vernacular commonplace: "Schame of a man ... is not ... ellis as in substaunce ... þan a drede of his vngloriyng." Reginald Pecock, *The Folewer to the Donet*, ed. Elsie Vaughan Hitchcock, EETS o.s. 164 (London: Oxford University Press, 1924), 99, lines 16–18.

22. Thomas Aquinas, *Summa Theologiae*, ed. and trans. Thomas Gilby (Cambridge: Blackfriars, 1968), 2a2ae.144.

23. Not even *verecundia* is free from the taint of shame. Felix Faber of Ulm, describing the sanitation problems on board a fifteenth-century pilgrim ship, refers to pilgrims who strip naked in order to avoid a soaking while visiting the toilet during a storm: "In this, modesty (*verecundia*) suffers greatly, which only stirs the shameful (*verecunda*) parts even more." Quoted in Philippe Braunstein, "Toward Intimacy: The Fourteenth and Fifteenth Centuries," in *A History of Private Life*, ed. Philippe Ariès and Georges Duby, trans. Arthur Goldhammer, vol. 2, *Revelations of the Medieval World*, ed. Georges Duby (Cambridge, Mass.: Belknap, 1988), 588.

24. Augustine, *City of God*, vol. 4, ed. and trans. Philip Levine (Cambridge, Mass.: Harvard University Press, 1966), XIV.17. Here and throughout, I have occasionally modified the English translation.

25. Ibid., XIII.3.

26. Plato, *Timaeus*, ed. and trans. R. G. Bury, rev. ed. (Cambridge, Mass.: Harvard University Press, 1952), 70d–71a.

27. Aquinas, *Commentary on the Nicomachean Ethics*, trans. C. I. Litzinger, 2 vols. (Chicago: Henry Regnery, 1964), 1:373. Latin text in *Sancti Thomae Aquinatis: Opera omnia*, ed. Petrus Fiaccadori (repr., New York: Musurgia, 1949), 21:152.

28. Aquinas, *Summa Theologiae*, 2a2ae.144.1, quoting Ambrose.

29. Chaucer, *Troilus and Criseyde*, I.178–80.

30. *Sir Gawain and the Green Knight*, lines 2371–2.

31. Linda Georgianna, *The Solitary Self: Individuality in the "Ancrene Wisse"* (Cambridge, Mass: Harvard University Press, 1981).

32. *Ancrene Wisse*, 161–62 (fol. 85b, lines 13–18).

33. Ibid., 169 (fol. 89b, lines 22–24).

34. Ibid., (fol. 90a, lines 4–6).

35. Ibid., (fol. 90a, lines 10–12).

36. This imagery of blood and tears occurs throughout the *Ancrene Wisse* and its related texts; see Elizabeth Robertson, *Early English Devotional Prose and the Female Audience* (Knoxville: University of Tennessee Press, 1990), 9–11.

37. Augustine, *De Doctrina Christiana*, 2.1; Latin text in Migne *PL* 34, col. 36.

38. Dante Alighieri, *The Divine Comedy*, ed. and trans. Charles S. Singleton (Princeton: Princeton University Press, 1970–1975), *Purgatorio*, v, 20–21.

39. Augustine, *De Doctrina Christiana*, 2.2.; Migne *PL* 34, col. 37.

40. Aquinas, *Summa Theologiae*, 2a2ae.144.1.

41. For the distinction between shame and guilt cultures, see *The Greeks and the Irrational* (Berkeley and Los Angeles: University of California Press, 1951), 1–63, where E. R. Dodds describes the evolution of the Homeric world from a shame culture to an Attic guilt culture. The highest good to the Homeric individual is honor (*tīmē*). Fear of its loss—shame (*aidōs*)—constitutes the most powerful moral force in one's choices, resulting in conformity and traditionalism. Bernard Williams, in *Shame and Necessity* (Berkeley and Los Angeles: University of California Press, 1993), 75–102, identifies guilt as a more abstract sense of justice; under Western modernity, it becomes autonomous from and dominates shame; it is deemed morally more advanced than the narcissistic self-preoccupation of shame because it is concerned with the victim rather than the perpetrator. No doubt owing to the phenomenological turn away from abstract being, we have of late reevaluated the philosophical implications of shame and the nature of knowledge itself. As Silvan Tomkins observes, it is questionable whether "anyone may fully grasp the nature of any object when that object has not been perceived, wished for, missed, and thought about in love and in hate, in excitement and in apathy, in distress and in joy.... Only an animal who was as capable as man could have convinced himself that the scientific mode of acquaintance is the only 'real' mode through which he contacts reality"; quoted in Joseph Adamson and Hilary Clark, eds., *Scenes of Shame: Psychoanalysis, Shame, and Writing* (Albany: State University of New York Press, 1999), 6.

42. Garrett P. J. Epp borrows the phrase from the Marines of Vietnam; see "Ecce Homo," in *Queering the Middle Ages*, ed. Glenn Burger and Steven F. Kruger (Minneapolis: University of Minnesota Press, 2001), 245.

43. Geoffrey Chaucer, *Canterbury Tales*, VI.121–26. See R. Howard Bloch, "Chaucer's Maiden's Head: *The Physician's Tale* and the Poetics of Virginity," *Representations* 28 (1989): 113–35.

44. *Middle English Dictionary*, s.v. "blishen."

45. Augustine, *City of God*, XIV.17, quoting Gen. 3:7.

46. *Fasciculus Morum: A Fourteenth-Century Preacher's Handbook*, ed. and trans. Siegfried Wenzel (University Park: Pennsylvania State University Press, 1989), pt. 7, pp. 650–53.

47. *Nota de confesione*, in *English Works of Wyclif Hitherto Unprinted*, ed. F. D. Matthew, EETS o.s. 74 (London: Trübner, 1880), 330.

48. Myrc, *Instructions for Parish Priests*, lines 773–84.

49. *Ancrene Wisse*, 175–76 (fol. 93a, line 29–fol. 93b, lines 1–7).

50. *Jacob's Well: An English Treatise on the Cleansing of Man's Conscience*, ed. Arthur Brandeis, EETS o.s. 115 (London: K. Paul, Trench, Trübner, 1900), pt. 1, chap. 28, lines 3–5.

51. *A Book of Showings to the Anchoress Julian of Norwich*, ed. Edmund Colledge and James Walsh (Toronto: Pontifical Institute of Mediaeval Studies, 1978), vol. 2, chap. 39, lines 9–10.

52. *Ancrene Wisse*, 162 (fol. 86a, line 15), 163 (fol. 86a, lines 22–27).

53. Ibid., 163 (fol. 86a, line 27, through fol. 86b, line 4).

54. Chaucer, *Book of the Duchess*, lines 959–60.

55. Aristotle, *Poetics*, ed. and trans. Stephen Halliwell (Cambridge, Mass.: Harvard University Press, 1995), chap. 7, 1450b.

56. Horace, *Ars Poetica*, ed. and trans. H. Rushton Fairclough (Cambridge, Mass.: Harvard University Press, 1926), line 188.

57. In *Le Jongleur Gautier Le Leu: Étude sur les Fabliaux*, ed. Charles H. Livingston (Cambridge, Mass.: Harvard University Press, 1951), 199–206.

58. In *The Literary Context of Chaucer's Fabliaux: Texts and Translations*, ed. Larry D. Benson and Theodore M. Andersson (Indianapolis: Bobbs-Merrill, 1971), 22–23, lines 242–50.

59. François Rabelais, *Oeuvres complètes*, ed. Mireille Huchon with François Moreau (Paris: Gallimard, 1994), 4.47, p. 648. See also the story of the lion who mistook a woman's "what-d'ye-call-it" for a wound, 2.15, pp. 269–71.

60. Ibid., 3.17, p. 404.

61. For discussion of the comic "Story of the Porter and the Three Ladies" in *One Thousand and One Nights*, which revolves around the (in)correct naming of the ladies' pudenda, see Lisa Perfetti, *Women and Laughter in Medieval Comic Literature* (Ann Arbor: University of Michigan Press, 2003), 203–38.

62. Chaucer, *Canterbury Tales*, V.719–26.

63. The word occurs in a number of instances in *Lollard Sermons*, ed. Gloria Cigman, EETS o.s. 294 (Oxford: Oxford University Press, 1989).

64. Dan Michel, *Ayenbite of Inwyt; or, Remorse of Conscience*, ed. Richard Morris, EETS o.s. 23 (London: Trübner, 1866), 177.

65. *Jacob's Well*, chap. 27, lines 23–24.

66. *Middle English Dictionary*, s.v. "colour," 2c(b).

67. "Gar nicht zu reden vom Ding an sich, vom horrendum pudendum der Metaphysiker!" [To say nothing of the "Ding an sich," that *horrendum pudendum* of the metaphysicians!], in Friedrich Nietzsche, *Götzen-Dämmerung oder Wie man mit dem Hammer philosophirt* (Leipzig: G. Naumann, 1889), 34; also Sheila Delany, *The Naked Text: Chaucer's Legend of Good Women* (Berkeley and Los Angeles: University of California Press, 1994), 1, 122.

68. Sigmund Freud, "The Antithetical Meaning of Primal Words," in *The Standard Edition of the Complete Psychological Works of Sigmund Freud*, trans. James Strachey, 24 vols. (London: Hogarth, 1953–74), 11:153–61, at 155.

69. *Confessio Amantis*, in *The Complete Works of John Gower*, ed. G. C. Macaulay, vol. 3 (Oxford: Clarendon, 1901), 7.1964–66.

70. Quoting Bloch, "Chaucer's Maiden's Head," 120.

71. Ibid., 123, paraphrasing Tertullian.

72. Michel, *Ayenbite of Inwyt*, 178.
73. *Ancrene Wisse*, 166 (fol. 88a, lines 14–16), 170 (fol. 90a, lines 14–17).
74. Chaucer, *Canterbury Tales*, 3.782, quoting Jerome.
75. Rabelais, *Oeuvres complètes*, 2.15, p. 271.

Contributors

Valerie Allen is associate professor of English at John Jay College of Criminal Justice, City University of New York. She contributes annually to the Chaucer chapter of *The Year's Work in English Studies*, has coedited the New Casebook *Chaucer* (1996), and has also published on women in Chaucer. Most recently she has published on the ethics of noise in the Middle Ages and on the tournament in late fourteenth-century England.

Elena Carrera is lecturer in Spanish at Oxford Brookes University. She has published several articles on Teresa of Avila and has contributed essays to volumes on women's writing in Spain and Brazil and to *Trajectories of Mysticism in Theory and Literature*, edited by Philip Leonard, as well as to a volume (forthcoming) on the emotions in early modern Europe and colonial North America. She is the author of *Teresa of Avila's Autobiography: Authority, Power, and the Self in Mid-Sixteenth-Century Spain* (2004).

Katharine Goodland is associate professor of English at the College of Staten Island, City University of New York. She has published essays on women and emotion in the *Journal of Religion and the Arts*, *Medieval and Renaissance Drama in England*, and *Early Theatre* and is completing a book entitled *Mourning Women in Early Modern English Drama*. She is on the editorial board of *Shakespeare Bulletin*.

Kristi Gourlay is pursuing a career in university administration at the University of Toronto. She has written on a range of topics including two papers on the didactic function of medieval unicorn tapestries published in the *Gazette des Beaux-Arts* and *Young Medieval Women*, edited by Katherine Lewis, Noel James Menuge, and Kim Phillips. She is currently working on a monograph based on her doctoral dissertation, "'Faire Maide' or 'Venomous Serpente': The Cultural Significance of the Saracen

Princess Floripas in France and England, 1200–1500," and a paper that examines Western representations of Eastern women in sixteenth-century travel literature.

E. Ann Matter is professor and chair of religious studies at the University of Pennsylvania. She is the author of *The Voice of My Beloved: "The Song of Songs" in Western Medieval Christianity* (1990) and coeditor of the collections *Creative Women in Medieval and Early Modern Italy: A Religious and Artistic Renaissance* (1994) and *The Liturgy of the Medieval Church: Essays for Teachers* (2001). She has written numerous articles on female religious of the Middle Ages, including an essay in the recent *Gender in Debate from the Early Middle Ages to the Renaissance*, edited by Thelma S. Fenster and Clare A. Lees.

James J. Paxson is associate professor of English at the University of Florida. He is coeditor of *Desiring Discourse: The Literature of Love, Ovid Through Chaucer* (1998) and *The Performance of Middle English Culture: Essays on Chaucer and the Drama in Honor of Martin Stevens* (1998). His essays on Chaucer, Langland, and medieval rhetoric have been published in *Style, Rhetorica, Rhetoric Society Quarterly, Exemplaria*, and the *Yearbook of Langland Studies*.

Lisa Perfetti is associate professor of French at Muhlenberg College. She is the author of *Women and Laughter in Medieval Comic Literature* (2003). Her writings on medieval women include an essay in *Bakhtin and Medieval Voices*, edited by Thomas J. Farrell, and articles in *Medieval Feminist Forum, Exemplaria*, and the forthcoming *Women and Gender in Medieval Europe: An Encyclopedia*.

Wendy Pfeffer is professor of French and chair of classical and modern languages at the University of Louisville. She is the author of *Proverbs in Medieval Occitan Literature* (1997) and coeditor of *Three Medieval Views of Women* (1989) and *Songs of the Women Trouvères* (2001). She has published in *Speculum* and elsewhere on lyric in the troubadours and trouvères, and has contributed numerous entries to *Medieval France: An Encyclopedia*, edited by William W. Kibler et al.

Sarah Westphal is associate professor of German at Rice University. She is the author of *Textual Poetics of German Manuscripts, 1300–1500* (1993) and a coeditor of *Sisters and Workers in the Middle Ages* (1989). Her publications on women in medieval fictional trials have appeared in *Essays in Medieval Studies* and *Zeitschrift für Literaturwissenschaft und Linguistik*. She has also coauthored an article on the implications of stories of violence against girls for contemporary legal theory in *Wisconsin Women's Law Journal*.

Index

Abu-Lughod, Lila, 18n.7, 20n.23, 22n.33
Addison, Joseph, 61n.25
Affective piety, 3, 15, 65–71, 80, 82–83, 117n.28
Ajuwon, Bade, 114n.6
Akbari, Suzanne Conklin, 149, 161n.60
Akehurst, F.R.P., 130
Alan of Lille, 24, 51, 57
Alexander VI (pope), 29
Alexiou, Margaret, 113n.2, 116n.22
Allegory, 44–62
Alliterative Morthe Arthure, 93
Allen, Valerie, 3, 7, 9, 12
Alumbrados, 64, 85n.6
Ambrose (bishop of Milan), 80
Ancrene Wisse, 193–94, 197, 201–2
Anderson, Gary, 114n.6
Andreasi, Osanna, 30
Angela of Foligno, 3, 13, 15, 63–89
Anger: appropriate response to, in women, 11, 141–42; associated with women, 44, 58–59n.3, 137–39; choler producing, 5; and class, 8, 19n.15; and climate, 8, 149; and crimes of passion, 135; discouraged in Christian devotion, 83; and ethnicity or race, 8, 148–49, 180–85; expressed with verbal insults, by women, 140; of female characters, erotic appeal of, 152–54; heroic, 171–72, 181; hot in men, cold in women, 5, 135, 139–40; in judicial and court records, 134, 139, 142; laughable, in women, 8, 150–51, 175, 180, 184; as legal position, 11, 172, 180, 183; motivated by the devil, 20n.22; and national character, 36; paired with grief, 103, 127; in *Psychomachia*, 44; in reaction to dishonor or insult, 135–38, 141–42, 171; righteous or justified, 11, 135, 139, 147, 151; sinful, 6, 23; visual representations of, 137–38, 176;

words associated with, 157n.26, 171, 188n.25
Apostrophe, 47–48, 91
Aquinas, Thomas, 3, 9, 194, 196, 198
Alan of Lille, 24
Arabs, 8, 148–49
Aristotle, 2: on anger, 136; and cosmology, 27; and humoral theory, 25, 134; on metaphor and simile, 50–52, 60n.17; on sexual difference, 4; on shame, 194; on *signa naturalia*; on women's emotionality, 65
Ashley, Kathleen, 116n.18, 117n.40
Astell, Ann, 113note
Augustine (bishop of Hippo), 3, 15, 24; *Confessions*, 64, 66, 69, 72, 82; *De Doctrina christiana*, 197; on sexual difference, 194; on shame, 3, 195, 203

Bakhtin, Mikhail, 54, 61n.24
Barthes, Roland, 61n.24
Barton, Richard, 135
Basil of Seleucia, 94, 95
Bataille, Georges, 51–52
Bayless, Martha, 161n.62
Becon, Thomas, 92
Beguines, 85n.12
Belardini, M., 41n.47
Bell, Rudolph M., 88n.38
Bellomo, Manlio, 185n.4, 188n.36, 189n.44
Bendelow, Gillian, 18n.8
Beowulf, 114n.7
Bernard of Clairvaux, 15, 66, 68, 78, 80
Bernardino de Laredo, 85n.5, 85n.7
Bernardus Silvestris, 24, 47, 57
Berneville, Gillebert de, 128–29
Bevis of Hampton, 141
Bloch, R. Howard, 208n.43, 210n.70
Blondel de Nesle, 124

Bloomfield, Morton, 37n.1, 52, 62n.25, 158n.32
Blush: from anger, 192; in confession, 197, 203; from fear, 193; from loss of honor, 196; meaning of, in Middle English, 198; from modesty, 192; restorative power of, 196; of romance heroes, 192; from shame, 9, 192, 197, 204
Boccaccio, Giovanni, 19n.16
Body: connected to emotion, 4–7, 58n.2; effect of emotions on, 75–76; as female, 4; and shame, 191–213; taboos against, 174–75; weakness of female, 5, 194, 195. *See also* embodiment; humors
Boethius, 38n.2
Bonaventure, Saint (Franciscan cardinal), 87n.36
Borgia, Lucrezia, 29
Børresen, Kari Elisabeth, 85n.9
Borromeo, Federigo (cardinal), 36–37
Bourdieu, Pierre, 20n.21
Bourke, Angela, 114n.6
Brigit of Sweden, 28
Bunyan, John, 44
Burns, E. Jane, 170, 184
Bynum, Carolyn Walker, 26, 28, 86n.18, 87n.37, 88n.38

Cadden, Joan, 18n.9, 19n.11, 20n.18, 25, 38n.6
Calderón de la Barca, 54
Calefurnia, 5, 11, 164–90
Camilla (*Roman d'Eneas*), 152–53
Carrera, Elena, 3, 7, 13, 14, 15
Caviness, Madeline, 170, 186n.11, 187n.16
Chanson de geste, 140, 150
Chanson de malmariée, 10, 11, 16, 125–26
Chanson de Roland, 114n.7, 137, 147, 148
Chartier, Alain, 128
Chaucer, Geoffrey: Alison (*Miller's Tale*), 202; Blanche, 202; Canon's Yeoman, 192; Criseyde, 192, 196; Franklin, 203; Friar, 157n.25; Griselda, 19n.16, 191–92; Lucrece, 192; Parson, 191; Summoner, 157n.25; Walter, 192–93; Wife of Bath, 142, 154
Chaude colle, 5, 135, 140

Christine the Marvelous, 28
Chrysostom, John, 86n.22
Civilizing process, 3
Cixous, Hélène, 170, 184
Class, social: and education, 65–66; role of, in emotions; 4, 7–8, 95–96, 111–12, 192–94
Clopper, Lawrence M., 59n.3, 95–96, 117n.28
Cognition: related to emotion, 4, 8
Cohen, Elizabeth S., 157n.23
Compassion: greater in women, 12, 94; of Jesus, 94, 96, 110; as positive Christian emotion, 84; of Virgin Mary, 93
Conceptual primitives, 20n.24
Conduct literature, 14, 133, 138–39
Confessio Amantis, 209n.69
Confession: in Council of Trent, 82; demeanor of priest during, 199–200; importance of shame in, 197, 205; "naked," 10, 200–2, 205; of women, 10, 193–94, 199–202
Conger, George Perrigo, 37
Constable, Giles, 41n.45
Contenance des fames, 119, 130
Corpus juris civilis, 173–74
Cosmology, 23–27: interiorization of, 36–37
Courtly love poetry, 13, 16, 64, 66, 77, 78, 121–22, 130
Cousins, Ewert, 40n.45
Crane, Susan, 21n.27
Culler, Jonathan, 48
Customary law, 5, 166–78

Damasio, Antonio, 18n.8, 19n.12, 20n.19, 21n.25
Daniel, Norman, 150, 160nn.58–59
Dante Alighieri, 197
Davis, Natalie, 139–40, 150, 151, 156n.5, 162n.70
Death: constructions of, 90–92; definition by Augustine, 195; as passage to life with God, 12; wish for, 92, 97, 103, 123
Deaux, Kay, 19n.15
de Blois, Robert, 132n.15, 138
Deguileville, Guillaume de, 44
De Lauretis, Teresa, 187n.22

De Man, Paul, 45–46, 56
Demers, Patricia, 59n.5
de Meun, Jean, 57
Demonic influence, 20n.22, 27, 32–37, 67: on women, 28
Derrida, Jacques, 43
Descartes, René, 29
Devotio moderna, 86n.13
Dido, 123, 182
Dionysius the Areopagite, 68
Dobozy, Maria, 167, 185n.6
Dodds, E. R., 208n.41
Doyle, Mary Agnes, 113n.2
Dronke, Peter, 26, 29, 59n.7, 91, 93
Duffy, Eamon, 115n.15

Ebenbauer, Alfred, 182, 190nn.59–62
Ecclesiasticus, 175, 176, 184
Elias, Norbert, 3, 18n.6
Elisabeth of Schönau, 28
Ellington, Donna Spivey, 116n.15
Elliott, Dyan, 25–26, 27, 29, 32, 37
Ellison, Julie, 20n.23
Embodiment: and belief in women's emotionality, 4–5; and female mysticism, 26, 39n.18, 65; personification, 43, 55–56; and privileging of women's emotion, 6, 28, 71; and stigma against women, 4–5, 14, 28, 47, 191
Emotion: basic, 20n.25; and behavior, 9; and class, 7–8, 95–96, 111–12, 192–94, 198; communal identity of, in Middle Ages, 4, 8–12; contrasted with feeling, 18n.8; cultural construction of, 10; and ethnicity 7–8, 148–49; 180–85; etymology of, 6; fake or insincere, 9, 124; and genre, 11, 16, 121, 130; greater displays of, by women, 13, 69; historical shifts in, 2, 16, 23; and language issues, 10, 20n.24, 157n.26; in legal descision making, 9, 164–65, 168, 173, 184; of medieval women, as described or mediated by men, 2, 39n.18; medieval views of, 2, 6, 23, 43–44; medieval women's understanding of their own, 12–15, 37, 57, 77–78, 120; mutability of, in women, 1, 119–21; in neuroscience, 18n.8, 19n.12; outlet for, in lyric, 127, 130; performative aspect of, 9, 13, 15, 32–33, 91–92, 198; and reason binary, 14, 65, 69, 164–65, 170, 176, 181, 184; standards, 4, 16, 17n.4; women's lack of control over, 1, 4–5, 71, 90, 97, 101, 138, 165. *Also see entries for individual emotions*
Emotionology, 17n.3
Enders, Jody, 173, 185n.3, 188n.30
Enide (Chrétien de Troyes heroine), 13
Envy, 6
Este, Alfonso d', 30, 32
Este, Ercole d', 29–32
Ethnicity, 8, 148–49, 180–85
Exomologesis, 65, 74

Fabliaux, 16, 170, 202
Fahnestock, Jeanne, 58n.1
Farce, 14
Farmer, Sharon, 21n.28
Farrell, Thomas J., 61n.24
Fassler, Margot, 59n.5, 59n.8
Fear: as basic emotion 20n.25; of God, 48, 72, 80, 81, 84; related to shame, 196
Feeling. *See* emotion
Fehr, Hans, 178
Ferrante, Joan, 57
Fierabras, 8, 133–63
Filipczak, Zirka, 24
Finch, A. J., 136
Fischer, Agneta H., 19n.15, 21n.26, 22n.30
Foehr-Janssens, Yasmina, 127
Francis of Assisi, Saint, 70
Frantzen, Allen J., 37note, 117n.35
Freud, Sigmund, 204

Galen, 24, 25, 58n.2, 134, 149
Galluzzi, Maria Domitilla, 29, 35–37
García de Toledo, 87n.26
Garin lo Brun, 138
Gender: and emotion, psychological studies of, 7, 13; medieval understanding of, 5, 25–26
Genre, 16, 121
Geoffrey of Vinsauf, 192
Georgianna, Linda, 207n.31
Gertrud of Helfta, 85n.11
Gestures, 91

Gombrich, E. H., 61n.25
Goodland, Katharine, 3, 7, 12, 15, 115n.14, 117n.31
Gosnai, Dame de, 128–29
Gosselin, Ronald, 136
Gourlay, Kristi, 3, 5, 8, 11, 15, 22n.34
Greenblatt, Stephen, 21n.27
Gregory, Saint, 66, 68, 80
Grant, Edward, 38n.2, 39n.20
Gravdal, Kathryn, 162n.70, 163n.75
Gray, Thomas, 44
Grief and grieving, 9; criticized in women, 15, 108–10; greater in women, 101, 112; inconsolable, 92, 93, 102–4; paired with anger, 127; performative aspect of, 91; physical expressions of, 126–27; and vengeance, 9; of Virgin Mary, 91, 99, 115–16n.15, 122. *See also* lament and lamentation; sorrow
Griffiths, Lavinia, 52, 62n.25
Griselda, 19n.16, 193
Guillaume de Lorris, 57
Guilt: distinguished from shame 198, 208n.41; in women's lyrics, 127–28
Gusick, Barbara, 110, 117n.40

Hadewijch of Antwerp, 78
Hamburgh, Harvey E., 116n.16
Hamilton, Alastair, 85n.6
Happiness: as "basic" emotion, 20n.25; of Christian soul, 47; differences across cultures, 10–11; in women's lyric, 129–30. *See also* joy
Harris, William V., 156n.5
Hass, Renate, 114n.7
Hate: discouraged in Christian devotion, 83; in legal proceedings, 9
Hildegard of Bingen: as melancholic, 25–26, 28; *Ordo Virtutum*, 3, 6, 14, 43–62; valorizing emotion, 14, 56; as woman writer, 14, 57, 85n.11
Hippocrates, 24, 25
Hogan, Patrick Colm, 21n.25, 22n.35
Holsinger, Bruce W., 59n.8
Holst-Warhoft, Gail, 113n.2, 114n.6
Honor, 8–9; in chivalric literature, 137; loss of, as motivation for vengeance, 135–38, 171; loss of, provoking shame, 192, 196; and sexual reputation of women, 11, 139, 193
Hugh of St. Victor, 66
Humiliation: producing anger, 136–37; of self, in Christian devotion, 70, 72, 74
Humility, 13; in repentance, 72–74
Humor, 150–52, 172, 184
Humors: and anger, 5, 135, 139–40; and cosmology, 24–26; and emotion, 3, 4–5, 19n.12, 23–26, 135, 196; and microcosm 6, 23–25; mind's ability to alter, 6, 28; and sexual difference, 4–5, 25–26; and shame, 196

Ignatius of Loyola, 33, 34, 36, 77
Imitatio Christi, 72–73
Iseut, 141–42
Isidore of Seville, 24, 25, 149, 161n.60
Iwein, 172

Jacquart, Danielle, 25–26, 29, 38n.6
Jaeger, C. Stephen, 17
Jerome, Saint, 30, 65, 73, 205
Jeu-parti, 10–11, 128–29
Joan of Arc, 28
Johanek, Peter, 189n.50
John of Trevisa, 191
John Scotus Eriugena, 38n.2
Johnson-Laird, P. N., 20n.25
Johnston, Alexandra, 96, 116n.15
Jones, George Fenwick, 157n.26
Joubert, Laurent, 19n.12
Joy: Christian views of, 7, 47, 68; and laughter, 19n.12; meaning of, in Old French, 10, 131n.14; produced by good blood, 19n.12; in religious experience, 68, 105. *See also* happiness
Juliana, Saint, 150–51
Justinian, 173–74

Kaeuper, Richard W., 137
Kant, Immanuel, 204
Kasten, Ingrid, 17
Kaufman, Nikolai, 114n.5
Keiser, George R., 115n.15
Kempe, Margery, 108

Kennedy, Gwynne, 17, 156n.5
King, Laura Severt, 118n.41
Kisch, Guido, 176
Kolve, V. A., 162n.69
Krueger, Roberta, 151
Kurtz, Barbara E., 61n.23

Lacan, Jacques, 51–52
Lambert of Ardres, 193
Lament and lamentation: and class, 7, 111–12; considered blasphemous, 91–94, 99, 104; and creation of community, 101; function of, 12, 91–92, 98, 101–102; as genre, 91–92, 113n.4; persistence into early modern period, 93; phases of, 93, 97; in repentance, 71–72; ritual, 7, 12, 91–92; of Virgin Mary, 91, 99, 115–16n.15; by women, criticized, 12, 90; by women, defended, 12, 98; by women, as resistance to male authority, 90, 112, 115n.14. *See also* grief and grieving; tears; weeping
Langland, William, 44; *Piers Plowman*, 44, 52, 57, 61n.25
Lanham, Richard A., 58n.1
La Tour Landry, Geoffroy de, 139
Laughter: and class, 7–8, 19n.17; and good blood, 19n.12; more frequent in women, 5; seat of, 19n.12; unbecoming in women, 7–9; in women's lyric, 131n.14
Lawton, David, 52, 62n.25
Lazarus plays, 7, 12, 15, 90–118; Chester, 95, 105–108, 112; Digby, 111–12, 117n.28; N-Town, 95–96, 97–102, 105, 108, 112; Towneley, 95, 108–110, 112; York, 95, 102–105, 108, 112
Leclercq, Jean, 37n.1
Lehmijoki-Gardner, Maiju, 30
Le Leu, Gautier, 202
Lerner, Gerda, 85n.8
Lesnick, Daniel R., 157n.18
Lewis, Jan, 17n.3
Loersch, Hugo, 178
Lombard, Peter, 70, 86n.22
Love: Christian views of, 7, 9, 31, 48, 73, 80; discerning, in Mechthild of Magdeburg, 69; of God, 67, 68–71; of God, related to courtly love, 78–80; in legal proceedings, 9; pain of, 121–22; in Song of Songs, 78–81; transformative power of, 80
Lutgard of Aywières, 28
Lutz, Catherine, 18n.7, 20n.23, 22n.33, 116n.21
Lydgate, John, 44

Maclean, Ian, 161n.60
Maggi, Armando, 30, 32, 36, 40n.38
Malleus maleficarum, 28
Manstead, Antony S. R., 21n.26, 22n.30
Marbod of Rennes, 138
Margaret of Cremona, 28
Maria Maddalena de' Pazzi, 29, 32–37
Marie de France, 22n.29, 157n.25, 159n.49
Marie of Oignies, 28
Martín, Melquíades Andrés, 85n.6
Mary Magdalene, 90–118; as model for women's emotional expression, 69, 70, 71, 74
Mary Magdalene (Digby play), 93. *See also* Lazarus plays, Digby
Matter, Ann, 2, 3, 6, 12, 15, 39n.29, 41n.47, 89n.46
McEntire, Sandra, 116n.20
McGinn, Bernard, 34, 39n.18, 40n.45, 84n.1
McInerney, Maud Burnett, 59n.7
McKeon, Richard, 60n.14
Mechthild of Hackeborn, 85n.11
Mechthild of Magdeburg, 3, 15, 63–89
Melancholy, 4, 6, 26, 28
Ménagier de Paris, 19n.16, 138
Meyerson, Mark, 140, 156n.14
Miller, William Ian, 9, 136, 159n.44
Mills, David, 95
Mimetic spirituality: of Ignatius of Loyola, 33, 77; increasingly interiorized, 34–37
Minnesang. *See* courtly love poetry
Misrahi, Catharine, 37n.1
Mooney, Catherine M., 39n.18
Mörin, Die 8, 178–85
Mourning. *See* lament and lamentation
Muir, Edward, 135, 140, 156n.8
Müller, Jan-Dirk, 171, 172

Index

Mustanoja, Tauno F., 114n.5, 114n.6
Myrc, John, 199, 207n.18

da Narni, Lucia Brocadelli, 29–37
Nelson, Charles, 170, 186n.11, 187n.16
Newbold, R. F., 136
Newhauser, Richard, 37n.1
Newman, Barbara, 25–26, 29
Nibelungenlied, 171, 181
Nicholas of Cusa, 27
Norman, Joanne S., 158n.28, 158n.33
Nussbaum, Martha, 176, 185

Oatley, Keith, 20n.25
Orderic Vitalis, 140
O'Reilly, Jennifer, 158n.30
Osuna, Francisco de, 86n.15

Pain (emotional): directed inward, 128; of love, 121–22; in prayer, 67, 70, 71, 73, 77, 79, 82; women's stronger expression of, 13, 121; words to express, in Old French, 120–21. *See also* sorrow
Parker, Matthew, 92
Parody, 149–50, 161n.62
Parzival, 182
Passion of Christ, 15, 28, 29, 99; emotions provoked by meditating on, 75–78; imitation of, 32, 34; as model for human love, 31; as vehicle for union with God, 78–81
Passion plays, 91, 93
Passions: classical and medieval understanding of, 3, 6, 23, 27, 194; distinguished from virtue, 198; and physical change in the body, 196
Paul (apostle), 30, 70
Paxson, James, 3, 4, 6, 9, 14, 61n.21, 61n.22, 61n.25
Pedagogy, for teachers of medieval texts, 15–16
Penitential manuals, 7, 9, 199–203, 205
Perfetti, Lisa, 112note, 131n.6, 163n.77, 187n.13, 209n.61
Personification: and embodiment, 4; as female, 4, 43–44, 54–56; in Hildegard of Bingen, 3, 43–62; and mimetic spirituality, 34
Petrarch, 19n.16
Petroff, Elizabeth, 65
Pfeffer, Wendy, 3, 8, 10, 13, 14
Phillippy, Patricia, 115n.11, 118n.42
Pizan, Christine de, 22n.31, 57, 94, 106–7, 127, 130
Plato, 23–24, 47, 196
Porete, Marguerite, 78
Pozzi, Giovanni, 32
Premonition, in women, 98
Prosopopeia. *See* personification
Prudentius, 44, 46, 137–38
Psychology, in early modern period, 26, 34–37
Psychomachia, 6, 44; Ira (character), 44, 46, 137–38. *See also* virtues and vices

Quilligan, Maureen, 61n.25
Quintilian, 55
Quinzani, Stefana, 30

Rabelais, 202, 205–6
Raoul de Cambrai, 142
Rasmussen, Ann Marie, 21n.28
Ratramnus of Corbie, 38n.2
Rawcliffe, Carole, 58n.2
Razzi, Serafino, 31
Reddy, William, 17n.4, 19n.10
Reiss, Timothy J., 21n.27
Repentance, 71–74. *See also* penitential manuals
Rhetoric: classical and medieval, 3, 43–62; colors of, 203
Richard of St. Victor, 85n.7
Richlin, Amy, 163n.75
Richmond, Velma Bourgeois, 114n.7
Riemer, Seth, 110
Robertson, Elizabeth, 297n.36
Roman d'Eneas, 152
Roman de Silence, 141, 150
Roman de Tristan, 141
Romance (genre), 66; anger in, 140–41; grief in, 126; shame in, 192
Romance of the Rose, 57

Rosaldo, Michelle Z., 20n.19
Rosenwein, Barbara, 17n.2, 18n.6, 19n.15, 37n.1, 155n.5
Rosmarin, Adena, 113n.4, 114n.6
Ruether, Rosemary Radford, 85n.9
Ruggiero, Guido, 136, 156n.9
Rummel, Mariella, 188n.24

Sachs, Hans, 175
Sachsenheim, Hermann von, 178
Sachsenspiegel, 5, 10, 15, 164–90
Sadness. *See* sorrow
Savonarola, Girolamo, 29, 30, 31
Scharfenberg, Albrecht von, 183
Schmidt, Margot, 87n.31
Schwabenspiegel, 166–67
Scott, S. P., 188n.39, 189n.42
Self: in Christian devotion, 2, 64, 197; concept of in Middle Ages, 10, 25–26; and shame, 198–99
Self-loathing, 13–14; and Christian humiliation, 74; in women's lyric, 127–28
Shakespeare, 115n.14
Shame: in Christian devotion, 65, 67, 70, 75, 80, 81, 84, 194–97; difficulty in ascertaining, 192, 197, 205; etymology of, 191; and gaze on the subject, 198–203; and genitals, 191–92; as involuntary passion, 9, 198; from loss of honor, 135–38, 192, 196, 207n.21; and Middle English *schameless*, 204; and modesty, 207n.23; and nakedness, 195, 200–204; as positive force for action in men, 192; related to virtue, 194, 198; sexual nature of, in women, 5, 192–94; versus guilt, 198, 208n.41
Sharon-Zisser, Shirley, 51, 60n.12, 60n.13, 60n.17
Sharpe, J. A., 157n.18
Sin, 6, 23, 71, 79, 101; in confession, 71, 194, 200–201; emotions viewed as, 23, 135; and movements of the body, 31, 195; original, 194–95. *See also* entries for individual emotions
Sir Gawain and the Green Knight, 12, 192, 196, 198
Siraisi, Nancy G., 156n.7, 161n.60

Smail, Daniel, 9, 22n.34
Smiles, 131n.14; interpreted by men, 132n.15
Solterer, Helen, 156n.15, 184, 188n.24
Song of Songs, 78–81
Sorrow: in Christian devotion, 65, 75–76, 84; of Virgin Mary, 99–100, 122; of women unable to decide their own fate, 124–25; in women's lyric, 130. *See also* grief and grieving; lament and lamentation; weeping
Sponsler, Claire, 116n.17
Stafford, Anthony, 115n.14
Stanbury, Sarah, 115n.15
Stearns, Carol Z., 17n.3, 18n.5
Stearns, Peter N., 17n.3, 17n.4, 18n.5
Sterling-Hellenbrand, Alexandra, 182
Strange, William, 52, 62n.25
Strocchia, Sharon T., 114n.6
Strohschneider, Peter, 189n.54
Strothmann, Friedrich Wilhelm, 178
Suicide, 13, 22n.29, 124
Sultan, Nancy, 114n.6

Tearing of garments, 12, 94
Tearing of hair, 94, 98
Tears: faking of, 9; in confession, 197; of devotion, 69, 77; of lament, 12; of Jesus, 95–97, 107, 110; of Margery Kempe, 108; of Mary Magdalene, 69; mixed with laughter, 1, 5, 123; of pain in love, 121; of supplication, 105; of Virgin Mary, 99–100. *See also* lament and lamentation; weeping
Teresa of Avila, 3, 14, 15, 36, 63–89
Tertullian, 65, 204
Teskey, Gordon, 62n.28
Thomas of Chobham, 12
Thomasset, Claude, 25–26, 29, 38n.6
Todorov, Tzvetan, 62n.26
Triandis, Harry C., 21n.26
Trouvères, 14, 119–32
Troyes, Chrétien de, 126–27

Unhappiness. *See* sorrow
Unruly woman, 151–52
Uterus, 5

Vanna of Orvieto, 28
Vaught, Jennifer C, 17n.2, 112
Vengeance: and grief, 9; women's role in inciting men to take, 140, 159n.44
Virgin Mary: grief/sorrow of, 99, 122; as model for women's emotional expression, 70, 74; mourning of, 91; as spiritual guide, 33, 34
Virtues and vices: in Hildegard of Bingen, 45–48; as guide to behavior, 6, 47; related to emotions, 6, 9, 14, 137–38; visual representations of, 195
von Eschenbach, Wolfram, 182
von Etzenbach, Ulrich, 183
von Repgow, Eike, 164–90

Wailing the dead. See lament and lamentation
Warrior women, 152–53, 181
Watts, Pauline Moffitt, 39n.21
Weatherbee, Winthrop, 24
Webster, 115n.14
Weeping: considered feminine, 13, 21n.29, 92; as expression of compunction, 93–94; of Jesus, 94, 96; leads to consolation, 72; promoted in Christian devotion, 70, 83; of women, criticized, 12, 94–95; of women, defended, 94, 107. See also tears
Welz, Dieter, 190n.56

Westphal, Sarah, 3, 5, 7, 8, 11
Wierzbicka, Anna, 20n.24
Wiesner Hanks, Merry, 165
Wiethaus, Ulrike, 39n.17
Willging, Jennifer, 155n.5
William of Auvergne, 27
William of Conches, 25
William of St. Thierry, 68
Williams, Bernard, 208n.41
Williams, Simon J., 18n.8
Wogan-Brown, Jocelyn, 163n.75
Women, medieval: inability to speak in public, 70–71, 82–83; lack of intellectual training of, 15, 70; legal status of, 5, 7, 129–30, 160, 165, 174–75, 178–79; seduction and abuse of, 179, 183–85; writing about their own emotions, 2, 12–15, 25–26, 65, 81–84
Woolf, Rosemary, 94, 116n.18
Wrath. See anger
Wycliffe, John, 199

Yvain, 126–27

Zarri, Gabriella, 30
Ziolkowski, Jan, 51
Zorn, 11; as battle of words, 172; of hero, 171, 181; as legal position, 11, 172, 180, 183; meaning of, in Middle High German, 171, 188n.25